Apr. 14-72.
To Jan from
Grandmother

ERNESTINE L. ROSE

And the Battle for Human Rights

Published under the Sponsorship of

EMMA LAZARUS FEDERATION OF
JEWISH WOMEN'S CLUBS

Commissioned in 1954 in Celebration of the 300th
Anniversary of Jewish Settlement in the U. S. A.

Ernestine L. Rose

AND THE BATTLE FOR

HUMAN RIGHTS

BY

Yuri Suhl

REYNAL & COMPANY

NEW YORK

FOR ISABELLE

HN
57
.S9

CONTENTS

PART ONE: 1810–1836

PART TWO: 1836–1869

PART THREE: 1869–1892

Illustrations following page 22

PREFACE

A CENTURY AGO the name Ernestine L. Rose was known to thousands in many parts of America. It was associated with such unpopular causes as Abolitionism and Woman's Rights; the advocacy of free public education; the principles of Robert Owen's utopian socialism; the Free Thought movement. And at a time when the dogmas of the church dominated the lives of the majority of the people she dared to challenge the prevailing concepts of religion.

All this made her a highly controversial figure. Clergymen denounced her as an Infidel. Newspaper reporters jeered at her foreign accent. Editors called her a menace and a foreign propagandist. Legislators quailed in her presence. Slaveholders nearly tarred and feathered her. But thousands flocked to hear her speak; and many who came to scoff remained to cheer and applaud. Even her enemies could not deny her rare gift of eloquence and her charm. On the platform she was queen and her large audiences did indeed bestow upon her the title: Queen of the Platform. But today Ernestine L. Rose is virtually forgotten.

Like her friends and colleagues, Susan B. Anthony, Elizabeth Cady Stanton, Lucy Stone, Lucretia Mott, she was totally dedicated; her life was in her work. Unlike them her work almost entirely overshadowed her personal life. But even her work has never been presented to the public in its fullest dimensions and in a comprehensive form. The few available accounts of her life, ranging in size from a mere paragraph to a chapter in a book, are sparse, sketchy and, in some instances, factually incorrect. This biography, the result of five years' work, is the first full-length account of her life.

The writing of this biography was rendered particularly difficult by the almost total lack of the basic materials which a biographer regards as his primary sources of information, such as: diaries, personal memoirs, family recollections, private correspondence and official records relating to such vital family statistics as deaths, births, marriages, etc. Her life lay buried in the crumbling pages of the newspapers and periodicals of her time; the stenographic reports of the conventions she attended; her speeches; her articles; the reminiscences of some of her contemporaries and the almost forgotten history of the woman's rights movement. It was these materials that yielded the bulk of the chronicle that makes up her life.

But some gaps even diligent research could not overcome. To mention but a minor one: All biographical references to her record her maiden name as Ernestine Louise Siismondi Potowski. But no Jewish girl born of orthodox parents in a ghetto in Poland would be named Ernestine Louise. This is, without a doubt, a later modification of the Hebrew name originally given her at her birth. Rather than indulge in guesswork and invent Hebrew equivalents for Ernestine Louise, this writer chose to use the available name even in the beginning years of her life. The same principle was applied throughout the book with regard to other blanks.

The dialogue is, in the main, genuine. Where direct quotation was lacking it was painstakingly reconstructed from her speeches and newspaper accounts of her utterances. Only in the first sixteen years of her life were liberties taken with the dialogue. But even there the invention is based on some known situation and supported by a study of the mores and manners that prevailed in her particular time and environment.

Despite the occasional lapses in her personal history, whether large or small, a life does emerge—fullblooded, vital, colorful. For she was a true child of the nineteenth century, a century, as characterized by one of her contemporaries, when the air was "thick with the flying splinters of exploded dogmas." * Ernestine L. Rose was one of the most indefatigable exploders of the dogmas of her time. Wherever she appeared the splinters were indeed flying thick.

---

* Rev. H. L. Ziegenfuss, "Women, Work and Wages," *Revolution*, August 18, 1870.

PART ONE: 1810–1836

"I was a rebel at the age of five."

ERNESTINE L. ROSE

Chapter I

PIOTRKOW

O N THE COLD WINTER DAY of January 13, 1810, the most
noteworthy event in the ghetto of Piotrkow, Poland,
was the birth of a girl. Word passed quickly from mouth to
mouth and soon the whole ghetto knew that Rabbi Potowski
had become a father. The people rejoiced. They were proud
of their rabbi. In learning he could compare with the best of
Talmudic scholars; and as for piety, one would have to travel
far to find his equal. Now came the fulfillment of fatherhood.
Fatherhood added stature to a man.

In the synagogue, that day, the worshippers crowded
around him, eagerly shaking his hand and offering congratulations.

"Mazeltov, Rabbi, mazeltov."

"With mazel we should live, blessed be the One Above."

Mixed with the well-wishing and congratulations was the
unspoken regret that the rabbi's first-born was a girl. A girl
was a millstone around your neck. You began saving for her
dowry almost from the day she was born, and your hair turned
gray with worry before you married her off. But a boy was
practically a born husband, and sought after from all sides.
Learning was for a boy; a girl's head was too weak for such
lofty matters as Torah. And who was privileged to say the
special prayer of kaddish after a deceased parent? A boy; a
girl was exempt from everyday prayers.

But why spoil a happy mood with unhappy thoughts? The
rabbi's wife was, after all, still a young woman; they might

yet be blessed with a son. At least it was certain now that she was not an *akureh*, a barren one. Where there is fertility, there is hope.

In accordance with Jewish tradition the little girl was given a name in the synagogue on the first Sabbath after her birth. When the services were over, some worshippers accompanied the rabbi to his home for a *lekach un bronfen* (honey cake and whiskey). But there was more than that on the table. The men ate and sang and never lacked for toasts as they raised their glasses to the rabbi and each other:

"May the children of Israel multiply."

"Amen."

"May they be redeemed from all evil."

"Amen."

"May they not know from want and sorrow."

"Amen, Father in Heaven."

In another room the rebbetzin lay in her maternal bed, curtained off with white sheets on which hung the *Shir Hamalos*, the Song of the Steps. These were thirteen Psalms which symbolized the thirteen steps of the Holy Temple. They were copied out painstakingly by hand for this occasion. It was believed that they could ward off all evil spirits that might seek to invade the maternal room. Only women were allowed in this room. They came to pay their respects to the rebbetzin and to catch a glimpse of the little one. To the newly-born they would say, "May your path be strewn with *mazel*;" and to the mother they would say, "May you live to lead her to the wedding canopy." And the rebbetzin, exhausted from the ordeal of birth, managed to nod and whisper for both of them, "Amen, God in Heaven."

For the ghetto the Sabbath was a day of complete rest not only from physical labors but from mental stresses as well. No Jew, however destitute, would desecrate the holy Sabbath with thoughts about such earthly matters as money or a livelihood. One day a week his worries were pushed out of consciousness and the Sabbath became a day of truce in the perennial battle with hunger. On that particular Sabbath the ghetto was enlivened by an air of festivity and everyone knew that this air emanated from the rabbi's house, and that it was bound up with the arrival of a new ghetto-dweller, a little girl named Ernestine Louise Potowski.

With the lighting of the *Havdalah* candle, the ritual that separates the holy Sabbath from the rest of the week, the ghetto returned to normal—to the skilled art of duelling with poverty and the plague of numerous taxes.

If a Jew managed to obtain a piece of kosher meat for the Sabbath—and what God-fearing Jew would consider any other kind of meat?—he had to pay a kosher-meat-tax. Part of the koshering ritual, before cooking the meat, consisted in sprinkling it heavily with salt, and so there was a salt-tax. One of the most sacred commandments that the Jewish woman observes is the lighting of Sabbath day candles on Friday, at the first sign of dusk. There was a tax on candles, too. A Jew was not drafted into the army but he had to pay a draft-exemption tax. He could not marry off a son or a daughter without paying a wedding-tax. Even in death there was no relief for there was also a cemetery- and funeral-tax. And there was always *Kahal*—the Jewish administrative body which was empowered to collect taxes, enforce decrees, and administer all secular and religious affairs of the ghetto. In many instances Kahal became a callous, corrupt and self-seeking clique, an added instrument of oppression. And because all public institutions as well as the clergy depended on Kahal for their financial support, a corrupt Kahal could misuse its powers and contaminate even the spiritual head of the community, the rabbi himself.

This, however, was not the case with Rabbi Potowski. He refused to accept a fee for his rabbinical services because he did not want material rewards to get between him and his spiritual duties. True, he did not have to depend on Kahal for his livelihood. His well-to-do father-in-law had given his daughter a handsome dowry and made it possible for the young rabbi to devote himself to Torah without the encumbrances of financial worries. Still money was money, a thing of allurement and temptation; and was it not written in the Talmud that one could judge a man's character by three things and one of them was his attitude to money? That was why the Jews of Piotrkow respected their rabbi, not only for his learning but also for his integrity. When they brought their disputes to him for arbitration they knew that his verdicts were based on his regard for justice; and in their grievances against Kahal the rabbi was on the side of the people.

Doing battle with hunger was only one part of the struggle for survival; doing battle with anti-Semites and pogromists was another; and still another was matching wits with the authorities in bypassing many of their restrictive decrees. As far back as the beginning of the fifteenth century, for instance, the Jews were officially banished from Piotrkow. But they managed to get around this decree by settling in the suburbs with the aid of some Polish landlords who, for a handsome profit, did not find Jewish tenants at all offensive. Later they were permitted to enter the city only to trade at the fairs. Gradually they found their way back altogether, and by the second half of the sixteenth century they had established a Jewish quarter inside the city.

At one time in the sixteenth century the Jews of Piotrkow had been forbidden to dress like Christians and compelled to wear yellow hats and badges to identify themselves as Jews. In 1810 their garb was, by their own choice, uniquely different; the wearing of the yellow hats and badges was only a painful memory. Progress had been made.

Life for the Polish peasant was not much brighter than life for the average Jew. On close observation one saw that the only difference between their respective lots was that of suffering misery in the countryside or in a city ghetto. The Jew was at the mercy of the corrupt and hostile government official and the peasant was at the mercy of his master, the landed aristocrat who could flog him at will. Whenever the bitterness of the peasant's life reached a point of overflow, he was manipulated by his real oppressors to engage in a kind of emotional blood-letting by spilling the life-blood of another victim of oppression—the Jew. The Jew, in short, was marked as the convenient scapegoat, and the all-powerful priest frequently led in whipping up the peasant's frenzy against him. For Jews the ringing of churchbells was always an ominous and fear-inspiring sound.

In 1810 there were still some Jews in Piotrkow who remembered the pogrom of 1740. It was carried out by the monks themselves. When the Jews took refuge in the synagogue the monks set the building on fire. When they were not making pogroms on Jews, they tried to convert them to Catholicism. They had more success with pogroms.

A favorite device of the monks for inciting the local population was the blood libel, a false charge that Jews required the blood of a Christian for ritual purposes on Passover.* One day they conceived the idea of perpetual incitement through the medium of art, with this canard as the theme. On the front wall of their monastery they hung a large oil painting depicting a ritual murder which was supposed to have taken place in Piotrkow sometime in the seventeenth century. The entire Jewish population with their rabbi at the head was shown participating in this ritual.

For a long time the Jews protested the display of this inflammatory piece of anti-Semitic propaganda, but to no avail. Finally, in 1825, and as a result of continued and vigorous

---

* The blood libel originated in twelfth-century England and nearly two hundred cases of this infamous charge have been recorded since then. One such case that drew world-wide attention was the Damascus affair of 1840, when Jews of that city were accused of the ritual murder of a Catholic priest and his servant. Many Jews died at the hands of inquisitors who through methods of torture sought to force confessions of guilt from them.

protests, they succeeded in having the painting removed.

Whenever the Jews ventured beyond the confines of the ghetto they took the risk of being attacked by the young priests and monks. Frequently these attacks developed into fierce street battles. The Jews were strongest when they were able to defend themselves on their own ghetto grounds. After such an encounter they would earn the respect of their attackers.

In a very definite sense the ghetto where the Jews lived was a prison within a prison, and their oppressors were themselves not free from oppression. In 1810 Poland was a thrice-dismembered country, groaning under the yoke of foreign domination. The monarchs of Austria, Prussia and Russia had divided Poland amongst themselves and had subjected it to their autocratic rule. Piotrkow belonged to that part of Poland which fell under the rule of Czar Nicholas I. These rulers did not always see eye-to-eye, but with regard to their Jewish subjects their differences disappeared and they spoke the common tongue of inhumanity.

Though theirs was an old community the Jews of Piotrkow could not regard the ghetto as their permanent home. On any day of the year either the caprice of a new ruler or the whim of an old one could render them homeless. Although their number, in 1810, comprised nearly half of the town's population, they were crowded into a small area, a ghetto that stood on a piece of marshy ground along the east bank of the river Strava. The streets were unpaved and the wooden, ramshackle houses, the small shops and the artisans' homes huddled closely together. Here the Jews of Piotrkow lived, worshipped, traded, worked, worried and hoped. Always they hoped for the day of deliverance.

This then was the world into which Ernestine Louise Potowski was born. And because her father was the rabbi, the spiritual head of the community, her home reflected every shade and nuance of this world, forever impressing upon her young and inquisitive mind the authentic images of the struggling life around her.

The coveted son did not come to the Potowski family and Ernestine remained the only child. They could, however, find some consolation in the thought that their daughter was a girl with a "boy's head" for learning. She insisted that Torah was not the exclusive province of the male, and, at a very early age, began to study the Scriptures in the original Hebrew. At a very early age, too, she revealed an astonishing penchant for clarity and logic. She read with a critical mind. This led her to ask such questions as, "What was the formation of the universe?" Or, "How did evil originate?" The rabbi grappled with these questions as best he could but when they grew both in volume and persistence he met them with reproof and the stock reply was that "little girls must not ask questions." This only led to the most annoying question of all, "Why must little girls not ask questions?"

Although she was unusually serious-minded for her age her reflective nature was well-balanced with a cheerful disposition. She did, however, prefer the company of her father, whom she loved and revered, to the usual playful diversions with friends her own age.

The rabbi, being orthodox in the extreme, fasted on Monday and Thursday of every week. This practice was undermining his health and Ernestine was pained to see her father look so pale and in poor spirits. One day she said to him, "Father, why do you fast?"

"To please God, my child," the rabbi replied.

"What pleasure does God get from your fasting, father?"

"To please God, my child, one must be willing to make sacrifices for Him."

She thought a moment and then said, "You know, father, what I think?"

"What, my child?"

"I think if God is pleased in making you sick He is cruel."

Another time, on a Saturday, the rabbi noticed that Ernestine was combing her hair. Aghast at seeing his daughter violating the Sabbath he cried, "Ernestine! What are you doing?"

"Combing my hair, father," she said calmly.

"Drop that comb at once! You're committing a sin against God."

Ernestine looked at her father, baffled and confused. The house had been thoroughly cleaned in honor of the Sabbath; she and everyone around her were dressed in holiday attire because of the Sabbath; why then must her hair be dishevelled on the Sabbath?

"Why is it a sin to comb my hair, father?" she finally asked.

"It is a sin against God, and ask no foolish questions," the rabbi said with all the authority at his command.

Apparently not satisfied with her father's reply, Ernestine said, "I shall ask Him myself." Whereupon she strode off to another room and addressed herself to God on this question. A moment later she returned and triumphantly announced to her father, "I asked God if it was a sin and He didn't say anything." And with that she considered the matter closed.

She was a rebel at the age of five; at the age of fourteen she was a heretic. Her heresies, however, did not consist of theological hair-splittings but concerned themselves with the right to question the soundness of prevailing concepts; the right to investigate the unknown; and the right to make reason and not faith the touchstone of one's convictions. She rejected as utterly false the notion that woman was inferior to man and insisted on equality for both sexes. She rebelled against the prayer daily said by men: "I thank thee Lord that thou hast not created me a woman," and she refused to say the woman's prayer, "I thank thee Lord that thou hast created me according to thy will."

At five her rebelliousness could be dismissed as the aberration of a precocious child; at fourteen it was regarded with alarm. In a circumscribed community where religious authority was supreme no one could hold to such heresies with impunity, not even the rabbi's daughter. The fact that she *was* the rabbi's daughter may have lessened the severity of the attacks upon her but it did not spare her entirely the pain of social ostracism. Even her friends found unpleasant ways of expressing their disapproval of her heresies. But this did not cause her to change her views or waver in her convictions.

When she was sixteen her mother died, leaving her a substantial inheritance of property. Her mother's premature death set off a series of events which, one year later, led her to make the most momentous decision in her life. But first it was her father who made a far-reaching decision.

As long as his wife was alive they both coped with their daughter's independence of mind as best they could, but alone it was more than the rabbi could manage. Ernestine became a problem that clamored for a solution, and the solution, he thought, was not far to seek: Marriage. What good Jewish daughter, at sixteen, was not already married? he asked himself. For the answer to that question he had but to look around him. Not only were girls that age married but many were already mothers. And here was his own daughter, a veritable feast for the eyes, a girl with a handsome dowry and a keen head on her shoulders (indeed, too keen for her own good!) and not even betrothed! And is it not right for a father to take matters in hand and do what he, in his wisdom, believes is best for his children? Let her become a wife and a mother and she will, with God's help, forget her heretical ideas soon enough.

Without informing Ernestine of his decision her father selected a groom for her, a man much older than she, offered him her inheritance as her dowry, and betrothed her to him. There was nothing unusual about this procedure. For generations fathers had met, with or without the aid of a professional matchmaker, and arranged amongst themselves the betrothals and marriages of their children without their knowledge and consent. Rarely, if ever, did a respectable father leave the choice of a marriage partner to the initiative of the principals themselves.

The news of her betrothal could not be kept from her forever and when she heard it her reaction was as emphatic as it was instantaneous. "Father, I will not marry him," she said.

"Why?" the rabbi demanded. "He is a pious and God-fearing Jew."

"That I am sure he is. But piety is no basis for selecting a husband."

"Is it perhaps because of his age that you hesitate?"

"It is because I do not love him, father. He is a total stranger to me."

"Love," the rabbi nodded sadly. Another one of his daughter's heresies. "Marriages are ordained in heaven," he said. "The matchmaker below is merely fulfilling the wish of the One Above. That was how your mother, may she rest in peace, and I got married. That is how all Jewish daughters get married. That is how the people of Israel have lived and multiplied for generations. And you wish to choose your own path?"

"If it be true, as you say, that marriages are ordained in heaven then the man I will some day select as my husband will also be heaven-approved. Isn't that so, father?"

"You talk of 'some day' as though one lived forever and time were standing still. You forget that you are already sixteen years old."

"And you, father, if you will forgive me, talk as though today I am still young and marriageable, and tomorrow I'll be a gray-haired old maid. I see myself not as being *already* sixteen but as being *only* sixteen."

"Only sixteen! Look around you and see, how many girls of sixteen will you find in the whole of Piotrkow who are not yet married or not betrothed to be married. I doubt if you will count them on the fingers of one hand."

"I do look about me, father; and I do see the life of these girls. They grow old before they grow young; they are children bearing children. The husband is off somewhere with his head in the Talmud or at the Hassidic rabbi's court singing and dancing while the wife is tied to the cradle and the stove. She will have her reward, of course. She will be his footstool in heaven. I will not live such a life."

"Each has been apportioned his task in life, and you, my daughter, will not change the order of things. Listen to reason; do as your father tells you."

"To reason I listen, but to unreason I will not. It is no use arguing, father. I will not marry that man."

"But the contract is already signed."

"I have not signed it and I will not honor it. I beg you, father, tell him that I regard this contract null and void."

"This I will not do."

"Then I will."

She went directly to the man's home and pleaded with him to release her from the engagement contract. He refused and, laughing in her face, reminded her that if she took the initiative in breaking the contract she would forfeit her dowry and he would come into possession of her inheritance. She was outraged by this threat and vowed never to submit to so flagrant an injustice. And yet she knew that the man could very well have his way if she did not take some decisive steps to thwart his plan.

Ordinarily such a matter would come before the rabbi for arbitration and both parties would be bound to abide by his decision. But what chance was there for a fair decision in a case where the rabbi himself was a prejudiced party to the dispute? There was only one course of action left for her now and that was to take the case to a Polish court. It was a painful decision to make, for this meant engaging her own father in litigation. But it would be a thousand times more painful to compromise and live with an injustice. Her mind was made up. In the nearby city of Kalish sat the High Tribunal of the Regional Polish Court. The value of her inheritance made her case eligible for litigation before that body.

It was a cold winter. The snows were high and the winds sharp and penetrating. But she would not be delayed. She hired a sleigh and driver to take her to Kalish.

Soon after they left Piotrkow the countryside burst upon them with its vast stretches of dazzling white. Farm huts, barns, trees and fields, all were under a blanket of fresh snow. And the air was crisp and exhilarating. But she could not abandon herself to the peace and serenity of the surrounding countryside. She had some serious thinking to do. She had decided to act as her own attorney and, being entirely unfamiliar with court procedures, she used the time to good advantage by going over in her mind the presentation of the case.

Time passed quickly for Ernestine. In her thoughts she was facing the august judges of the High Tribunal. Over and over again she argued her case before the imaginary court, carefully choosing her words and hearing her voice rise and fall with the proper tonal emphasis. Indeed, she was so lost in thought that it took her some time to realize that the sleigh had come to a sudden and abrupt halt.

The sleigh had broken down and they were in the middle of nowhere. The driver set to work to repair the damage, with whatever tools he had at hand. Time dragged on. The winter day was short. Soon it would be getting dark and the end of the repairs was not yet in sight. After five hours of work the driver was able to announce that he was ready to resume the journey. The cheering news came not a minute too soon. From a distance they could hear the yelping sound of hungry wolves, a not uncommon occurrence, in those days, during a rigorous Polish winter. They clambered into the sleigh and sped off to safety in the nick of time. Ernestine heaved a deep sigh of relief. After this, she said to herself, facing the judges in the court will be easy.

The Regional Tribunal of Kalish had before it a case that was unusual from beginning to end. The litigants involved were Jews, a rare occurrence in a Polish court; and the plaintiff was a sixteen-year-old girl who, when asked where her attorney was, pointed to herself. But the honorable judges were apparently so impressed with the argument presented by this young pleader for justice that they gave her a favorable decision. When Ernestine left the courtroom she was in possession of a legal document that fully endorsed her claim to her inheritance. It represented more than a personal victory to her; it was a triumph of justice. For it was not for the property as such that she had taken the drastic step of engaging her own father in litigation. It was for the *right to ownership* that she fought, and won. But now, holding the victory in her hand, what was she to do with it? During her uneventful journey back to Piotrkow she arrived at a decision. Having established the principle of justice she would now turn the property over to her father.

In the meantime the rabbi, too, had made an important decision. While his daughter was away extricating herself from a potential marriage he had made a marriage of his own. When Ernestine returned to Piotrkow her father presented her with a stepmother of her own age.

The sixteen-year-old rebbetzin and her sixteen-year-old stepdaughter, though both children of the ghetto, were in all other respects worlds apart. Moreover, the teen-age bride lost no time in asserting her authority as the new mistress of the house. The rabbi was called upon to play the role of peacemaker and was frequently torn between conflicting loyalties to daughter and wife. The situation at home became untenable. It soon became clear to Ernestine that there was no room for her and her stepmother under the same roof.

In a larger sense there was no room for Ernestine under *any* roof in Piotrkow. In the ghetto she was a heretic in a community of unbending orthodoxy; outside the ghetto she was a Jew in a world of gentiles whose anti-Semitism was not a matter of speculation, only a matter of degree. But beyond Piotrkow there was a great wide world beckoning with its infinite opportunities for growth and development. She decided to investigate that world. She took enough money with her for travel expenses and the first difficult period in a new land. She bid farewell to her father and left Piotrkow never to return again.

Chapter II

BEYOND THE GHETTO WALLS

HER DESTINATION was Berlin, Germany, which, next to Paris, was the foremost cultural center of Europe. We do not know by what means she traveled, how long the journey took and whether the trip was dull or eventful. But the answers to these questions are hardly as important as the fact that in 1827 a Jewish girl of seventeen set out alone to go from Poland to Germany and got there safely.

An even more astonishing aspect of this trip is that it took place at all. When one considers the traveler's age, sex and social status, one is inclined to wonder where this youthful ghetto-dweller had acquired the self-reliance and intellectual resourcefulness to plan and execute this daring feat. Courage and imagination she apparently possessed; but who in that narrow ghetto life gave her courage direction and her imagination wings? Who fed the fires of her curiosity and kindled within her the vision of a world beyond the ghetto walls? These are questions that demand to be answered if we are to understand better both her unorthodox behavior prior to her departure and her decision to break out of the ghetto.

But in this, as in some other instances touching on Ernestine's life, we cannot always point to a specific individual or concrete event for the answer to a vital question. We can only describe in general terms the various social forces at play in her environment at a given time, and assume that her character and mental growth were influenced by them.

In nineteenth century Poland Jews lived behind two walls—

an inner, spiritual wall which they regarded as vital to their survival as a people; and an outer, physical, wall imposed upon them by a hostile officialdom and calculated to isolate them from the rest of the nation. But no wall is apparently thick enough to withstand the penetration of new and invigorating ideas.

The spirit of the French Revolution with its concomitant quest for knowledge and change, which swept through the continent of Europe, did not bypass the ghettos of Poland. In the beginning of the nineteenth century this spirit gave rise to a new movement in Jewish life known as Haskalah (Enlightenment) which sought to raise the social and economic level of the Jewish massses.

When the Maskilim (Enlightened Ones) appeared on the scene two sects were already contending for the spiritual hegemony of the Jewish community, the Hassidim (Pietists) and the Misnagdim (Opponents). The Hassidim attracted many followers to their movement with their claim that the Hassidic rabbi was a Tzadik (A Righteous One) capable of performing miracles. The average Jew in the Poland of those days was so hopelessly entrapped in his daily struggle with misery and hunger that only a miracle, he felt, could lighten the burden of his existence. The Tzadik held out that promise to him.

Another attraction of Hassidism which brought thousands to its fold was the sect's radical departure from the established concept of piety. A Jew, the Hassidim insisted, did not have to be a Talmudic scholar or versed in Torah in order to achieve communion with God. What mattered was how one felt about God. Prayer charged with feeling, devotion and faith based on feeling, these were the surest paths to the ear of the Almighty.

The Misnagdim regarded this new approach to piety as a serious threat to the basic tenets of Judaism and sought desperately to halt its rapid spread among the people. A bitter battle ensued between the two factions, which smouldered for decades.

The proclaimers of Haskalah, although outnumbered by either of the other sects, continued to be a progressive force within the ghetto. Through the medium of satiric plays and songs the Maskilim flayed the Hassidim for the superstitions they fostered among the masses and exposed the sham of their "miracle-making" rabbis. They advocated a modernization of dress, a knowledge of the language of the land in which the Jews lived, and the learning of trades. Generally they sought to bring a breath of worldliness into the stifling ghetto life. They were opposed not only by the Hassidim; the Misnagdim, too, regarded these "enlightened ones" as advocates of heretical ideas. When it came to battling Maskilim, the Misnagdim and the Hassidim joined forces against a common adversary.

But the Maskilim persevered. Under the very vigilant noses of the Hassidim, "heretical" pamphlets and books were passed surreptitiously from hand to hand. Secular knowledge was purveyed under the counter even at the risk of social ostracism and bodily harm. Lessing's *Nathan der Weise* and Schiller's *Wilhelm Tell* were avidly read and discussed. And if a treatise on astronomy, or a manual on geography, fell into the hands of a Maskil, the ghetto wall cracked ever so widely, and for some it cracked wide enough to peer out and discover the life beyond it. However modest the program of Haskalah may have been it was part of the social ferment of a continent. And when the whole continent was marching forward even Piotrkow could not lag too far behind.

Considering Ernestine's alive imagination and intellectual curiosity it is not idle to speculate that she sought out these "heretical" books and pamphlets and read them in the seclusion of her own room even while her father, the rabbi, was swaying over the Talmud in his study. If she was at all aware of the social stirrings within her immediate environment it is only logical to assume that that awareness led her to the camp of Haskalah, the force of enlightenment inside the ghetto that opened a path to the secular world.

But there were also stirrings outside the ghetto that were of vital concern to the ghetto dwellers. A spirit of nationalism was abroad in Poland. The Poles hated their foreign oppressors and the Jews shared that hatred with them. History had taught them that the more liberal the regime the greater their chances for survival. They had a personal stake in Poland's freedom and independence. That was why many Jews fought on the side of Napoleon in his drive against Russia, in 1812. Like their Polish compatriots they saw him as the liberator of the oppressed, the man who would free Poland from foreign domination. Even long before the "Little Corsican" had turned his eyes eastward, legends had sprung up in the ghettos, especially in some Hassidic circles, about the "invincible king of France" who feared no one and brought rulers and nations to their knees.

Even though as early as 1806, when Napoleon brought his conquering armies directly into Poland, he had cynically betrayed the Pole's yearning for independence by playing off the invaders of that unhappy land one against the other to his own advantage, the Poles still cherished the dream that he would liberate them from their oppressors. So in 1812, when his armies actually marched to Moscow, a wave of patriotism swept through Poland, especially in that part of the country known as the Duchy of Warsaw which Napoleon had formed in 1807. Side by side with French, Westphalian and Polish troops, Jewish soldiers fought bravely and gave their lives for what they hoped would lead to Poland's independence.

Ernestine was only two years old when a contingent of Napoleon's retreating army overran Piotrkow and pogromized the ghetto. She was five when the victors, Russia, Austria and Prussia, met at the Congress of Vienna, formed the Holy Alliance, and redivided Poland. But whoever the ruler and whatever the division, Poland yearned to be free and independent.

The Czarist police were forever on the alert against any expression of that yearning. In 1823 the Polish poet and patriot, Adam Mickiewicz, was arrested for revolutionary activities and subsequently deported to Russia. Mickiewicz was very popular among the Polish youth and university students. After his arrest he became their symbol of Polish resistance to Czarist oppression. Inspired by the poetry and patriotic fervor of their hero-poet, they banded together in various secret societies to work and plan for the day of Poland's liberation.

Ernestine was thirteen at the time of Mickiewicz's arrest. It is not far-fetched to assume that a girl of her intellectual curiosity and innate sense of justice was acquainted with his poetry, and may even have had some contact with enlightened Polish youth where a common bond existed.

In later years she once referred to herself publicly as being "a daughter of poor crushed Poland, and the downtrodden and persecuted people called the Jews." Clearly, even in her girlhood, her vision of freedom encompassed not only her people but all of Poland.

When she arrived in Berlin she learned that although she had traveled a long way from Piotrkow the ghetto was not far behind her. Polish Jews were not welcome in Germany and the Prussian government had devised special laws to restrict their movements in that land. A Polish Jew could not remain in Germany unless a Prussian citizen and property holder offered security for him. Even then his stay was limited and he was not allowed to engage in any kind of business.

According to one contemporaneous account, Ernestine could have obtained such security had she applied for it, but instead she applied for and obtained an audience with the Prussian king before whom she argued the injustice of this decree, urging him to abolish it. The monarch, this account states, was so impressed with the eloquent presentation of this young pleader that although he did not abolish the restrictive measure he did make a concession to Ernestine. He granted her permission to remain in Germany for as long as she wanted and to engage in whatever business she desired. It was not the victory she had aimed for but it was a triumph nevertheless.

In Berlin she rented a room and began to plan for some kind of income that would provide both freedom from economic worry and freedom of movement. But where did one find so ideal a combination? She literally had to invent it.

She had observed that long after a meal had been consumed a variety of smells and odors set off by the cooking of it still clung to the apartment. Soon another meal was in preparation and a house was never really rid of unpleasant smells. Now if there were some kind of chemically treated paper which, when burned, would dispel the unpleasant odors and at the same time supplant them with pleasant ones, that would be quite a novelty, would it not? It was a thought worth putting to the test of experimentation. This she did and succeeded in inventing just such a paper.

In Piotrkow they might have laughed at this thought. Who in the ghetto was worried about smells resulting from cooking when the primary worry was to find something to cook? But in cosmopolitan Berlin this novel idea apparently had some merit. The invention was a success and her economic problem was solved. But she knew that freeing apartments of unpleasant smells would not free the world of the evils that afflict it. Her goal, though still vague and undefined, was that of the social reformer. The invention of the paper was merely a stepping stone in that direction. Now she was able to devote herself to what she really wanted to do—study life in Germany at first hand.

As she traveled through the various German states Ernestine discovered that poverty and oppression were not the exclusive monopoly of Czar Nicholas I. The German peasant was no better off than was the peasant in Poland. If he let the industrial revolution lure him to the city his lot as a factory worker was not an improvement over that of the farmer. His workday was fourteen and sixteen hours long and still he was unable to

Ernestine L. Rose
Portrait by Grozlier, 1857

A Jew of Warsaw and his Wife
Early 19th Century
Jewish Scientific Institute

A Hasid and his Wife
Early 19th Century

Jewish Children of Poland
Early 19th Century
Jewish Scientific Institute

A Jewish Coachman of Poland
Early 19th Century

THE BROADWAY TABERNACLE

Prints Division, New York Public Library

Mrs. Fawcett Mrs. Mark Pattison Mrs. Ernestine Rose Miss Lydia Becker Miss Rhoda Garrett
Women's Rights—A meeting at the Hanover Square Rooms

A LECTURE

ON

WOMAN'S RIGHTS,

DELIVERED BEFORE THE PEOPLE'S-SUNDAY MEETING, IN
COCHITUATE HALL, BOSTON, ON SUNDAY,
OCTOBER 19TH, 1851.

By MRS. E. L. ROSE.

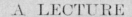

Ernestine L. Rose
with best wishes.

BOSTON:
PUBLISHED BY J. P. MENDUM, INVESTIGATOR OFFICE.
1886.

Cover of Susan B. Anthony's copy of Mrs. Rose's speech delivered
at Worcester and Boston, 1851

ERNESTINE L. ROSE

LUCRETIA MOTT

PAULINA W. DAVIS.

ELIZABETH C. STANTON.

SUSAN B. ANTHONY.

ANTOINETTE B. BLACKWELL.

ANNA DICKINSON.

OLIVE LOGAN.

THE CHAMPIONS OF WOMAN'S SUFFRAGE.

Original farmhouse at Mottville, N.Y. built 1834–purchased by
John Collins in 1843 for Skaneateles Community

provide for the basic needs of his family. Children as young as five and six years of age were sent to factories to supplement their father's earnings. They worked from sun-up to sundown. Frequently it was fear of the overseer's lash that kept them awake on the job.

Everywhere Ernestine turned she saw evidence of the iron rule of the landed aristocracy and the autocratic princes. In the eyes of the rulers the word freedom assumed a treasonable character and had to be uttered with caution. University professors were spied upon by the police and their liberal utterances reported to the authorities. A teacher whose political views were regarded as being radical was dismissed from his job. Over him hung the official threat of the Carlsbad Resolutions: "No teacher who shall have been removed in this manner shall be again appointed to a position in any public institution of learning in another state of the union." A German novelist named Fritz Reuter was not cautious enough and so he landed in prison. His sentence was thirty years. His crime? He was a member of a students' club which the authorities regarded with suspicion. When he was amnestied in 1840 he had this to say about his arrest: "What had we done to deserve this? Nothing! All we had done was to talk in our clubs about Germany's unity and freedom . . . Yet people are surprised that we became democrats! When we were imprisoned we weren't democrats, but when we came out we were democrats."

Life had not always been so oppressive in Germany. In the first decade of the century, the German people had enjoyed a brief burst of freedom. Under the impact of the French Revolution and Napoleon's onrushing armies the rulers of Germany had been compelled to grant concessions to the people in the form of significant social reforms. Serfdom was abolished, religious and legal equality was proclaimed, and the power of the clergy and landed aristocracy greatly diminished. Even the centuries-old ghetto walls came tumbling down and the Jews were accorded the rights and the dignity of full citizen-

ship. But after Napoleon's downfall and the Congress of
Vienna and its creature, the Holy Alliance of Russia, Austria
and Prussia, these reforms were all but wiped out.

As in all periods of political repression a scapegoat was
found on whom to blame the difficult times. In this particular
period the passions of the populace were inflamed against the
French and the Jews. The French were in France, but the
Jews were close at hand. And so they were pushed back into
the ghetto, anti-Jewish manifestations broke out in various
parts of Germany, and the virus of anti-Semitism polluted the
air. In this respect Berlin was not so far from Piotrkow after
all.

And so at the age of nineteen, the ghetto provincial, the
Jewish girl from Piotrkow, was a much-traveled, well-in-
formed young lady with an easy cosmopolitan manner. She
had become highly proficient in the German language and
was as meticulous in her dress as she was in her speech. Her
two years in Germany had been used to good advantage. She
was now ready to see what life was like in other European
countries. In June of 1829 she left Germany. Her first stop
was Holland. One account states that at this time she sailed
for England from Germany and was shipwrecked on the way,
but was fortunate to escape with her life and a little money.
It may be that because of this shipwreck she landed in Holland first.

Her stay in Holland was brief but eventful, that is, if talking face-to-face with a king is regarded as an event. Once
again we find Ernestine involved in what appears to be an
incredible situation. The same account that relates her experience with the King of Prussia also tells of her meeting with
the King of Holland. And if we are to believe the one, we
have no reason to discount the other. According to this account Ernestine is alleged to have become interested in the
case of a poor Dutch sailor's wife, the mother of four children, who was the victim of a gross miscarriage of justice. She

had been thrown into prison for a crime she had not committed. This, at any rate, was the sailor's claim as he tried, unsuccessfully, to obtain his wife's release. Ernestine became interested in the case and personally investigated the facts. When she was satisfied that the victim was innocent she drew up a petition in the woman's behalf and presented it to the King. It is not known in what language Ernestine pleaded with the monarch, but whatever the language her arguments were certainly persuasive. For the King ordered that the woman be immediately released, and the distraught family was reunited.

The rabbi's daughter from Piotrkow, it seems, was beginning to have a way with kings. She had met two so far and was soon to meet a third. This time, however, not in the role of pleader for justice but as spectator, an eyewitness to an historic event. From Holland she went for a short visit to Belgium and from there to France.

In the year 1830 the European continent rumbled with revolt. Even the wily and ubiquitous Metternich, with all the repressive forces of the Holy Alliance at his command, could no longer stifle the rebellious spirit of the people. The cry was "Freedom from Tyranny" and once again France led the way. In July of that year the people of France drove Charles X from the throne and erected barricades in the streets of Paris. Ernestine was in France during those historic days and mingled with the excited multitudes of the tumultuous French capital.

Together with thousands of other onlookers her eyes turned to the balcony of the Paris Hotel de Ville, where General Lafayette presented Louis Philippe as the new ruler of France. A thunderous cheer rent the air. As Ernestine watched this ceremony she turned to a friend and said, "That man, as well as Charles X, will one day have good reason to wish himself safely off the throne of France." She was not quite twenty when she uttered those words. Time proved them to be prophetic. Fourteen years later the validity of her observation was borne out by the revolutionary events of 1848.

The French revolution of 1830 touched off a series of uprisings in other parts of Europe. In December of that year Poland was in revolt. Poet Adam Mickiewicz was in Paris at the time, rallying support for the Polish nationalists. Finally he himself attempted to return to his homeland to join the insurrection. But he did not get beyond Poznan, where he was stopped by the Prussian authorities. Ernestine, too, tried to get back to Poland to fight, with weapon in hand if need be, to liberate her country from Czarist oppression. She was not permitted to advance beyond the Rhine city of Coblenz where she was threatened with arrest by the Austrian police if she insisted on going farther.

Without military aid from abroad the Polish revolt collapsed. By themselves the insurgents were no match for the Russian army. The Czar crushed the uprising and loosed a wave of terror over Poland. But Polish patriots at home and abroad kept the flame of their country's liberation burning bright. Mickiewicz returned to Paris and Ernestine went to London.

Chapter III

LONDON—YEARS OF DECISION

FROM PIOTRKOW Ernestine brought a knowledge of Hebrew, from Berlin a knowledge of German; and in London she earned her livelihood tutoring in these two languages while she herself studied English. And since bad odors are offensive in any country, she supplemented her earnings by selling the odor-dispelling paper she had invented in Germany.

While revolution swept the continent of Europe, England in 1830 was comparatively calm. But it was an uneasy and deceptive calm. There were no barricades on the streets of London, but in rural areas not far away, agricultural workers smashed machinery; a rash of minor riots broke out in other parts of the country and rumors flew thick and fast that a mass revolt was gathering momentum.

The governing aristocracy was in a grip of fear. The July events in Paris now loomed threateningly ominous before them. The fever of revolution has been known to travel longer distances than the width of the English Channel. To make sure that what happened in Paris would not repeat itself in London, the government instituted at once a series of repressive measures. But the clamor for reform would not be stilled by the clang of prison doors. A revolution more thoroughgoing and more far-reaching than that symbolized by barricades was already sweeping all of England. It was the revolution of social reforms. Labor unions and reform societies sprang up overnight. Workers turned out by the thousands to listen to radical speakers calling for universal suffrage, liberalization of election to Parliament, higher wages and shorter hours. The country was in a state of social ferment. Clearly it was a time for reformers. And it was at this time that Ernestine met Robert Owen, the foremost social reformer of the day.

He was past sixty then and she about twenty-two. It was an auspicious meeting for both of them and marked the beginning of a lifelong association. The aging reformer found in Ernestine a young and dedicated disciple and a fiery advocate of his principles; and Ernestine, standing at the crossroads of her life, found in Owenism a social philosophy that gave her both a program and direction. Henceforth Owenism was to be at the core of all her thinking in the sphere of social reform.

By the time she had met him, Owen was already a legendary figure not only in his native England but on the whole continent and on the other side of the Atlantic as well. The essence of his social philosophy which he expounded in his many tracts and public addresses is that man is the product of his environment; he is not responsible for what he is because he is what he is made to be by circumstances beyond his control. Speaking of man, Owen said, "Surround him with evil circumstances or conditions and his thoughts and conduct must become evil; while when surrounded through life with good conditions only, his thoughts and conduct must be good."

This was not an entirely new theory. But Owen put it to the test; he clothed it in the flesh and blood of practice; he consciously set out to create an ideal environment in miniature to show its beneficial effects on man. It was the success of this unique social experiment that brought him fame and recognition, and carried his ideas forward to the level of a movement known as Owenism.

Owen began his experiment in 1800 when, as a young man of twenty-nine, he stood on triple thresholds—the nineteenth century, the industrial revolution, and a brilliant career as a successful cotton manufacturer and social reformer. The three became interlocked when in January of that year he took over the part ownership and supervision of the New Lanark cotton mill in Scotland. He himself preferred the term "government" as a more fitting description for his supervisory duties in the mill. "I say 'government'" he wrote in his autobiography, "for my intention was not to be a mere manager of cotton mills, as such mills were at this time generally managed; but to change the conditions of the people who, I saw, were surrounded by circumstances having an injurious influence upon the character of the entire population of New Lanark."

Conditions in the New Lanark that Owen took over in 1800 were typical of a community that clustered around a cotton mill in the era of the industrial revolution. The workers lived in extreme poverty and squalor, in many instances an entire family sharing one room. Illiteracy was widespread, drunkenness and vice the popular escapes from an oppressive life. But nothing, perhaps, reflected more keenly the callousness of the rising manufacturing class than their inhuman exploitation of children. Children five and six years of age were compelled to put in a fourteen- and fifteen-hour workday in a cotton factory. Even the coal operators found them a lucrative source of profit. It was not unusual for boys and girls as young as six and eight years of age to work the long nightshift in the underground coal mines, hauling on their fragile backs buckets of coal weighing fifty pounds each.

A cry of indignation against this heartless treatment of children arose from many quarters. These unforgettable lines are from Elizabeth Browning's poem "Cry of the Children,"—

> "For oh!" say the children, "we are weary
> And we cannot run or leap;
> If we cared for any meadows, it were merely
> To drop down in them and sleep."

Owen built new homes for the workers; opened stores where they could buy food supplies of a better quality at reduced prices; instituted improved working conditions in his own mill and succeeded to a large degree in eliminating the evil of drinking. Consistent with his belief that, "To form the most superior character for the human race, the training and education should commence from birth of the child . . . ," Owen established the Rational Infant School in New Lanark, perhaps the first such school for working-class children in all of England.

The success of the experiment surpassed his own expectations. The fame of New Lanark spread far and wide. Sociologists, educators, and even royalty beat a path to its doors to observe Owen's social theories in actual operation.

Encouraged by the success of his experiment, he held it up as an example for others to emulate. He pleaded with his fellow manufacturers to pay at least as much attention to their human potential as they did to their mechanical equipment, pointing out that even from a business standpoint it was more profitable to have healthier and happier workers than overworked and unhappy ones. His plea fell on deaf ears. Owen recalled to them the depression of 1806 when practically all the mills and factories, including his own, were shut, yet he had continued to pay his workers a full salary for several months while the mill was idle, and his books still showed a profit in the end. But the manufacturers remained unmoved.

He then sought to ameliorate labor conditions for children through legislative channels. He prepared a bill which would forbid employers to hire children under ten and reduce the workday of children under twelve to six hours. The bill also contained a provision for a certain amount of education for these children.

Sir Robert Peel introduced the bill in Parliament and the manufacturers at once raised a clamor against it on the ground that the government had no right to interfere with their private business affairs. Indeed, so strong was their resistance to this bill that they succeeded in blocking its passage for four years. It was introduced in 1815 and when in 1819 it was finally passed it had been so revised as to render it ineffective.

In 1824 Owen abandoned his business in order to devote himself entirely to the implementation of his social theories. He conceived the idea of a model community on a much bigger scale than New Lanark and chose the New World as the ideal laboratory for the future world. In that year, when he arrived in America, he was an honored celebrity and was accorded the rare privilege of addressing both houses of Congress. From Washington he proceeded to Indiana where he bought from the Rappists, a religious sect, the Harmony community, an area of thirty thousand acres of land, for the sum of $150,000. He renamed it "New Harmony" and at his very first public gathering at New Harmony Hall he stated the reason for this purchase. "I am come here to this country," he said, "to introduce an entire new system of society; to change it from an ignorant, selfish system to an enlightened social system which shall gradually unite all social interests into one, and remove all causes for contests between individuals."

New Harmony was a failure. After sputtering along for three uncertain years, the colony expired. But the experiment was continued by nineteen other Owenite communities, some of which were initiated by splinter groups from New Harmony. But by 1830 these too had ceased to exist.

Upon his return to England in 1829, Owen witnessed a resurgence of interest in his social theories. The seeds he had planted in the New Lanark days were not lost. There were various cooperative societies and there were some leading economists who urged the inclusion of Owenite principles in the program of the emerging unions. Owen who hitherto had shied away from the trade unionist theory of achieving a better life for the workers through struggle and legislation and had hoped to establish his utopia with the cooperation of philanthropists and enlightened capitalists, now sought to combine the trade unions with the cooperative societies so as to insure "for the productive classes a complete dominion over the fruits of their own industry."

He now began to work for this plan with the zeal and dedication that were characteristic of him. He traveled, lectured, and organized unity congresses. It was during this period of heightened activity in his life that Ernestine met him. He was impressed with this young immigrant from Poland and invited her to address a meeting of workers in one of the large palladiums in London. She accepted the offer and was a huge success. Despite her foreign accent and halting English she enthralled the audience with her sincere passion and fiery oratory. Owen was so pleased with his new disciple that he called her affectionately "my daughter." This period marked the beginning of Ernestine's career as a public speaker.

In 1835 Robert Owen effected a sweeping change in the Owenite movement when on May first of that year he formed the Association of All Classes of All Nations. With the formation of this organization Owen broke whatever ties he still had with the trade union movement and swung away completely from the concept of class militancy as a path to social welfare. The Association's goal was an ambitious one. Through its program and elaborate organizational structure it aimed at the salvation of mankind by entirely peaceful means.

Though Ernestine's precise role in the formation of the Association is not known, we have it from her own lips that she participated in its birth. In a speech she delivered in Albany in 1854 she said, as quoted in the *Albany Morning Express*, ". . . I stood on the woman's rights platform before that name was known, and twenty years ago I presided over an association for the protection of human rights which embraced all colors, and nations, and sects, and I stand on the same platform still."

A separate section of the program adopted by the Association is devoted to: Religion of the New Moral World. Ernestine fully subscribed to these principles. This was also her religion—the only religion, she felt, worthwhile practicing:

The religion of the New Moral World consists in the unceasing practice of promoting the happiness of every man, woman and child, to the greatest extent in our power, without regard to their class, sect, party, country or colour.

There will be therefore no worship—no forms and ceremonies—no temples—no prayers—no gloom—no mortification of the flesh or spirit—no anger on account of religious differences—no persecutions. But friendship, and kindness, and charity for the Jew and Gentile. All that will be required by man for the Glory of God, will be to make himself and all the other living things, as happy as possible.

In the New Moral World to produce happiness with others will be the only religion of man; and the worship of God will consist in the practice of useful industry; in the acquisition of knowledge; in uniformly speaking the truth; and in the expression of joyous feelings which a life in accordance with nature and truth will be sure to produce.

Sometime between the years 1832 and 1836 Ernestine met her future husband, William Ella Rose, jeweler and silversmith. They were married in a civil ceremony. Mr. Rose was also a disciple of Robert Owen and, most likely, they had met each other in the Owenite movement. Beyond these scant facts the circumstances surrounding their meeting and marriage remain shrouded in obscurity. The only additional fact related to their marriage that we know is that the groom was three years younger than the bride.

1836 marked the end of the first decade of Ernestine's life outside the ghetto of Piotrkow. But it was more than a rounded figure in the passage of time. It was a high watermark in her continuous search for a social philosophy that would assure mankind a life of dignity and abundance. She found this philosophy in Owenism. Behind her were ten years crowded with travel, study and experiences of which the period in London was by far the most meaningful; before her was a lifetime to live and a world to remake; beside her stood a man who was not only a husband but an ideological comrade-in-arms. William Rose shared his wife's devotion to the cause of human happiness and encouraged the full flowering of her talents as a social reformer. 1836 was also the year of a momentous decision in the life of the young couple. They decided to go to America.

PART TWO: 1836–1869

"Ernestine L. Rose is one of our best."

LUCRETIA MOTT

"Ernestine L. Rose . . . —a kind of Thomas Paine among her sisterhood."

THEODORE TILTON

"Brave and fearless of all Women,—Mrs. Rose"

SUSAN B. ANTHONY

Chapter IV

ARRIVAL

I T WAS MAY, 1836. It was Spring not only on the calendar but in the very marrow of their bones. Ernestine was twenty-six, William twenty-three; their marriage was still very young and they were on the way to the youngest of all countries—America.

America was many things to many people but above all it was the land whose birth-cry was Freedom. That cry rang around the world and shook the foundations of the earth: "We hold these truths to be self-evident: That all men are created equal . . ."

In far-off Poland, in the ghetto of Piotrkow, she had heard the echo of that cry and from then on America never ceased to lure her to its legendary shores. She had traveled much before she set out for the New World. But all her travels, it seemed, were but a prelude to the present journey, a grand rehearsal for the greatest adventure of her life—America.

There would be no relatives to meet her at the landing, and yet it was not as though she were a stranger coming to a strange land. She felt a strong kinship to America and she spoke of it with a deep sense of pride. Had not a son of oppressed Poland stood at the very birth of this nation? Had not General Thaddeus Kosciusko fought side by side with General George Washington to make America possible? General Kosciusko was a military man and so he fought with musket and cannon. But she was a reformer. Her battlefields were the vast marshes of ignorance, bigotry and superstition. Against these she had rebelled all her life. But her greatest battles were yet to be fought; and her instruments of warfare—logic, wit and eloquence—were yet to be perfected.

As she stood beside her husband, scanning from a distance the slowly emerging outline of the Empire City, the long journey to America was rapidly coming to an end. Soon a new journey would begin, the journey called America.

Perhaps no other city in the world was growing and expanding as rapidly as New York in 1836. More than 1600 new buildings were erected that year alone to meet the steady rise in the city's population. One important factor in this phenomenal expansion was, of course, the continuous stream of new immigrants, most of whom settled in New York. Together with Ernestine and her husband, close to sixteen thousand new immigrants arrived there in the month of May. The population of New York City, in 1836, was well over a quarter of a million. But the space comprising the city's business and residential areas was hardly big enough to accommodate its inhabitants. Beginning at the Battery, Broadway extended northward for a distance of about three miles, while the city's distance from east to west was altogether about two miles.

In the spring of 1836 a writer complained in the *New York Mirror* that "Broadway has ceased to be Broadway. It is nearly as much of a mere crowded thoroughfare as Fleet Street, London. During the winter it has been almost blocked with omnibuses, carts, sleighs, carriages, barrows, etc., etc." He predicted that New York would some day build "tunnels" as one solution to the problem of congestion.

But prolonged traffic jams were not the city's only affliction in those days. In 1836 a visitor from nearby New Jersey spent three days in New York and was so disgusted with the city's appearance that upon his return home he dashed off the following letter to the local newspaper, the *Salem (N.J.) Post:*

The city of New York is in all probability the most filthy city in the United States. To a person accustomed to the pure atmosphere of the country, the effluvia arising from the carcasses of dead hogs, dogs and cats, (with which many of the streets are ornamented) the effect is sickening in the extreme.

Every few rods a leakage in the gaspipes emits a stench insufferable. The scrapings of the gutters and the rubbish and excrescence of kitchens, are suffered to lie in the centre of some of the principal streets, basking in the noonday sun, to the great annoyance of the inhabitants and the pedestrian.

A walk through some parts of Broadway (the pride of the Gothamites) may, without exaggeration, be compared to a promenade over a *rotten oyster-bed!* We spent three days in this promising city last week and really blessed our stars when circumstances allowed us to bid adieu to this metropolis of rubbish, stench and dandies.

How New York compared with the London they had just left behind them, or the various European capitals where Ernestine had lived since her departure from Piotrkow, we can only speculate. We do know, however, that they made their permanent home in New York for the next thirty-three years, the duration of their stay in this country.

Their first residence, as recorded in the New York directory for the year 1837, was at 484 Grand Street, now a part of Manhattan's Lower East Side—but then a fashionable residential section. When they moved to that address and where they lived the first days after their arrival, we do not know. Had they been so inclined, they could have stopped at the famous Astor House which opened for business in May of 1836. The rate was very reasonable—three dollars a week for room and board.

In the directory Mr. Rose is listed as silversmith. The shop and their residence were at the same address.

Chapter V

1836

ERNESTINE ARRIVED amidst the noise and tumult of an election year. Andrew Jackson was finishing out his second and last term in the White House and Van Buren was grooming himself to be the next president. And although Jackson was bowing out, the Jacksonian Era which he had ushered in was not bowing out with him. It was, in fact, at its height. His administration was characterized by such expressions as "kitchen cabinet," "shirt-sleeve diplomat" and "to the victors belong the spoils;" but of far greater significance for the future of America was the fact that it became synonymous with such concepts as "Jacksonian Democracy," and "the age of the common man."

It was during this period that suffrage for the white male became universal; and what until recently had been the privilege of the taxpayer and property owner now became the right of the farmer, the laborer, the mechanic. Thus, with the ballot in hand, the laborer secured a voice in the affairs of his government. It was the people who had swept Jackson into office and, after staging one of the noisiest inaugural ceremonies in the history of Washington, surged triumphantly into the White House with their muddy boots to continue the celebration. They may not have displayed their best manners when they upset the punch bowls on the White House rug, and their behavior came pretty close to the description of one socialite eyewitness who saw them as a "noisy and disorderly rabble . . . ," but who could weigh their absence of good manners against their own presence in the White House? They were celebrating not merely an election victory but the emergence of the Common Man on the stage of history. That was in 1829; in 1836 Jackson was still "a son of the soil," honest, brave and incorruptible, and the concept of Jacksonian Democracy had penetrated deeply into American consciousness.

And there was prosperity in the land. The West was expanding at a feverish tempo, doing a "land office business," and in the East factories were going up and industry was making gigantic forward strides. True, somewhere in the financial folds of the nation's economy there already lurked the panic of 1837, but that was still a whole year off and, anyway, that was to be Van Buren's headache.

In 1836 two events occurred which played a significant role in providing a spiritual base for the rising structure of the young American democracy. One was the publication of a book, the other the banding together of a group of individuals for the purpose of holding informal discussions. The Symposium, they called it.

The title of the book was *Nature,* a collection of essays by Ralph Waldo Emerson who was then thirty-three years old. The members of the Symposium were poets, philosophers, scholars and preachers from the New England area. They became known as the Transcendentalists. Henry Thoreau was one of them; Theodore Parker was another; foremost among them was young Emerson.

However diverse may have been the individual temperaments of these people and their approach to the vital questions they discussed, they were held together by a unity of purpose: to heighten man's consciousness both with regard to his spiritual potential and his social responsibility. Man, they felt, possessed infinite possibilities for growth and development; he was nature's highest expression and had within him the divine spark. Therefore his place in the scheme of the universe should be a central one.

Emerson's essays as well as the writings and lectures of his co-transcendentalists were permeated with a deep sense of humanism and reflected a strong affirmation of the dignity of man. The transcendentalists were scathing critics of those forces which in their drive for material gains trampled on man's spiritual values. They attacked everything in which they saw a stumbling block to man's self-realization. They were foes of conformity.

"I embrace the common," Emerson said. "I explore and sit at the feet of the familiar, the low. Give me insight into to-day, and you may have the antique and future worlds. I speak of the politics, education, business, and religion around us without ceremony or false deference."

"It seems so easy for America to inspire and express the most expansive and humane spirit; new-born, free, healthful, strong, the land of the laborer, of the democrat, of the philanthropist, of the believer, of the saint, she should speak for the human race."

America was not merely a young country; it was a New World, and in the center of that new world stood man in all his dignity and glory. The Dignity of Man—the Rights of Man—the Dawn of the Common Man—philosophers expounded it, reformers argued it, poets sang it, people believed in it. It was in the air.

But there was also another side to the picture of the Common Man. While the philosophers were concerned with the enrichment of his soul, he was trying desperately to keep body and soul together. In the year 1836, when prosperity was at a peak, the Common Man, the man who made the wheels go round, was toiling from dawn to dark, often as long as fifteen

hours a day, in factories that were poorly lighted, poorly ventilated and a hazard to life and limb for a wage that was not
enough to keep him and his family properly fed and clothed.
But as inadequate as were the wages of the workingman, those
of the working woman were even less adequate.

The novelist Nathaniel Hawthorne, himself a Jacksonian
Democrat, left a vivid description of a seamstress's life in those
days: ". . . this crowd of pale-cheeked, slender girls who disturb the ear with the multiplicity of their short dry coughs . . .
seamstresses who have plied the daily and nightly needle in
the service of master tailors and close-fisted contractors until
now it is almost time for each to hem the borders of her own
shroud." An alarming number of those "pale-cheeked" girls
looked to prostitution as a way of easing their economic
pressures.

Here, as elsewhere, the rising manufacturng class had no
qualms about making profits from child labor. Children under
fifteen would put in a ten-hour day and more in a dirty, ill-
ventilated factory for a mere pittance. The free public education which an enlightened democracy gave them with one
hand, a ruthless exploitation took away with the other.

To better his lot, the workingman organized and went out
on strike. For that he was hailed into court and charged with
"conspiracy to raise wages." The laws, he discovered, were
heavily weighted on the side of the employer, but experience
taught him that organization was, in the long run, the most
effective solution to his problem.

In the summer of 1836 the journeyman tailors of New York
found themselves in precisely such a situation. They resorted
to the strike as a means of improving their living conditions.
The employers responded by taking them into court, and the
court ruled in favor of the employers. But the tailors would
not be intimidated. If on the Sunday afternoon of June 5, a
few short weeks after her arrival, Ernestine Rose had taken a
stroll to City Hall Park, someone would probably have

pressed the following handbill into her hand. Headed by a drawing of a coffin, the handbill read:

THE RICH AGAINST THE POOR!

Judge Edwards, the tool of the aristocracy, against the people! Mechanics and working men! A deadly blow has been struck at your liberty! The prize for which your fathers fought has been robbed from you! the freemen of the North are now on a level with the slaves of the South! with no other privilege than labouring, that drones may fatten on your life-blood! Twenty of your brethren have been found guilty for presuming to resist a reduction of their wages! and Judge Edwards has charged an American jury, and agreeably to that charge, they have established the precedent that workingmen have no right to regulate the prices of labor or, in other words, the rich are the only judges of the wants of the poor man. On Monday, June 6, at ten o'clock, these freemen are to receive their sentence, to gratify the hellish appetites of the aristocrats! On Monday, the liberty of the Workingmen will be interred! Judge Edwards is to chant the requiem! Go! Go! Go! every freeman, every workingman, and hear the hollow and the melancholy sound of the earth on the coffin of equality! Let the courtroom, the City Hall, yea! the whole park be filled with *mourners;* but remember, offer no violence to Judge Edwards, bend meekly, and receive the chain wherewith you are to be bound! Keep the peace! Above all things, keep the peace!

On that Monday a crowd of about twenty-seven thousand people gathered in City Hall Park and burned the Judge in effigy. That evening the Board of Aldermen met informally and passed a resolution granting the mayor full authority to offer a reward for the apprehension of the author, printer, publisher or distributor of the handbill.

William Cullen Bryant, editor of the *New York Evening Post,* sided with the tailors. "They were condemned because they had determined not to work for the wages offered them!" he wrote in a stinging editorial. "Can anything be imagined more abhorrent . . . If this is not Slavery we have forgotten the definition. Strike the right of associating for the sale of labor from the privileges of the freeman, and you may as well at once bind him to a master or ascribe him to the soil . . ."

But if the slavery of the northern factory was abhorrent, how much more so was the slavery of the southern plantation? In 1836 the traffic in human beings whose skin was black had reached an all-time high. The cries of the slaves at the auction block and the crack of the overseer's whip fell, for the most part, on deaf or indifferent ears. Northern manufacturers as a class lent moral and active support to the slave owners. Most other Americans, whether because of apathy or fear of social ostracism, remained silent on the issue of slavery. There was, however, a small minority that took a forthright stand on this evil. They were the abolitionists. Their spokesman was William Lloyd Garrison, that "flintiest character amongst the New England militants."

In the first issue of the abolitionist newspaper *The Liberator* (January 1, 1831) Garrison wrote "I will be as harsh as truth, and as uncompromising as justice." Ernestine must have heard of this dealer in harsh truth long before she came here, but in 1836 she had no idea that some day they would be friends, that they would share the same platform on many occasions; and that Garrison would hold her in high esteem. In 1833 the American Anti-Slavery Society came into being in Philadelphia, and a year after that the Female Anti-Slavery Society was founded in Boston, all carrying the harsh truth about slavery to the American public. And large segments of that public carried this harsh truth right to Washington in the form of a flood of anti-slavery petitions. Congress was alarmed and appointed a committee to look into the matter. On the twenty-sixth of May, 1836, the committee brought in its report. "Whereas, it is extremely important and desirable that the AGITATION on this subject should be finally ARRESTED, for the purpose of restoring tranquility to the public mind, your committee respectfully recommends the following resolution:

> *Resolved*, That All Petitions, Memorials, Resolutions and Propositions Relating In Any Way, Or To Any Extent Whatever To The Subject of Slavery, Shall Without Being Printed or Referred, Be Laid On the Table, and That No Further Action Whatever Shall be Had Thereon.

This Resolution was adopted by a vote of 117 Yeas against 68 Nays.

The *Anti-Slavery Examiner*, published in New York, had this to say about the Resolution:

> If Congress may thus dispose of petitions on one subject, they may make the same disposition on any other and every other subject. Our representatives are bound by oath, not to pass any law abridging the right of petition, but if this resolution is constitutional, they may order every petition to be delivered to their doorkeeper and by him to be committed to the flames; for why preserve petitions on which no action can be had? . . . The men who perpetrated this outrage had sworn to support the Constitution, and will they hereafter plead at the bar of their Maker that they had kept their oath, because they had abridged the right of petition by a *resolution*, and not by law!

One of the most colorful and controversial women in America in 1836 was Frances Wright, more familiarly known as Fanny Wright. A Scottish noblewoman of striking appearance, and a protege of General Lafayette, she could have lived a life of ease and respectability within the upper circles of the aristocracy of her day. She chose instead the thorny and unpopular road of the social reformer.

She came here in 1827 and was the first foreign woman to lecture publicly in this country at a time when even native women did not dare take to the platform. She spoke from a wide range of knowledge, and with a rare force of eloquence, on such subjects as: Education, Anti-Slavery, Women's Rights. Thousands flocked to hear her.

She was not satisfied with merely talking about freeing the

Negro slave; she wanted to demonstrate with some concrete
example the possibility of his freedom. And so she bought
two thousand acres of land in Tennessee, and about forty Negro slaves from the slaveholders of that state, and set up what
she called the Nashoba Colony.

Her aim was to model it after the New Harmony colony
in Indiana as it was administered by her friend Robert Dale
Owen, the son of Robert Owen. When the Nashoba experiment failed she took the Negroes, at her own expense, in a
special boat to Haiti, where they would be free, and gave
them each a sum of money to assist them in a new start in life.
Though in a practical sense Nashoba failed as an experiment
in freedom, in a moral sense it could not be regarded a total
failure for it boldly dramatized the issue of slavery and kept
it alive before the eyes of the nation.

In 1829 Fanny Wright was passionately involved in the
municipal elections in New York where she threw her support
on the side of the Workingman's Party. In the *Free Enquirer*
which she then edited, she wrote, ". . . it is labor rising up
against idleness, industry against money; justice against law
and against privilege." The opposition vilified her and a hostile
press denounced her as an "infidel" and a "red harlot of infidelity."

But a carpenter named Whitman apparently thought so well
of Fanny Wright that he took along his young son, Walt, to
her lectures. Years later, reminiscing about those meetings,
Walt Whitman wrote: "She has always been to me one of the
sweetest of sweet memories, we all loved her; fell down before
her; her very appearance seemed to enthrall us . . . graceful,
deerlike . . . she was beautiful in bodily shape and gifts of
soul."

It would be difficult to imagine two more dissimilar back-
grounds—in terms of ancestry, environment and education—
than those of a Scottish noblewoman and a rabbi's daughter
from a ghetto in Poland. Yet, as social reformers in America,
Frances Wright and Ernestine Rose had more in common

with each other than each had with any other woman of her time.

Following in Fanny's footsteps, Ernestine became the second foreign woman in this country to speak from a public platform. Like her forerunner, she too spoke on education and anti-slavery and pioneered in the subject of woman's rights. Though each had her own individual style of oratory, both held their audiences spellbound.

Both women envisioned a new form of society as the ultimate solution to mankind's ills; a society based on the principle of human equality and a community of property. Their social philosophy was rooted in Owenism. Ernestine was under the influence of Owen the father, and Fanny worked in close association with Owen the son. For their radical views and their courage to express them publicly they were attacked with equal vehemence and ferocity. There is, after all, little difference between being assailed as a "red harlot of infidelity" and being reviled as a "woman a thousand times below a prostitute."

Judging from their respective photographs, one would not hesitate to describe Fanny as beautiful in the classical concept of feminine beauty, while Ernestine's face, though striking in its expression of strength and determination, had a decidedly masculine quality. But her contemporaries, foes and friends alike, gave lavish praise to her physical charm and spoke of her as the beautiful and exotic Polish lady.

The two women moved in the same free thought circles and, on at least one occasion, they shared the same platform. Both in the lecture hall and in print, Ernestine paid generous tribute to her friend Frances Wright for her pioneering efforts in causes they both espoused.

When Frances Wright died in 1853, at the age of 57, Ernestine Rose was at the height of her career as lecturer and social reformer. By then she was known as the "Queen of the Platform" and was a prominent leader of the woman's rights movement which was already claiming substantial gains in the sphere of woman's rights. Years later, when the time came to write the history of that movement, the editors (Susan B. Anthony, Elizabeth Cady Stanton and Matilda Joslyn Gage) themselves veterans in the struggle for woman's rights, listed three main causes that led to the formation of the woman's rights movement in America. One of these causes was the educational work done by two pioneers—a Scottish noblewoman named Frances Wright and a Jewish woman from Poland named Ernestine Rose.

In 1836 Ernestine Rose found that, with regard to legal rights, the married woman of America was not much better off than the married woman of England. Both were governed by the same feudal statute of English Common Law. Their legal status was summarized by Sir William Blackstone in the following words: "By marriage, the husband and the wife are one person in law; that is, the very being or legal existence of the woman is suspended during her marriage, or at least, is consolidated into that of her husband under whose wing, protection and *cover*, she performs everything."

The colonies had fought a war of independence and had freed themselves from British domination, but sixty years after that war some archaic relics from the Common Law of England were still on our statute books. A married woman's legal rights were practically nil. In the eyes of the law she was in a class with the minor and the idiot. If she was attacked, robbed or insulted and sought redress through the courts, her husband had to institute legal suit for her. She herself could neither sue nor be sued.

Not having a legal existence, she did not have the right to elective franchise. The state did, however, accord her the status of taxpayer. Woman was compelled to support a machinery of government in which she had no voice and to accept as binding the authority of a set of laws which affected her well-being without giving her the slightest say in the formulation of those laws. It was men who voted into office the men who made the laws that benefitted men. It was indeed a man's world.

But man claimed that woman too had her world—the home. Her home, she was told, was the kingdom where she reigned supreme. In an editorial entitled "Woman," *Godey's Lady's Book*, the most widely read woman's magazine of the time, declared that "of every domestic circle woman is the centre. Home, that scene of purest and dearest joy, home is the empire of woman. There she plans, directs, performs . . ."

But what if she wanted to prepare herself for a professional career such as medicine, law, engineering or the ministry? Such an idea would be nothing more than wishful thinking. The institutions of higher learning were closed to her on the assumption that her mind was too dense to absorb such advanced academic subjects, and she was barred from industry, commerce and politics on the grounds that her nature was too gentle and refined to partake in the rough and tumble life of these competitive fields.

If economic necessity compelled her to go to work, there were only three jobs considered as proper employment for her—domestic worker, seamstress or school teacher. But the mere fact that most of the school teachers were women relegated the teaching profession to an inferior position, and a teacher's salary was exceedingly low. Her lot as a factory worker was even more deplorable.

And if he wanted to, her husband could come to her employer at the end of the week and claim her entire salary. Legally speaking she was a minor, and a minor could not be trusted with such important matters as money.

If a marriage ended in divorce it was the husband who automatically received legal custody of the children; and if the court ascertained that the father was morally or mentally unfit to discharge this responsibility, the guardianship of the children was passed on to the father's parents—but not to the mother or her parents.

If a husband died without leaving a will, his wife and minor children could not even lay claim to all the household possessions. The lawmakers of New York State took great pains to itemize in exact detail a list of things the wife could legally call her own under these circumstances.

The following is an extract from the Statutes:

1st. All spinning wheels, weaving-looms, or stoves put up for use.

2nd. The family Bible, family pictures, school-books and books not exceeding in value fifty dollars.

3rd. Ten sheep and their fleeces, and the yarn and cloth manufactured from the same; one cow, two swine and the pork of such swine.

4th. All necessary wearing apparel, beds, bedsteads and bedding; the clothing of the widow and her ornaments proper to her station, one table, six chairs, six knives and forks, six tea-cups and saucers, one sugar-dish, one milk-pot, one teapot, and six spoons.

But what of the woman who lived in comfortable economic circumstances, the wife of the businessman or professional? She occupied a more glorified position in her "natural sphere" but only externally so. Basically, her life was shallow and her freedom illusory. True, she could afford to hand over her broom to a servant, her pantry keys to a housekeeper and her children to a governess. But this merely elevated her to the position of overseer. Her authority over her household employees was supreme, but her dominion did not extend beyond the doorstep of her home.

She had more leisure time on her hands than had her poorer sister, but to what use was she able to put it? She could while away the hours at the spinning wheel, or busy herself with embroidery, or meet with other ladies of her class for afternoon tea and complain about the inadequacy of the servants, make small chitchat or plan the next charitable function. Such activities could hardly stimulate the full development of her mental faculties. The husband was still the "monarch." It was he who had the final say over all important matters. The "kingdom" she ruled was legally in his possession even though she may have brought it with her into their marriage. She was a bird in a gilded cage, but in a cage nevertheless.

This then was the prevailing condition of the married woman in the New World in the year 1836. To Ernestine Rose this condition constituted a form of slavery, one of tyranny's many guises that had to be exposed and combatted out of existence.

But where to begin? How to move that twin mountain of deep-seated prejudice and backward laws? Until now there was only the lone, though eloquent, voice of Frances Wright. She, too, had been speaking publicly on the subject of woman's rights. All this was important; theory had to lay the basis for action. But from what quarter would that action come and in what form? These questions were at least partially answered that very same year.

Chapter VI

"WE HAVE RIGHTS ENOUGH"

O N MAY 20, 1836, Judge Thomas Herttell, formerly judge
of the Marine Court of New York and now a member
of the New York Legislature, rose in the House of Assembly
to introduce the following resolution:

Resolved, That a select committee be appointed to inquire
and report to this house, at the present or succeeding session of
the legislature, what provisions, if any, will be proper and necessary to be made by law, the better to protect the rights and
property of married women from injury and waste by means
of improvident, prodigal, intemperate and dissolute habits and
practices of their husbands.

Judge Thomas Herttell was not only a legislator, he was a
reformer as well and had publicly taken a forthright stand on
various social issues. His opponents called him "infidel" but
his New York City constituents kept returning him to Albany
as their representative. Once, when he felt that the Supreme
Court of New York State had made an erroneous decision,
he wrote a pamphlet entitled:

*The Demurrer; or, Proofs of Error in the Decision of the
Supreme Court of the State of New York, Requiring Faith in
Particular Religious Doctrines As a Legal Qualification of
Witnesses; Thence Establishing By Law A Religious Test
and A Religious Creed* (1828).

Compression was definitely not one of his Honor's more
recognizable virtues. But his lack of brevity was easily offset
by his more admirable quality of courage. In 1836 it took a

considerable amount of that quality for a legislator to introduce even this mild resolution in behalf of the married
woman's property rights. One could well imagine the astonished look on the Assemblymen's faces. This was not one of
Judge Herttell's usual crusades. This one was too close for
comfort. What was their venerable colleague (he was sixty-
five then) trying to do? Undermine the marital structure?
Disturb the harmonious balance of the husband-wife relationship?

Judge Herttell proceeded with caution. He assured his
colleagues that in introducing his resolution he did not expect
them to swing into action at once. All he wanted to achieve at
the present time, he told them, was to place it on the legislature's journals in "the hope that it may elicit public attention
to the subject matter of it." A more modest goal one could
hardly imagine. He was aware, he said, that some people
viewed with alarm any new law that tended to disturb the
status quo, and so he wanted them to know that he was not
proposing a new law, but "an innovation" on an old unjust
law. One of the evils which these bad laws were breeding, he
pointed out, was the mercenary marriage.

At one point in his speech the passionate reformer in him
had apparently overwhelmed the calm legislator and he cried
out, "The whole fabric of our present judiciary must be de-
molished and all the rotten rubbish of obsolete . . . forms and
proceedings of feudal times . . . must be swept away." These,
he said, he would replace with a judicial system that was more
in harmony with the spirit of our constitution and "with the
equal rights and liberties of the people . . ."

Soon thereafter the Legislature recessed for the summer and
the lawmakers returned to their respective constituencies,
leaving Old Man Herttell's resolution safely behind them. But
upon their return to Albany the legislators had to face an even
more determined Herttell. Having laid the groundwork with
his resolution, Judge Herttell now proceeded with the next
step. He introduced a bill entitled: *An Act For The Protection*

And Preservation Of The Rights And Property Of Married Women. The substance of the bill was expressed in five brief clauses. The sixth and final clause read: "This law shall take effect immediately after the passage thereof."

It turned out to be one of the longest "immediatelies" in the Judge's experience as a legislator. It took twelve years of hard campaigning before the bill was finally passed in the spring of 1848. When he had introduced the resolution in 1836, all that he had hoped it would accomplish at the time was "to elicit public attention to the subject matter of it." But the public was sound asleep on the subject and only a true reformer would undertake the herculean task of rousing it from its deep and apathetic slumber. That reformer was here. It was as though Ernestine Rose had come at precisely that time so that her arrival in New York would coincide with the introduction of Judge Herttell's Property Bill.

She drew up a petition in support of the bill and set out to collect signatures on it. Who, she thought, would be more eager to sign such a petition than women who had all to gain from the passage of this bill? But it was not so. She went from house to house, knocking on doors; and when she explained the purpose of her presence, the doors slammed in her face. In five months' time she had collected many calluses on the soles of her feet, many insulting remarks and all of five signatures! The men would greet her with ridicule and say that "the women had too many rights already." And the women, whether from fear or ignorance, would echo their husbands and say, "We don't want any more rights—we have rights enough."

Though she was not given to moods of defeat, Ernestine had to admit that the women's reaction to the Property Bill was "indeed discouraging, for the most hopeless condition is that when a patient loses all sensation of pain and suffering." But she did not consider her efforts a total loss because, "by depicting their condition to themselves," she said, "by holding before them the mirror of facts, it had the wholesome effect of an irritant, and roused to some extent, at least, their dormant energies."

She sent off the petition with the five signatures to Albany and then set out on a new round of house-to-house canvassings for more signatures to be sent to next year's legislative session, and to the one after that.

For Ernestine Rose, the adventure called America had begun.

Chapter VII

"AGITATE! AGITATE!"

I NTRODUCING A BILL was a relatively simple matter; securing
its passage was quite another story. Judge Herttell did
not underestimate the resistance with which the legislators
would meet his proposed measure. And so when he rose in
the Assembly to argue in behalf of his bill he had before him
a well-documented address that filled an eighty-page pamphlet.

The main weight of his argument rested on the premise
that "The common law of England, by which the property of
married women is taken from them and given to their respective husbands, is *not* and never was constitutional law in this
state." He took as his authority for this statement the state
constitution itself and quoted: ". . . all such parts of the
'common law' and such of the said acts and parts thereof as
are repugnant to the Constitution are hereby abrogated." Did
anyone doubt, asked Mr. Herttell, that this "common law"
as applied to the rights of married women was repugnant to
the constitution?

Again he returned to the state constitution: ". . . no member of this state shall be disfranchised or deprived of any of
the rights and privileges secured to any citizen thereof, unless
by the law of the land or the judgement of his peers." Was a
female a member of this state or was she not, inquired Mr.
Herttell? Let the honorable lawmakers answer that question.
And as for the law of the land, he added, let the constitution
speak for itself: ". . . no person shall be deprived of life, lib-

erty or PROPERTY without due process of law . . ." Would
the gentlemen of the Assembly say that a married woman was
not a person? Judging from what some men were doing these
days, one would indeed be hard put to say what a woman was.

Men, he said, are doing "the retailing of tape, taste [sic],
pins and needles; and men-milliners and *men-midwives* are by
no means rare characters."

But there were those who contended that if such a bill were
passed it might give rise to marital conflict, shatter marital
bliss. Such anxieties, Mr. Herttell assured them, were entirely
groundless. He reminded his skeptical listeners that in the state
of Louisiana married women enjoyed the same property rights
that the law granted to men and unmarried women. Had anyone heard that because of this fact the institution of marriage
was crumbling in the state of Louisiana?

Or take the Quakers. Here was a sect that refused to recognize the validity of the "common law," simply disregarded it.
For years married Quaker women continued to own and manage their property as they saw fit. Yet, "in no community of
mankind has there been more domestic peace, harmony and
happiness or less of family contention, disorder, demoraliza-
tion and misery, than in that of the Society of Friends."

The legislators listened politely, but Mr. Herttell might as
well have addressed himself to vacant chairs. If they were at
all moved by their colleague's eloquent plea the record fails
to reflect it. But the official *Journal* of the Assembly does tell
a revealing story. It is the story of how the first bill to secure
property rights for married women of New York State began
its long hopeless journey on the parliamentary treadmill, going from committee to committee. And when its originator
succeeded in steering it out into the open and holding it
there long enough to force a showdown, the Nays invariably
outnumbered the Ayes and the parliamentary hocus-pocus began all over again. It is a story of strangulation by committee.

During the sessions of 1838 and '39, Mr. Herttell was absent
from the Legislature and so there was no one to disturb the

serenity of the Assembly with that nuisance of a property bill
for married women. But in 1840 Mr. Herttell was back again
in Albany and on January 13, one week after the Assembly
had convened, he served notice that he would "bring in a bill
to restore to married women their rights of property, as guaranteed by the Constitution of this State." Three days later he
did introduce his third property bill entitled: *An Act for
the More Effectual Protection of the Right of Property of
Married Women, and to Enable them to Devise their Estate.*
It was also Mr. Herttell's last term in the Assembly. When he
went home to New York his bill was still pigeon-holed in
committee.

In the meantime Ernestine Rose was still knocking on doors
and with each year the door-slammings grew fewer, the number of petitions larger and the signatures more numerous.
Prejudice against the bill was still widespread and stubborn
but it no longer dominated the field. Many women became
aware of the promise that this bill held out for them and some
translated that awareness into concrete and active support for
the measure.

Paulina Wright (who later became Paulina Wright Davis)
had, independently of Ernestine Rose's efforts, succeeded in
collecting some signatures on a petition in western New
York. She now joined forces with Ernestine. Sometime afterwards Elizabeth Cady Stanton also became interested in the
Property Bill. For these three women this was the beginning
of a life-long association as founders and leaders of the
woman's rights movement.

Beginning with 1840 they took the campaign straight to
Albany, appearing before various legislative committees to
argue for the passage of the Married Woman's Property Bill.
Ernestine Rose herself addressed such committees on at least
five different occasions.

One day, support for the bill came from an unexpected
quarter. The landed Dutch aristocracy that had settled in
New York State, especially the fathers of married or mar-

riageable daughters of that group, wanted to get on the statute books a law that would grant married women the right to retain their inheritance in their own names. Their eagerness to see the enactment of such a law did not stem from any reformatory motives on their part. They were motivated by a prudent self-interest, a desire to protect their own wealth.

The rate of dissipation was high among the young men of that class and fathers frequently saw the accumulations of a life-time which their daughters inherited squandered by dissipated and irresponsible husbands. They wanted to make sure that their daughters and grandchildren would be the ultimate benefactors of their wealth. Under existing common law this was not possible. And so the wealthy Dutch conservatives and the radical reformers joined hands across the chasm of divergent interests, for the purpose of achieving a common goal.

Ernestine Ross and her co-workers welcomed that support and did not underestimate its importance. But Albany's resistance to the enactment of the Married Woman's Property Bill was so stubborn that even with so influential an ally in their campaign, they could not relax their agitation for a single legislative session.

By 1841, the sentiment in favor of such a bill had apparently become so widespread that a New York Assemblyman named O'Sullivan introduced a bill entitled: *An Act to Establish and Protect the Right of Private Property of Married Women, and in the event of Separation Between Married Persons, To Establish the Respective Rights of Parents to the Guardianship of Children.* It met the same fate as had all of Mr. Herttell's bills on this subject.

There was, however, a new element in the picture worth mentioning—the report. Apparently the petitions that the Legislature had received during its 1842 session were, in terms of their number and geographic representation, not to be dismissed with a mere legislative formality. This time, the Judiciary Committee felt that in dismissing these petitions it had to *say something* about them, lay them to rest with an appropriate funeral oration. And so the committee issued a report which may be described as a masterpiece of ambiguity and evasion.

REPORT

Of the committee on the judiciary, on the petitions to extend and protect the rights of property of married women.

Mr. O'Sullivan, from the committee on the judiciary, to which were referred sundry petitions praying for an alteration of the existing laws so as to extend and protect the rights of property of married women,

REPORTS:

That the constant pressure of other duties upon the time and attention of this committee, together with their knowledge of the hopelessness of any legislation on this subject, at the present session, under the heavy accumulation of business piled up for action on the tables of the House, has prevented their bestowing upon these petitions the consideration necessary to enable them to mature any measures to carry into practical effect the prayer they urge. They deem it, however, due to the subject not to return them to the House without an expression of their unanimous opinion in favor of a more liberal extension of the rights of married women, in accordance with the general object proposed by these petitioners, though how far it might be proper to go in securing to them the separate possession and control of property, must of course be a subject of much diversity of individual opinion. The present state of the statute and common law in force amongst us unquestionably operates in many cases to the great wrong and oppression of women, and in many respects their condition would be much improved and elevated, and the happiness and well-being of the marriage relation probably benefited, by some considerable extension and protection of their rights of property. In a change so important and delicate, in what may be regarded as the very fundamental institution of society, as it is certainly the most sacred and precious, no degree of caution can be too great, to guard against rash derangement of whatever may be good in the existing settled order of things. Consistently with this principle of prudence they yet think that something of a safe and salutary character could be done and ought to be done, to engraft at least partially upon the hard and stubborn trunk of the common law the more liberal principle in relation to this subject of which a successful precedent has long been held out to as in most of the codes of other countries founded on the civil law. The task of digesting and framing such a measure they are constrained, however, to leave to future legislation, and for the present to content themselves with asking to be discharged from the further consideration of these petitions, and that this report be printed.

[Assembly, No. 189. April 12, 1842]

If this report had any effect on Ernestine and her co-workers it was only to intensify their petition campaign. During the next legislative session when yet another Property Bill was defeated in committee, the legislators needed a ten-page report to explain their action. One of the arguments they advanced was that if married women were granted the right to their own property our marital structure would disintegrate and we would "rival France and some of the other continental nations in the laxity of our morals." And lest there be any doubt as to what the honorable lawmakers meant by laxity of morals they hastened to be a little more specific on this matter. Out there in France, they said, where married women have their property rights, they have " 'left-handed marriages' and 'mariages à la St. Jacques,' which are but open and barefaced states of concubinages, and prostitution has proceeded step by step until it is in fact legitimatized and made respectable, if not honorable . . . With these facts staring us in the face, it can hardly be said that the giving to the married woman rights, separate from her husband, has tended to elevate her in her own estimation or the estimation of others, or has added to her dignity, her purity or her usefulness."

But these dire threats to the future of our marital institution failed to hold back the steady flow of petitions to Albany. By 1845 the campaign had been carried beyond the cities and towns and into the smaller communities on a county level. Indeed, so great was the pressure on the legislature from many parts of the state that between 1846 and 1847 alone four different bills were introduced in the House, relating to property rights of married women.

The petitioners were in a bitter mood. A petition received by the Assembly on March 15, 1848, and signed by forty ladies from the counties of Genesee and Wyoming, New York, expressed the state of mind of thousands of women. It ended on this note of sarcasm:

> Our numerous and yearly petitions for this most desireable object having been disregarded, we now ask your *august* body to abolish all laws which hold married women more accountable for their acts than *infants, idiots and lunatics.*

This was the last petition recorded in the Assembly Journal. Three weeks later a married woman's property bill was finally passed.

AN ACT FOR THE MORE EFFECTUAL PROTECTION OF THE PROPERTY OF MARRIED WOMEN

Passed April 7, 1848

The People of the State of New York, represented in Senate and Assembly, do enact as follows:

I The real and personal property of any female who may hereafter marry, and which she shall own at the time of her marriage, and the rents, issues and profits thereof, shall not be subject to the disposal of her husband nor be liable for his debts and shall continue her sole and separate property as if she were a single female.

II The real and personal property and the rents, issues and profits thereof of any female now married shall not be subject to the disposal of her husband; but shall be her sole and separate property as if she were a single female except so far as the same may be liable for the debts of her husband heretofore contracted.

III It shall be lawful for any married female to receive by gift, grant device or bequest, from any person other than her husband and to hold to her sole and separate use, as if she were a single female, real and personal property and the rents, issues and profits thereof, and the same shall not be subject to the disposal of her husband, nor be liable for his debts.

IV All contracts made between persons in contemplation of marriage shall remain in full force after such marriage takes place.

About six months after this event, on October 1, 1849, Judge Thomas Herttell died. He was seventy-eight. As a personal tribute to him and as a way of keeping his memory alive in the hearts of his countrywomen, his wife, Barbara Amelia Herttell, made a provision in her will for the republication in pamphlet form of the eloquent argument her husband made before the Assembly when he introduced his first property bill in the winter of 1836-37.

The passage of the Married Woman's Property Bill represented a significant victory in the emerging struggle for women's rights. But those who campaigned for the Bill had no illusions as to its shortcomings. Years later when Ernestine Rose recalled those early winter days when she went from house to house with a petition in her hand, and of the widespread campaign that developed from those early steps, she spoke with the restraint of a realist about the hard-won Property Bill. "This was not much, to be sure," she said, "for at best it was only for the favored few and not for the suffering many. But it was a beginning and an important step for it proved that a law had to be altered and some others might need it just as much. It is a curious fact," she observed, "that as soon as that law passed every one considered it not only perfectly right, but wondered how it ever could have been otherwise!"

She spoke of the "wide field of labor" the passage of this

Bill had opened up for the reformer, which in turn had led to greater achievements and to more profound changes in public opinion. "Agitate! Agitate!" she said, "ought to be the motto of every reformer. Agitation is the opposite of stagnation— the one is life, the other death."

Another twelve years had to pass and more of the Ernestine Rose type of agitation had to be employed before the legislators granted the married women of the state a more comprehensive property bill and an equal right to the custody of their own children. This episode will be dealt with more extensively in another chapter.

Chapter VIII

LECTURES, DEBATES AND COLOGNE WATER

GOING FROM HOUSE to house and from door to door with a petition in her hand was only one of Ernestine's many interests during her early days in this country. The America of the 1830's presented a fertile and challenging field for a social reformer of the Owenite school. The married woman's property bill was but a small, though significant aspect of that challenge. She had hardly set foot on American soil and she was already lecturing on the social evils of the time and painting a vision of a new society, free from poverty, oppression and injustice.

Among the first to offer her a public platform was a group of freethinkers who had banded together in an organization called "Society for Moral Philanthropists." The main activity of the Moral Philanthropists consisted in sponsoring public lectures and debates. Their guiding spirit was Benjamin Offen, a self-educated shoemaker, who came here from England in 1824 at the age of fifty-two. He was a man of considerable intellectual qualities and was described as ". . . a master of pointed logic, unsparing wit and telling humor." He was a permanent lecturer at the society. For this he received two hundred dollars a year, not enough to live on but just enough to divert him from his shoemaking. Offen's favorite theme was a critical evaluation of the Bible and he could match his knowledge of this book with that of any clergyman.

The society's busiest day was Sunday when it dispensed

culture in three separate shifts. Lectures on theology and readings in the morning, debates in the afternoon and more lectures in the evening. The lectures were usually well attended and as many as two thousand would come to hear a debate. Frances Wright and Ernestine Rose were among the society's featured speakers.

In the summer of 1837 Ernestine participated in a debate with the rather incredible title of: "To What Extent May A Community of Property Be Applied To The Happiness Of Mankind?" Incredible, too, was the duration of the debate; it continued for thirteen weeks. In this verbal marathon Ernestine held her own throughout while new opponents kept throwing their hats into the ring, some at the rate of one a week. In describing this novel event the *New York Beacon* wrote: "Last week the Polish lady [Ernestine Rose] found a new and able opponent, logical and systematic in his reasoning and deficient only in energy; he, however, could only make a beginning, and therefore we yet expect a continued and interesting debate."

The Moral Philanthropists were mocked, derided, and denounced by the clergy and the reactionary press as a band of infidels whose avowed aim it was to undermine religion and shake the pillars of orderly society. Because they held their lectures and debates in Tammany Hall they were called the Tammany Hall infidels. The shrillest voice in this denunciatory chorus was that of James Gordon Bennett, editor and publisher of the pro-slavery *New York Herald*. One Sunday Mr. Bennett paid a personal visit to Tammany Hall and then reported to his readers: "What trash! what blockheads! what genuine asses!"

But despite these attacks on them the Moral Philanthropists continued to flourish and attract large audiences until the panic of 1837 caused a sharp drop in audience attendance and forced them to curtail their program. But they quickly regrouped their forces, changed the name of the organization, found a new headquarters and were in business again.

As far as is known the Tammany Hall infidels formed the circle of friends and acquaintances in which Ernestine moved during her early period in this country. These radical free-thinkers were her kindred spirits; people who in their own way sought to elevate man to a higher level of existence; people who had the courage to hold unpopular views, and the moral fibre to persevere in the face of persecution. The fact that they were branded as infidels only attracted her to them all the more. For she knew quite well that when the epithet "infidel" was hurled at the freethinker the odium attached to it was aimed at the social reformer.

Today the word "infidel" leads a retired dictionary life, rarely venturing beyond the confines of its definition: an un-believer; a disbeliever; one who does not accept Christianity. But in the 1830's, infidel was a busy epithet, an ugly stigma capable of inflicting serious damage to the reputation of its victim. A person thus branded could lose his job, be socially ostracized and even suffer physical harm. Originally employed by the church to denounce the faithless, the word, in a period of religious intolerance, easily became a weapon in the arsenal of bigotry. Ernestine herself witnessed how profoundly religious people who became active Abolitionists because they regarded slavery as a violation of the highest principles of Christianity were branded as infidels by the pro-slavery forces of the North as well as the South. She had before her the living example of her friend Frances Wright who had been vilified as an infidel from the moment she stepped onto a public platform. And so she too bore the stigma, not as a cross of martyrdom but as a badge of honor.

During her first few years in America Ernestine was known mainly to her fellow freethinkers and to that small segment of the public that heard her lectures in New York and in other parts of the state. To the general public, however, she was still an unknown and the metropolitan press had not yet taken note of her activities. Even the *New York Beacon*, a free thought weekly supported by the Moral Philanthropists, for some inexplicable reason referred to her as "the Polish lady" rather than by her name. Once she caused an incident which held an audience of several thousand spellbound and was the talk of New York for many days afterwards. But the *Herald* which printed a full account of the incident guessed that she was a French lady, and the *Beacon*, as usual, merely described her as a Polish lady and so the public was left in the dark and did not know that the heroine of that dramatic episode was Ernestine Rose.

That incident happened on December 14, 1837. For days in advance the New York newspapers had carried notices about a public meeting that was to take place on that day at the Broadway Tabernacle, a Congregational Church on the northeast corner of Broadway and Anthony (now Worth) Street. The purpose of the meeting was to find ways and means of improving conditions in the common schools, or public schools, as we now say. It was called for seven o'clock but so great was the public interest in that meeting that the large auditorium began to fill long before seven. It was estimated that about five thousand people crowded into the Tabernacle that evening. Ernestine was glad that something was at last being done to raise the level of the common schools. Free secular education was one of the key points in her program of social reform, and a frequent topic in her own lectures. She regarded it as a primary duty to support such a meeting and considered herself lucky to have found a seat in the gallery.

The prime mover of this assembly was J. Orville Taylor, a young educator and indefatigable worker in behalf of an improved common school system. He was the first speaker and began by telling an anecdote appropriate to the subject of the evening. One day, he said, he was walking with another person along the street when they came upon a warning written on a board:—"All dogs found on these premises will be shot." Whereupon his companion commented, "Those dogs will be badly off who cannot read." Encouraged by the audience's response he told another one: Dr. Johnson was once asked,

"Who is the most miserable man?" He replied, "He who cannot read on a rainy day." Mr. Taylor then plunged into his subject in earnest and for a full hour described the terrible condition of the common schools. "They are badly located," he said, "often upon a damp, unhealthy site; in many cases dilapidated, the door off its hinges and the casement broken in others. Upon entering I have been obliged to step back, so bad has the confined air been in places which are miserably ventilated."

Another prevailing evil of the present common school system, he said, was the low quality of the teaching; and for this he blamed, partly at least, the inspectors who were wont to hire a teacher not for his qualifications but because he was willing to work for very little. If a man offered to teach for ten dollars a month he would be hired, whether he knew grammar or not. "He will do very well for us," the inspectors would say, ". . . we can do without grammar, there are few of us who know it." And so out of eighty thousand teachers in the United States there were not even a hundred qualified for their job. Why, even a man who tended pumpkins and took horses to water got thirteen dollars a month! "As is the teacher," Mr. Taylor said, "so will be the child, and as is the pay, so will be the teacher." The result of all this, Mr. Taylor said, was that "At present nothing is taught to make a man—he is only taught to be a quack; hence we have quacks in literature, quacks in the press, quacks in medicine. And they're all quacking, quack, quack, quacking."

And was the picture any brighter with regard to education for women? Not at all. On this subject Mr. Taylor, though far in advance of other educators, fully shared the limitations of his day. One could almost see Ernestine wince as she heard him say, "As regards female schools, they are also very deficient; they do not make housewives; how few are turned out of them who can make a pudding?"

He was followed to the rostrum by Rev. Breckenridge, a prominent Presbyterian minister of Kentucky. For the first few minutes the clergyman dwelt on the subject of the evening. He told the audience that out of the 4,500,000 children in the United States a full million were deprived of education; he also told them that there was a gang of boys in New York, fifty of whom had organized themselves into a kind of syndicate for planned robbery and murder. But from this point on he abandoned the topic of the evening and launched into a violent attack on infidels. He also reviled Thomas Paine for his *Rights of Man*, which he called a source book for the enemies of religion. "But now is the time," he cried out with fervor "and the common schools are the machines through which these heaven-daring doctrines must be met and effectively put down. For if infidelity continues to prevail, as it does now," warned the minister, "we must perish and should deserve it. I for one am ready to fight the infidels with their own weapons!" And so on and on he went, tilting swords with infidelity instead of coming to grips with the real problems of the common schools. When he had finished Ernestine rose to her feet and her voice rang out from the gallery, "Will the chairman permit me to ask the gentleman who has just closed a question in relation to his remarks on infidelity?"

All heads turned upward. They saw, standing on the gallery, a young woman, immaculately dressed, her flowing black ringlets framing a handsome face. This woman dared to speak out in public; dared to question the words of a minister! A hush fell over the assembly. It was as though the entire audience were holding its breath in tense expectation of the next move.

Suddenly a loud, shrill voice broke the silence. A woman sitting near the pulpit cried, "Infidel! Infidel!" and all heads now craned forward. The two accursed words set off a wave of excitement. Within a matter of minutes pandemonium broke loose in the hall. Cries, like pointed darts, came flying from all sides.

"Throw her out!"

"Infidel!"

"Tammany Hall!"

"Turn her out!"

"Send her to Tammany!"

"Order! Silence! Chair!"

The cries were drowned out by an ever-mounting din of hissing, hooting, stamping and shouting, and in the midst of this deafening roar someone cried out, "The walls are cracking!"

But up in the gallery Ernestine was still standing, waiting calmly for the tumult and confusion to subside. To everyone's surprise Reverend Breckenridge stepped forward and asked that the woman be allowed to state her question. When the tumult died down she said, "Sir, I labor under a disadvantage, being both a woman and a foreigner. But I can assure you that only a sense of duty and a regard for the truth impelled me to rise and intrude upon this audience. I have in mind a truth and a knowledge without mystery, mixture of error and the fear of man. And now my question: will the Reverend gentleman be willing to fulfill the promise he has made, to fight the infidels with their own weapons?"

The excitement which had been checked temporarily while Ernestine spoke now burst afresh upon the animated assembly. Once again all heads turned upward, to the gallery, to catch a glimpse of the lady who actually dared to challenge a man of the cloth. And once again the clergyman stepped forward, this time to give his reply. Raising his voice to make himself heard Rev. Breckenridge said, "The principles of my Christian religion forbid me to fight with a woman." He received several rounds of applause and sat down.

Some religious publications viewed this incident with alarm. If a woman could dare challenge the words of a minister, and in a church at that, then the world was indeed on the brink of catastrophe.

Years later Ernestine herself recalled this incident at large public meetings where she was among the featured speakers. At one such meeting she told her audience that the voice which had been raised at that Tabernacle meeting "had never ceased and . . . had been echoed and echoed until it found a voice in this community."

That was twenty-one years after the Tabernacle meeting when she was a well-known public figure. But at the time of its occurrence the Tabernacle incident was just one more episode in her life as a social reformer during her first years in America when she went about quietly but busily, trying to improve the lot of her fellow beings. As she wrote to Susan B. Anthony many years later about that period, "Yet in spite of hardships, for it was not easy to travel at that time as now, and the expense, as I never made a charge or took up a collection, I look back to that time, when a stranger and alone, I went from place to place, in the highways and byways, did the work and paid my bills with great pleasure and satisfaction . . ."

But how could the wife of a silversmith afford to pay her own expenses entailed in the social reform work she was doing? True, her husband was more than a competent silversmith. His work bore the stamp of an imaginative craftsman with a flair for the creative. But it takes time for a newcomer in a new land, even if he is highly skilled in his field, to build up a dependable following. How then did the Roses manage financially in those days? At least part of the answer to this question can be gleaned from the following curious but enlightening item that appeared in the *New York Beacon* on March 13, 1838:

Mrs. Rose and Cologne Water

Mrs. Rose, an interesting Polish lady of education and great accomplishments, and who is already partially known to the readers of the *Beacon*, from the part she has taken in some liberal public meetings, now manufactures Cologne and other German waters.

This is a bold and dignified step. Cologne waters are imitated by novices; they are bad, but the manufacturers import French and German labels and have bottles manufactured in imitation of foreign bottles, and thus pass off their trash for a genuine article. Mrs. Rose has similar bottles and could get similar labels, and effect an exact imitation; but she assures that her Cologne water is genuine or the same in composition with the *best* imported, and infinitely superior to what is sold in New York as Cologne water. She therefore boldly challenges comparison and invites inspection, which deserves to be crowned with success.

Mr. and Mrs. Rose keep a small Fancy and Perfumery store, 9 Frankfurt Street, near Tammany Hall; he repairs jewelry, watches, ornaments and trifles which nobody else thinks of; while she manufactures German waters and offers them for sale, wholesale and retail, and for exportation, of course. Our fancy friends should call and see.

Gilbert Vale
Editor

It is not known how successful this enterprise was and to what extent Mr. Vale's personal endorsement of the waters helped boost their sales among friends, both fancy or otherwise; but it does throw an additional light on the many-faceted personality of Ernestine Rose. In New York, as in Berlin a decade earlier, when she was hard pressed for money she turned inventor. There, and later in London, it was her own brand of odor-dispelling paper that enabled her to study and pursue her search for a social philosophy that redounded to the benefit of mankind; and here it was her own brand of cologne water that aided her in bringing that philosophy to the towns and hamlets of America.

Chapter IX

THE DREAM THAT WAS LOST

B Y 1843 ERNESTINE ROSE had been to many points in New
York State on lecture tours, but in October of that year
she made yet another trip up-state which may be regarded as
one of the more important events in her life. Her destination
was a little village, fourteen miles south of Syracuse, with the
intriguing Indian name of Skaneateles; the purpose of her journey was to participate in the founding of a new experimental
community on a farm two miles north of that village. Despite
the bad weather, her poor health and the prospect of a long
and arduous journey ahead of her Ernestine was in high
spirits.

This was the period in American history when utopian
visionaries were busy trying to transform the New World
into the Ideal World. Their blueprints may have differed but
their goal was the same—to establish the millennium on earth,
here and now. An inspired leader, a handful of dedicated followers, a plot of land and a new experimental community was
begun. Emerson summed it up this way, in a letter to his
friend, Carlyle, written in 1840: "We are all a little wild here
with numberless projects of social reform. Not a reading man
but has a draft of a new community in his waistcoat
pocket . . ."

Knowing something of her social outlook, her dreams and
aspirations, one might say it was inevitable, in the 1840's, for
Ernestine Rose to be "a little wild" in this respect. About
twenty years earlier her mentor, Robert Owen, had been the

first to establish a community on socialistic principles in the New World. Now it was the disciple's turn to experiment with the dream of the ideal society. The fact that Owen's New Harmony experiment had failed and that in a matter of five years (1825-1830) about twelve other Owenite communities had met a similar fate did not deter Ernestine and the reformers of her circle from trying to achieve in the forties what their predecessors had been unable to do in the twenties.

The seeds of utopian socialism which Owen had planted in the 1820's may not have flowered into a single sturdy tree, but neither had they shriveled up completely. They were continually watered and kept alive by the lectures of Frances Wright, Ernestine Rose and other reformers of their type who, in turn, stimulated the imagination of less radical social thinkers. By 1840 the soil was ripe for a new wave of utopian experiments. This time the followers of the French utopian, Charles Fourier, burst upon the scene with their "Phalanxes," the most famous of which was Brook Farm in Massachusetts. Among its supporters were some of the leading intellectual figures of that time. George Ripley, Ralph Waldo Emerson, Theodore Parker, Nathaniel Hawthorne, John Greenleaf Whittier, Margaret Fuller, Elizabeth Peabody, Charles A. Dana and George William Curtis were all, to a greater or lesser degree, associated with Brook Farm. Albert Brisbane was the first to introduce Fourierism to America; the influential Horace Greeley became one of its most vocal advocates.

Although Owenites and Fourierists had much in common in their vision of a cooperative society, they differed sharply on two basic principles. Owenites believed in the abolition of individual property rights and in the benefits mankind derived from industrialization and scientific knowledge. Fourierists, on the other hand, clung to individual property rights and viewed industrialism as a great evil. They believed instead in a return to an agrarian, handicraft economy. Amidst the many Phalanxes that had sprung up in the 1840's the Skaneateles Community was the lone Owenite outpost; it was also the last.

The prime mover of the Skaneateles experiment was John Anderson Collins, a general agent for the Massachusetts Anti-Slavery Society. In the summer of 1843 the utopian socialist in him got the better of the Abolitionist. Upon completing his assignment for the Anti-Slavery Society he resigned and, together with some of his fellow utopians, issued a call to a two-day convention to be held in the middle of October on Mott-ville farm, the actual site chosen for the new experimental community. In his call Collins spoke in grandiloquent terms of his new venture. They would be laboring, he said, not "for the benefit of any particular class, but for the entire race—not to concentrate our efforts upon any one manifestation of evil, but to remove the sources of all our social discord—not merely to contend with effects but to battle against causes."

On a dreary October day in 1843 a large group of men and women came to Skaneateles in response to that call. They came from small neighboring communities, nearby Syracuse and other points in central and western New York; they came from Massachusetts, New Hampshire and as far west as Cincinnati. On the morning of October 14, they crowded into the large barn of the Mottville farm. They were disappointed that the bad weather did not permit them to hold their meeting outdoors as they had originally planned; they could have enjoyed the beautiful scenery while they talked of the beautiful life they were going to build on this very spot.

But their disappointment did not linger long. What did it matter that the barn was dimly lighted and a chill wind was blowing in through the cracks in the walls and the roof? What did it matter that some had to sit on the floor with only a layer of hay to separate them from the damp ground? These were minor inconveniences when compared to the high and noble purpose for which they had gathered. They had come here to create an oasis of brotherhood amidst a cold and selfish world; to proclaim to the entire human race that the earth could be a blooming garden of happy beings instead of a vast desert of unfulfilled lives. They had come here to lay the foundation for a model community that would show the world how man could build a paradise on earth.

Collins was the first speaker. He was on familiar Owenite ground when he said that man was shaped by circumstances and in order to free him from evil one had to free him first from evil circumstances. Here, on this land, he proposed to do just that.

He was followed by Ernestine who spoke on the subject of association. Association, she said, is written in man's nature but begins to be stifled in the cradle. To attain perfection man must resolve within himself the following three contradictory tendencies: the *selfish*, the *social* and the *universal*. Of man it must be said, "Thou shalt not be happy short of the universal happiness of every human being." The present irrational society looks on man as a stranger; the true society recognizes the brotherhood of the race. This perfection of mankind is impossible of attainment under the present society but will be achieved only when food, clothing and shelter are as free as the sunlight or the air. Then freedom and equality will abolish intemperance and slavery of every kind.

This, in essence, was what she said, as reported by the *Herald of Freedom*, a reform weekly published in Concord, N.H. whose editor, Nathaniel Peabody Rogers, attended the convention. The reporter concluded his account by saying that the enthusiasm created by Ernestine's speech "was truly astonishing; it was the breaking forth of humanity in a concentrated form."

She spoke again that evening, appealing for funds with which to build the new community. "The declaration that 'man is born free and equal,'" she said, "is a dead letter until now. He is born free and equal, he dies free and equal, but he does not live free and equal."

Whatever the occasion for a gathering may have been, Ernestine never missed the opportunity to speak on the subject which was the major interest of her life—woman's rights. Here, too, she appealed to the women to become aware of their degradation and their rights. According to the *Herald of Freedom* report, "It was a most effective appeal and met its response in the tears of the whole audience."

When the convention settled down to tackle practical matters that were basic to the existence of the new community, Collins and some of his friends displayed the characteristic weaknesses of the utopians, which eventually led to the undoing of the experiment. Even so practical a matter as the land deed came in for a lengthy discussion. Should a deed be taken out for the community farm or not? Collins and some others were against taking out a deed. They argued that since they were against ownership of private property the possession of a deed would represent a violation of that principle. Another reason for their reluctance to take out a deed was that it would bring them into direct contact with the law. They regarded the governmental structure as an instrument of oppression; therefore, resorting to any of its branches, even on the level of taking out a property deed, would be tantamount to recognizing its validity. Ernestine sided with those who argued that this was carrying principle to an impractical extreme. They succeeded in swinging the convention over to their point of view.

But deed or no deed, Skaneateles, as a community experiment, was doomed from the very start. The seeds of its failure were inherent in its program. The idea that several hundred individuals could erect a successful model for an ideal society to be emulated by the rest of the world was, at the most, naive. The world was either skeptical of, or downright hostile to such experiments. Even the respectable Fourierist Phalanxes who had the active support of some of the leading literary figures of the day did not last very long; the chances of survival for an Owenite community were even slimmer.

The Community's views on government, religion, property and marriage, as formulated by Collins, were so far out of step with prevailing concepts of these basic issues that many in the nearby communities turned their backs on these utopian visionaries; nor did all within the experimental community see eye to eye on these principles. The least troublesome of the Articles was probably the one on Dietetics, which stated that "a vegetable and fruit diet is essential to the health of the body and the purity of the mind, and the happiness of society . . ."

Under pressure from without as well as within, Collins revised his statement of principles but in his new version which he called Creeds he swung to the other extreme. "Our principles are as broad as the universe," he said, "and as liberal as the elements that surround us . . . We estimate the man by his acts rather than by his peculiar belief." But despite these vague generalities, aimed at pleasing everybody and offending no one, the neighboring communities continued to regard Skaneateles as a "No-God," "Free-Love" community; and dissension within the ranks of the Community itself continued to plague the experiment. After three years of strains and stresses it collapsed.

For Ernestine those were a busy three years. In addition to all her other activities she worked for the new project with characteristic zeal and dedication. One month after the Skaneateles Community was officially established she went out on the road with John Collins, lecturing and holding community meetings for the purpose of rallying moral support and raising funds for the infant Skaneateles experiment. One such meeting was held at the home of Lucretia and James Mott, the leading Quakers of Philadelphia. After several weeks of traveling together, Collins returned to Skaneateles while Ernestine continued to be the Community's roving ambassador.

Between December 1843 and April 1844 she saw very little of home and husband. She was on the road lecturing and on a single topic: social reform. Her main point of concentration that winter was Massachusetts, a Fourieristic stronghold with Brook Farm as its model community. She spoke several times at Amory Hall in Boston where such celebrated figures as William Lloyd Garrison, Wendell Phillips, Ralph Waldo Emerson and Charles A. Dana lectured at its Sunday Forum.

She also spoke at the famous Faneuil Hall and the Marlboro Chapel. On several occasions Collins came from Skaneateles to share the platform with her and supplement her talk with an up-to-the-minute account of life in the experimental community. Her last lecture in Boston was announced for April 3, and she had been home hardly a month when Collins issued a call for a four-day Social Reform Convention to be held in Boston, beginning on May 28, with Ernestine Rose featured as one of the main speakers. In the summer of 1844, together with her husband, she helped in the formation of the New York Universal Reform Society whose main objective was to pour new life blood into the tottering Community. William E. Rose was its vice-president and Ernestine Rose its treasurer. Since the advent of Skaneateles social reform was for Ernestine more than a topic for a lecture; it was a veritable crusade.

But despite all these efforts to keep it going the Skaneateles experiment failed in May 1846. Oddly enough, in a strictly financial sense, the Community was very much in the black at the time of its demise. It was estimated that the property was worth twice as much as when it was bought, and the Community was able to pay off all its debts. Why then did it fail? The answer to this question is perhaps best formulated by Morris Hillquit in his *History of Socialism in the United States*. ". . . the cause of failure of all communistic experiments," Hillquit wrote, "is one—the utopian character of the fundamental idea underlying their existence."

With the end of the Skaneateles Community, also came the end of John Collins as social reformer. Eventually he made a public statement in some newspapers that he was no longer involved in social reform undertakings. One socialist paper chidingly remarked that he now embraced "the decencies and respectabilities of orthodox Whiggery."

But Ernestine Rose continued to travel the "unrespectable" road of social reform. Even as the Skaneateles Community was in the last throes of its existence, Ernestine was conquering new territories for her advanced theories of society and woman's position in it. In March 1846, two months before the collapse of Skaneateles, she toured the state of Michigan, lecturing in Detroit, Ann Arbor and other cities. She spoke twice at the Hall of the House of Representatives on the subjects: "Science of Government" and "Antagonisms in Society." Then the House of Representatives passed a special resolution expressing high praise for her oratorical skill, eloquence and grace of delivery. The women of Michigan never forgot her visit to their state. Years later they reported: "The agitation on the question of woman suffrage began in this state in 1846 with the advent of Ernestine L. Rose."

And there was still the Married Woman's Property Bill to be won in her own state; and political equality to be won for all the women of America; and the scourge of slavery to be wiped off the face of the land. The road of social reform seemed to be a long and unending one. Somewhere along this road she lost a dream by the intriguing Indian name of Skaneateles. It was a sad and painful loss, but there was no time for looking back and no time for tears.

Chapter X

INFIDEL CONVENTION

O N SUNDAY, MAY 4, 1845, an unusual event took place in
New York City. Over two hundred infidels from fourteen states gathered at Coliseum Hall, 450 Broadway, for their
first national infidel convention. They had come from as far
south as Alabama, as far west as Indiana and as far north as
Vermont. In addition to the delegates there were also some
two hundred guests present. The atmosphere in the hall was
charged with an air of expectancy and exultation. Never before had so many of the persecuted, the vilified, the misunder-
stood been assembled under one roof. For the moment at least
the loneliness of isolation fell away from them and they were
intoxicated with the strength of their numbers.

As Ernestine looked about the crowded room she saw many
familiar faces. Seated with the large delegation from Massachusetts were two of her very good friends: Josiah P. Mendum, publisher of the *Boston Investigator*, the most influential
free thought weekly in the country, and its editor, Horace
Seaver. And there, with the New York delegation, was Dr.
Samuel Ludvigh, editor of the German weekly, *Die Fackel*
(The Torch); and sitting not far from him was another editor,
Gilbert Vale, of the *New York Beacon*. In fact, all the luminaries of the free thought movement were present at Coliseum
Hall that morning. But the most distinguished delegate of all
was the delegate from England, the seventy-four-year old
veteran of social reform, Robert Owen. For Ernestine, more
than for any one else in that hall, his mere presence was an

added reason for the prevailing mood of elation. Here, sitting beside her, was her friend and teacher, the man who, next to her father, had had the most profound influence on the entire course of her life!

And this time the reporter for the *New York Herald* did not have to guess who she was. In his account of the first day's proceedings he wrote, "Seated by our side was the venerable Robert Owen, and the highly accomplished, talented and intellectually beautiful Mrs. Rose."

Most of the morning and afternoon sessions were devoted to the usual convention business—the election of various committees and officers. Ernestine became a member of the committee to draft the preamble, constitution and by-laws of the new organization about to be formed. Thomas Herttell, former New York State Assemblyman and author of the first married woman's property bill, was elected president of the convention. But the seventy-four-year old jurist was too ill to attend the opening session; he did come the following day to deliver the principal address. The minutes of the convention show that at the evening session "the large hall of the Coliseum was crowded to suffocation."

Robert Owen was the first speaker. The essence of his remarks was that "truth without mixture of error" . . . and "knowledge instead of mystery" would raise society to a higher level. He was followed to the rostrum by Ernestine Rose who, in the short space of a few paragraphs, expressed the basic tenets of her social philosophy with rare clarity and force.*

The next day the *New York Herald* began its report of the first day's proceedings as follows:

> It was a lovely Sabbath morning yesterday—the sun shone in all its splendor, and the whole earth seemed to rejoice with great, unbounded gladness, and send forth a hymn of thanksgiving and praise in token of its joy.

---

* For text of speech see Appendix pp. 279-80.

There was one spot, however, in this vast metropolis, where an assemblage was congregated for far different purposes . . . with the avowed object of upsetting all earth's theological systems— all sanguine of success—all eager to proceed to the business of demolition.

But the reporter engaged in a little demolition of his own when sneeringly, and with obvious malicious intent, he quoted Mrs. Rose's remarks in dialect, changing the th's into d's, the d's into t's and the w's into v's. He did report accurately that "Mrs. Rose concluded and sat down amid thunders of applause."

Very early in the proceedings the convention ran into a stumbling block which was nearly its undoing. It was a question over names. There were some delegates who, for very practical reasons, did not want their names publicly associated with an infidel convention even though they had traveled long distances to attend it. The chairman, a Mr. Bell from Kentucky, summarized the touchy problem clearly and succinctly. "There were circumstances surrounding many infidels," he said, "which no spirit of independence could surmount; and when they saw their wives and little ones depending for bread upon their own cowardice, they would shrink from avowing their real sentiments until a more favorable opportunity." The convention found a compromise. It voted, "that members of the convention who wish to have their names suppressed have leave to withdraw them forthwith, and that all names not so withdrawn shall be regarded and disposed of as the property of the convention."

But the matter was far from settled. Now another problem arose, the problem of finding a suitable name for the newly emerging organization. One delegate proposed that the word "Infidel" be eliminated from the organization's name altogether because it "conveyed unpleasant and even *false* impressions to many." He suggested the word "Materialist" as a substitute.

The committee to draft the preamble, constitution and by-laws, of which Ernestine was a member, had also grappled with this question and came up with "The Society for the Promotion of Universal Mental Liberty." So now there were some who objected to the absence of the word "Infidel" in the name. Outspoken among these was Dr. Ludvigh who said, "I am from Europe and fear nothing in the shape of hard names . . . Let us take the name 'Infidel' and be known by it . . . I prefer wisdom and courage to cunning and prudence."

The convention was now hopelessly divided between those who were for, and those who were against the use of the term "Infidel," with each side clamoring for attention, eager to make itself heard. Proposals and counter-proposals came flying from all parts of the hall. Why not "Free Enquirer," suggested one? "Naturalist" called out another. And one enthusiastic Infidel-ite cried out, "Give us the name Infidel and we . . . could soon make it so honorable that the other sects would seek to steal it from us." At one point Robert Owen took the floor and said:

> If you wish to remain an isolated, insignificant sect, keep your name—*it means nothing*. But if you wish for progress, change it to its true signification. If you belong not to this Society for the Promotion of Universal Liberty, then I belong not here; for I claim the right for myself and race to express my convictions. The title of the Committee will convey this to the world. We have had repulsion long enough. The name Infidel is also repulsive. Many would wish to join your society, but cannot because they will not connect their wives and children with an Infidel society. If you take the name proposed by the Committee, 10,000 will flock to you. Your progress would astonish the world. I am desirous you should become the nucleus of the world for progress of society. If you refuse to constitute this nucleus, we must form another Society.

Despite the weight of prestige behind Owen's remarks the speaker that followed him insisted on retaining "Infidel." In no time he was opposed by another delegate who was convinced that "Mentors" was the best possible substitute. It was getting late and still there was no solution in sight. A motion

to adjourn until 7 o'clock in the evening came as a welcome
relief.

When the convention reconvened it faced the discouraging
prospect of seeing an entire evening session lost on the discussion over a name. To forestall this possibility it was voted,
"that the discussion on the 'name' shall close in one hour."
The hour was fast slipping away and there was no decision in
sight. A motion was made and voted on, "to call the list of
delegates upon the question, and that a majority of all the
names shall be necessary to a choice."

Result: no choice. "Society for the Promotion of Universal
Mental Liberty" polled 50 votes; "Infidel," 46; and sundry
others, 7. The chair announced that the hour was up and the
convention voted an additional half hour to continue the discussion. In the meantime Ernestine Rose had undergone a
change of mind.

> "It might seem strange," she said, "that a member of the Com-
> mittee, in favor of the largest mental liberty, should decide
> against the name of the Committee. But after considering all the
> bearings of the names, it seems that the name given us in
> derision is, after all, the best, if only for this reason—to show
> the world that even nicknames can be lived down, or made
> respectable and fashionable; perhaps society may then say, 'It
> is no use to give them nicknames for they adopt them and
> make them honorable.'

> "We are not unfaithful to our principles; and if society will let
> us move on, it will soon see the inconsistency of applying any
> nicknames. I have a preference for the name of the Committee,
> but it seems a violation of the trust of those friends who had
> been sent here to form an Infidel Convention and Society, and
> why? That it may be a name for all Reform. I do not wish to
> wear the name; but if given to us, let us adopt it and make our
> enemies ashamed of the hour they ever applied it to us. There is
> a false meaning and a true meaning. I know of no reason why
> I should now be ashamed of it."

Horace Seaver of the *Boston Investigator* sided with Ernestine. Already there were some who wanted to take the

floor and oppose him. Just then a New York delegate saved the day (or was it the night) by suggesting a compromise: "The Infidel Society for the Promotion of Mental Liberty." With a sigh of relief the convention adopted this name by an overwhelming majority.

With the vexing problem of the name out of the way, the convention was at last able to turn its attention to other business. It adopted a Preamble, a Constitution and ten Axioms. The first axiom read: "Unlimited and inviolable freedom of thought can alone prevent prejudice and insure peace and harmony of the mind."

By coincidence the American Anti-Slavery Society was celebrating its eleventh anniversary at the Broadway Tabernacle on the last day of the infidel convention. The chairman of the convention took time out from his duties to go to the Tabernacle and address the Anti-Slavery Society. Although it was customary for that Society to begin its anniversary meetings with the reading of a portion from the Bible, they saw nothing incongruous in receiving greetings from an infidel convention.

Not every Abolitionist was an Infidel, but it was a rare Infidel who was not an Abolitionist. And in the eyes of the pro-slavery advocates they were all a bunch of Infidels anyway.

In the fall of that year Ernestine's health broke down. The strain of her many social reform activities had finally taken its toll. She was badly in need of rest and was advised to go somewhere far away from the pressures of the petition campaign, the Skaneateles Community and the lecture platform. She chose Louisville, Kentucky, as the ideal place for such a vacation.

But Ernestine could not conceive of herself as traveling all the way to Kentucky for the sole purpose of improving her health when all along the way there were so many communities waiting to be enlightened on such vital questions as education, slavery, the Skaneateles Community and woman's rights. And so she made many stops enroute to her destination to lecture on these subjects. This, no doubt, gratified the social reformer in her but it must also have further undermined her health.

The journey was an ill-fated one. Out West she contracted the ague, a form of malarial fever which threw its victim into a state of hot and cold sweating fits, or shivering chills. As soon as she was able to, she started homeward but got only as far as Buffalo. There she became so violently ill that she could not continue her journey. The fever had settled on the brain, producing a state of delirium. For a while she hovered between life and death, and hope for her recovery was very slim. Finally she rallied, thanks to the excellent care of a Quaker family who had opened their home to her, and a devoted friend from Syracuse who had come especially to Buffalo to nurse her back to health.

As late as August, 1846, the ague was still plaguing her. She was compelled to turn down an invitation from friends in Boston to attend a celebration in honor of Abner Kneeland, a former editor of the *Boston Investigator*. In the letter expressing her regrets she wrote, "the nature of that most annoying complaint is such that the least over-exertion, or excitement, will invariably bring it on again . . . it requires great caution to prevent a relapse. The journey to Boston would, I have no doubt, do me good . . . But I *dare* not trust myself among you—*your spirit* is too stirring not to move mine when among you . . ."

In December of that year her friend J. P. Mendum, after visiting her, wrote back to Boston: "Mrs. Rose is still a victim of the fever and ague, which she formed an acquaintance with at the West; but she is not confined to the house." Despite her weakened condition caused by this disease, her most active and vital years still lay ahead of her.

Chapter XI

ALMOST TARRED AND
FEATHERED

FEW KNOWN ABOLITIONISTS ever ventured below the Ma-
son-Dixon line except when on a mission for the Underground Railway, in which case their identities and activities
were cloaked in utmost secrecy. Vigilance Committees who
took the law into their own hands had sprung up all over the
South. There was a price on Garrison's head. Senator William
C. Preston of South Carolina once said, "Let an Abolitionist
come within the borders of South Carolina; if we catch him,
we will try him, and notwithstanding all the influence of all
the governments on earth, including the Federal government,
we will hang him."

In 1847 an Abolitionist did come within the borders of
South Carolina and she did not keep her whereabouts a secret.
That was Ernestine Rose. She went there for her health and it
nearly cost her her life because even on slave territory she
would express herself freely on the evils of slavery.

People came to inquire why she had come to Charleston.
Her reply did not satisfy them. A young lawyer who stayed
at the same hotel where she stopped engaged her in a conversation about slavery.

"We don't want the North," the young man said, vehemently, "we are independent of the North, and we can afford
to dissolve the Union today."

Ernestine listened for some time and when he had talked

himself out, she gave him the following lecture: "I do not wish to have the Union dissolved," she said calmly; "I would like to stick to you because you need us. Wherein could you be independent of the North? Who are your teachers and professors? Northern men. Who weaves your cloth and bedecks you? Northern men. Just remember, my dear sir, that from your head to your feet you were manufactured at the North, directly or indirectly. From him who first taught you your alphabet to the professor who gave the finish to your education and taught you to make black appear white, they were all Northern men. Nevertheless, I don't want to see the Union dissolved. For as long as we are united we have an influence over you; indeed, you stand so greatly in need of us that I should be very sorry to leave you."

The young man shook his head unhappily. He had spoken to Northerners before, that is, Northerners visiting the South, and they all seemed to profess some sympathy to the South's point of view on the issue of slavery. But this Northerner was different. A very peculiar Northerner, indeed.

Another Southern gentleman had the misfortune to ask her what she thought of the South, particularly how she viewed South Carolina; she did not hesitate to tell him.

"I am sorry to say," she replied, "that you are a century, at least, behind in the means of civilization."

He wanted to know why she thought so, and she said, "The only civilization you have exists among your slaves; for if industry and the mechanical arts are the great criterion of civilization, then certainly the slaves are the only civilized ones among you because they do all the work."

The gentleman thought she was maligning the South. Ernestine thought she was merely stating a fact. "In Charleston and Columbia," she pointed out, "the slaves are painters, glaziers, carpenters and masons; in fact, all the trades are filled with slaves. The owners cannot do any kind of manual labor because it is disgraceful, so that everything is done by slaves."

The man lost his temper and with it his gentlemanly propriety. "Lady," he said, "you can thank your stars for being a woman."

"I always thank my stars for being a woman," she retorted quickly, "but I am curious, Sir, why do I have to thank my stars in this particular instance?"

"I'll tell you why," he said; "our state has made provisions for many cases, but not for all. For instance, when we catch a good Abolitionist we give him a coat of tar and feathers."

"Well, Sir," she said, "I am an Abolitionist in the fullest sense of the word, and be I a woman or not, you are so exceedingly lazy and inactive here that it would be an act of charity to give you something to do, were it even to give me a coat of tar and feathers. My dear Sir, you have to thank yourself for this altercation; I did not begin it; I knew your weak spot and did not wish to touch it. You thought that I would be a coward and recreant in my sentiments. I tell you, Sir, that if I had never been an abolitionist before, I would have become one here, and you would have helped to make me one."

The gentleman, too furious for words, now strode off in a fit of anger. But his threat was almost made good. Ernestine Rose came very close to being tarred and feathered.

What she saw of slavery at first hand by far exceeded the horror and revulsion of all that she had known of this evil prior to her visit to the South. Indeed, so shocked was she by what she saw that she placed a notice in a Charleston newspaper inviting the public to a lecture.

The very idea of a woman speaking in public was enough to attract a large audience. But the public that came to satisfy its curiosity at seeing a woman on a lecture platform did so at the expense of being subjected to a most vigorous attack on the institution of slavery. Had the hated Mr. Garrison himself addressed them on this subject he could not have shocked them more. The audacity of this Northern abolitionist so stunned her listeners that for a while it completely immobilized them. When they awakened to what had been done to them, the speaker's sex probably saved her from being strung upon the nearest tree. As it was, it took some swift action on the part of influential friends to get her safely out of Charleston.

Chapter XII

"INSURRECTION" AT SENECA FALLS

THE YEAR 1848 was crowded with events of national and international significance. Europe was once again rocked by violent revolution and, once again, it was France that sparked the conflagration which spread to most of the continent. Ernestine Rose hailed the uprising in France as ". . . the pure and magnanimous spirit of an oppressed nation struggling for freedom."

In this country a new president, General Zachary Taylor, was sent to the White House; a new state, Wisconsin, was admitted to the Union; and an old issue, slavery, was hotly debated by the Senate and the House. The debate centered around the Clayton Compromise; the Senate passed it, the House tabled it. Another item of interest that captured the nation's imagination that year was the news that gold had been discovered in Sacramento, California. For Ernestine Rose, 1848 was a year of triumph. The battle for the Married Woman's Property Bill which she had initiated twelve years earlier was at last won.

But in the quiet village of Seneca Falls, N. Y.—population 1500—all these important events were, for a few weeks at least, overshadowed by a major event of its own. On July 14, the villagers were startled out of their complacency by a strange item that appeared in their semi-weekly journal, *The Seneca Falls Courier*. It was a call to a woman's rights convention "to discuss the social, civil and religious condition and rights of woman. . . ." The event was to take place in less than a week (July 19 and 20) in Wesleyan Chapel. The first day of the convention was reserved "exclusively for women . . . ," but the second day was open to the general public which was invited to hear Lucretia Mott from Philadelphia, "and other ladies and gentlemen."

For the next five days the citizens of Seneca Falls did not lack a topic for conversation. A woman's rights convention! And of all places, in their own village! The call appeared unsigned because its authors did not dare to sign it, but the villagers guessed that their own Elizabeth Cady Stanton probably had a hand in it. Her radical views on such issues as temperance and slavery were well known in those parts. But they hardly suspected that the strange event they were discussing would give their village a permanent niche in history; for what was soon to take place in Seneca Falls was the first woman's rights convention ever to be held, not only in the United States but anywhere in the world.

In the meantime Lucretia Mott, her sister, Martha C. Wright, Elizabeth Cady Stanton, Mary Ann McClintock and Jane Hunt, were trying to formulate a program for the convention and were having a hard time of it. They had no previous experience in such matters and the problem of encompassing the vast subject of woman's rights in clear and comprehensible terms seemed staggering. For long hours they argued, debated and discussed; and out of these deliberations emerged a happy thought—they would pattern their declaration of principles after our own Declaration of Independence. The framework was there, tried and tested by time, and with some changes most of the words were there too.

> We hold these truths to be self-evident: that all men *and women* are created equal; . . ."

The history of mankind is the history of repeated injuries and usurpations on the part of man *toward woman*, having in the direct object the establishment of an absolute tyranny over her. To prove this let the facts be submitted to a candid world.

They listed eighteen such facts and put at the head of the list what they regarded as the main grievance.

He [man] has never permitted her to exercise her inalienable right to the elective franchise.

They called their document a Declaration of Sentiments and sighed with relief. With a genuine sense of modesty they viewed their accomplishment as being the best under the circumstances. They would have been astonished to hear that they had written a program for the woman's rights movement that was to be valid for the next two generations. Ernestine Rose regarded this Declaration as "no less great, noble and important, than the first honorable Declaration of Independence . . . even more farsighted and sublime."

These accolades came later; but they were desperately in need of some cheering word now, at the time of their greatest trial. Even at this late hour they were beset by doubts and anxieties: had they, perhaps, gone too far? had they, perhaps, acted too hastily? Who were *they* to call a woman's rights convention?! Oh, if they could only call off the whole affair even now, how relieved they would be! But the morning of the nineteenth was already here and there was nothing else to do but to go and answer their own call to a woman's rights convention.

On the morning of the nineteenth a large crowd had gathered in front of Wesleyan Chapel, waiting impatiently for someone to open the door. No one had apparently made arrangements for that detail and so someone had to climb in through the window and open the door from the inside. Another detail the women had overlooked was that of the chairman. Not having had any previous experience with the running of a convention it did not occur to them, until the last minute that they needed a chairman. The problem was solved on the spot when Lucretia Mott prevailed upon her husband, James, to take the chair. Those in the audience who had come to scoff—and there were many such—were no doubt amused by the spectacle of seeing a woman's rights convention presided over by a man. But once the meeting got underway even the scoffers were swept along by the earnestness of the occasion.

The Declaration of Sentiments, read by Elizabeth Cady Stanton was, after a thorough discussion from the floor, adopted unanimously, but the resolutions did not have such smooth sailing. The main stumbling block was clause number nine which read as follows:

> *Resolved*, That it was the duty of the women of this country to secure to themselves their sacred right to the elective franchise.

There were some in the hall who hesitated to endorse this clause on the grounds that the people were not yet prepared to take so radical a step as to grant woman the right to vote. But Elizabeth Cady Stanton held to the view that unless woman attained an equal voice in the shaping of the country's laws the best-sounding resolutions in her behalf would not be worth the paper they were written on. The tide of the general sentiment, however, seemed to be against her. Even Lucretia Mott wavered on this point. For the moment it seemed as if this key clause would be voted out of the resolutions.

At this critical juncture in the debate the delegate from Rochester asked for the floor. He was Frederick Douglass, who only ten years ago had been a slave in Maryland and was now the respected editor of the abolitionist weekly, *The North Star*. Douglass made an eloquent plea in behalf of woman's right to the elective franchise. He was the only delegate in that hall to give his unequivocal support to the ninth clause. When the resolution was finally taken to a vote it was adopted in its entirety.

Toward the close of the two-day proceedings there was enthusiasm in the hall and a feeling of good will for the cause that had brought this meeting together. One hundred people, thirty-two of whom were men, endorsed the Declaration by signature. All agreed that the convention was a huge success; and the citizens of Seneca Falls returned to their usual tasks somewhat enhanced by the feeling that something important had happened in their midst and that they had been privileged to be part of it.

Then came the shock. The initiators of the convention were still basking in the warm glow of their first triumph when the reaction of the press burst upon them with the fury of a violent storm: "Revolution . . ." "The Reign of Petticoats" "Insurrection Among Women." These were some of the shriller warnings sounded by newspapers in various parts of the state. The *Albany Advocate* went so far as to envisage the complete collapse of the world. It stated grimly that since the advent of Seneca Falls ". . . the order of things established at the creation of mankind, and continued six thousand years, would be completely broken up . . ."

And there were brickbats from other quarters too, brickbats wrapped in the clerical tissue of sanctimony. The clergy took Seneca Falls as a topic for a sermon and intoned, "Blasphemy!"

The organizers of the convention were stunned by this violent reaction; and the signers of the Declaration were confused, bewildered and frightened. Many began to withdraw their signatures. They wished to forget the entire affair as though it were a bad dream.

But to many women around the country the event at Seneca Falls was a hope and an inspiration. In an isolated area in Western New York a woman named Emily Collins was so inspired by what had happened in that small village that she called together some of her women neighbors and formed the Equal Suffrage Society, the first organization of its kind.

It is one of the ironies of history that a reform movement which embraced half of the country's population and revolutionized the relationship between men and women for generations to come was launched in a small village and with very little advance preparation, almost by accident, one might say. Had Elizabeth Cady Stanton not settled with her family in Seneca Falls, and had her good friend, Lucretia Mott, not come to nearby Auburn that summer to visit her sister, Martha Wright, and attend an annual meeting of Friends in that part of the state, the first woman's rights convention would have had to wait for a more auspicious time to make its bow to history. But that it had to come sometime there is no doubt, for in its deepest sense the Seneca Falls event was rooted in the historic necessity of righting an age-old human and social wrong; and though chance and coincidence played their role, its immediate origin could be traced to another important event that occurred on another continent and in another summer eight years earlier.

In June 1840 Abolitionists from various parts of the world had gathered in London, England, to attend a World's Anti-Slavery Convention. With the American delegation came several duly accredited women delegates, one of whom was Lucretia Mott, 47-year-old social reformer, whose guiding principle throughout her life was, "Truth for authority, not authority for truth." The convention refused to honor their credentials on the ground of their sex. This precipitated a storm which lasted an entire day. An eyewitness describing Freemason's Hall that morning wrote: "The excitement and vehemence of protest and denunciation could not have been greater if the news had come that the French were about to invade England."

When the question was finally taken to a vote the overwhelming majority decided against the women. Their status at the convention was reduced to that of spectators. They were obliged to take their seats in the gallery, "behind a bar and a curtain."

Seated in the gallery next to Lucretia Mott was a young woman she had met on the boat going over. Her name was

Elizabeth Cady Stanton; her husband was a delegate to the convention. They had only recently been married and they considered this trip their honeymoon. The two women were drawn to each other at once and though she was not a delegate Elizabeth shared her older friend's outrage at what she had seen happen in Freemason's Hall.

And just when the convention thought that it had finally disposed of the explosive woman question and was about to settle down to business the incident was revived again. William Lloyd Garrison, who was delayed in transit and arrived late at the convention, was so shocked at the treatment accorded the American women delegates that he demonstratively took his seat in the gallery near them. This noble expression of solidarity with the wronged and humiliated greatly cheered the women but was very embarrassing to the convention. After all, Mr. Garrison was America's foremost Abolitionist and he was scheduled to deliver a major address at this world gathering. Yet there he was, a silent spectator in the gallery! Something had to be done. Messengers were sent up from below to plead with him to come down, and whenever a speaker mentioned his name the entire convention rose to its feet, turned toward the gallery and gave him a standing ovation. But all these efforts to lure him down were of no avail. If the convention would not change *its* mind and seat the women properly, he would not change *his*.

Soon all of London was talking about Mr. Garrison sitting in the gallery. Newspapers interviewed him; Lady Byron came to sit at his side; the Duchess of Sutherland commissioned the famous painter, B. R. Haydon, to sketch him; and the American women delegates were, of course, eternally grateful to him for his uncompromising stand in behalf of equality.

In their London experience the women saw reflected their *true* position in society. How much better off were they, they asked, than the slave they tried to liberate? Elizabeth Cady Stanton and Lucretia Mott walked for hours through the streets of London, talking about just this question. They agreed that it was high time for a woman's rights movement and decided that upon their return to America they would take the initial steps in that direction.

Eight years had gone by since that London episode. The young bride was busy raising a family, and the older woman was engulfed in her various social reform activities. Woman's rights as a subject for thought, discussion and correspondence was always with them; but woman's rights as a movement still had to await its day. That day came in the summer of 1848 when the Motts visited the Stantons in Seneca Falls. Elizabeth and Lucretia fell to reminiscing about London and, recalling their vow to do something, decided that the time was now.

These were the circumstances that led to the first organized expression of a woman's rights movement. The American woman's struggle for equality was born out of her participation in the struggle against slavery; and as these struggles extended into ever-widening areas of the population the bonds between the two movements grew ever stronger and the leaders of one were also the leaders of the other.

In terms of historical sequence Seneca Falls marked the transition from the sporadic agitation of a few individuals to a mass movement, galvanizing thousands into action. Until then Ernestine Rose and a handful of brave women had made speeches about woman's rights; from then on they made history.

Considering what has happened since Seneca Falls, the cry of "Revolution!" with which a hostile press greeted the first woman's rights convention was not so far-fetched after all. The forces which Seneca Falls set in motion did indeed revolutionize the relationship between the sexes for generations to come. Today, more than a hundred years after that event, psychologists, as well as sociologists and historians, are still evaluating the effects of Seneca Falls on our present-day society.

Chapter XIII

THE ROSE OF AMERICA

JANUARY 29, 1850 was a busy day for William Rose. On that day he found little time to spare for the work bench of his jewelry repair shop. His entire attention was claimed by the almost forgotten hero of the American Revolution, Thomas Paine, whose 113th birthday it was that day. For the past twenty-five years freethinkers in various parts of the country had been observing Paine's birthday with an annual public celebration. In New York William and Ernestine Rose had been especially active in the planning and arranging of these Tom Paine birthdays. Today's, the twenty-fifth, was to be marked by a special gala affair, a supper and ball to be held at the Chinese Museum, on Broadway between Spring and Prince Streets.

The celebration got off to an early start with a salute to Paine at the Battery around eleven in the morning. No guns boomed in salute on that occasion. Instead, several short speeches about the author of the *Crisis* papers were "fired" at the small crowd. Then copies of Paine's pamphlet *Common Sense* were distributed free of charge and the audience was urged to come to the Chinese Museum in the evening. With the first phase of the celebration over, the crowd quickly dispersed. A sharp January wind came blowing across the water and no one wished to remain standing in the cold a minute longer than was necessary.

From eight o'clock on that evening, all of Broadway's traffic seemed to be heading in one direction—Spring and Prince streets. An almost endless caravan of cabs, coaches and even private conveyances drew up in front of the Museum to let out its well-dressed passengers. Altogether about eight hundred ladies and gentlemen paid a dollar each to celebrate Tom Paine's birthday. An air of spirited gaiety pervaded the elegant Museum ballroom as the dancing couples swayed animatedly to the tunes of the schottische, the polka, the Polish mazurka or the Viennese waltz. As busy as William was he found time to dance with Ernestine, who loved dancing. They did not have many social evenings out together, but when they did they made the most of it.

Ernestine and William knew most of the celebrants. They were freethinkers from the New York area, many of whom they had known since the days of the Moral Philanthropists, or Tammany Hall Infidels, as they were then called. A person whose absence was felt by many at the ball that night was the shoemaker-freethinker, Benjamin Offen, who might well be described as the father of the Paine birthday celebrations in America. Offen had died in May, 1848. Ernestine and William, who knew him well, also knew the history of these annual Paine events, a history that dated back to 1824, the year Benjamin Offen arrived in New York from England.

Offen, who admired Paine as a champion of human liberty, was shocked to find that in this country the man who wrote the *Crisis* papers and helped turn the tide of the War of Independence was either thoroughly forgotten or thoroughly despised as an "atheist" or "infidel." Why such bitter feeling toward one who did so much for the attainment of America's freedom, Offen asked. The answer was not hard to find. Those who feared the popularity of Paine's political principles were bent on destroying his reputation and they very nearly succeeded.

Offen and his friends decided that on the next January 29, they would celebrate Thomas Paine's birthday with a public dinner. He and two others took it upon themselves to find a suitable tavern for the occasion. But they soon learned that they had undertaken a difficult assignment. Wherever they went the answer was, "No, we cannot get up a dinner in memory of that infidel Thomas Paine."

After a succession of failures they tried their luck with a Mr. Sykes of the New York Hotel on Williams Street. Mr. Sykes' reaction was a refreshing contrast to that of his colleagues. Upon checking his appointment book he said, "Yes, we can accommodate you. The price is three dollars per dinner, including wine."

But by this time Offen was inclined to proceed with caution. "Mr. Sykes," he said, "may I suggest that before you give us your final answer you take a little time to think it over. This is, after all, not an ordinary engagement."

Mr. Sykes was somewhat annoyed at Mr. Offen's suggestion.

"I am a servant of the public," he said. "I entertain parties of every creed. I ought to know my business without any dictation from you."

"True, sir," Mr. Offen insisted, "but you perhaps are not aware of the consequences to yourself. Therefore I wish you would take time and not finally close the concern."

Reluctantly, Mr. Sykes yielded. He agreed to give the matter some more thought and promised to let the committee know of his decision that evening.

The decision was "no." "I have consulted some of the patrons of the hotel," Mr. Sykes wrote in his message, "and they advised me to do no such thing. But please do not consider this a refusal. I will consult others of my customers and if a majority do not object I will then fulfill my engagement and you shall hear from me again at your next meeting."

The committee did hear from Mr. Sykes again, and again the answer was "no." Only this time the hotelkeeper could not hold out to them even the hope contained in his first reply. "My patrons generally say," Mr. Sykes informed the committee, "that they would rather present me with one hundred dollars each, than have my house disgraced by getting up a public dinner for the friends of that infidel Thomas Paine."

As if this blow were not enough, a serious defection occurred in the committee's own ranks. One of its most devoted members, a young counsellor, panicked and withdrew from the committee for fear that further association with it might hurt his career. But the rest of the members were determined to go through with their plan.

The proprietor of Harmony Hall, on the corner of William and Duane streets, came to their rescue. He had the reputation of being a liberal Scotsman and he lived up to it. He was willing to take the risk of getting up a Thomas Paine dinner. That was on January 29, 1825. By the time Ernestine and William arrived in America in 1836 these Paine dinners had become an established institution. From a report in the *New York Beacon* we learn that in 1843 the dinner was held at the Shakespeare Hotel and that "Mrs. Rose addressed the audience in a style of argument and eloquence seldom equaled, not easily surpassed, in which she introduced a spice of satire which some gentlemen not attended by their ladies could readily appreciate." Unfortunately the *Beacon* did not quote a sample of Ernestine's spicy satire and did not describe the reaction of those ladies who did attend with their gentlemen.

In 1844 the celebration took place at Union Hall, on the corner of Henry and Oliver streets, and was sponsored by the Society of Socialists which was founded by Robert Owen. There too Ernestine addressed the celebrants "in a ready, extemporaneous and eloquent manner," and William offered a toast in rhyme:

> Health to the sick, honor to the brave;
> Success to the lover; and freedom to the slave.

Although the drink of the evening was lemonade the affair was a gay one; Ernestine and William sang a duet.

But the 1850 celebration was by far the largest and most elaborate of all. "We never saw on any occasion a more brilliant assembly," reported the *Herald*, "young and old mingled together in harmony and cheerful concord, gaily and merrily dancing to the harmonious sounds of a splendid band of music seated aloft . . ."

Dancing continued until about eleven o'clock "with uncommon animation and vivacity." Then the guests were called to supper. The potency of the drinks is not revealed but we learn that "the supper was furnished in an upper room of the building, over the large ball room, and was laid out in superior style, with viands of all kinds, of the most exquisite *gout*, and prepared with the best skill of the culinary artist . . ."

After all the toasts had been made, the president of the ball, William Allen, called upon the guests to refill their glasses and, alluding to oppressed Poland, said: "When I think of the once happy but now fallen country of Kosciusco, Pulaski and their dauntless associates . . . a strong sympathy and respect is produced in me for all who can trace their origin to that land of sorrow, and more especially to those who inherit the spirit of Kosciusco, whether they be male or female. I will therefore propose as a sentiment the name of Mrs. Rose—she was the morning glory of Poland; the lily of England; and she *is* the rose of America." This toast was loudly applauded and Mrs. Rose addressed the crowded assembly.*

When Ernestine finished "the thunders of admiration and applause were almost deafening." The dance was resumed and continued until dawn, when "the pleased and cheerful company departed, to meet again *nisi* on this day next year."

An interesting sideline to this particular Paine celebration is the fact that it was drawn into the perennial feud between James Gordon Bennett and Horace Greeley. Mr. Greeley who had been invited to the celebration chose to decline the invitation publicly via a long editorial published in the *Tribune* that day. "We shall not attend . . ." wrote Mr. Greeley and proceeded to explain why. "We never liked Paine . . ." He did pay generous tribute to Paine for his sizeable contribu-

---

* For text of speech see Appendix, pp. 280-81.

tion to this country's independence; nevertheless he found his writings "grossly distasteful . . ."

The next day the bellicose James Gordon Bennett came to Paine's defense with an equally long editorial in the *New York Herald*. It was obvious that he was motivated not so much by a love for Paine as by a hatred for Greeley. He called the *Tribune* an "infidel newspaper," and accused Greeley, Brisbane and Dana of scattering "the seeds of disunion, infidelity, disbelief in the Bible, and every manner and device of the arch-fiend Satan . . ." Emerson who was currently lecturing in New York was also included in the company. Bennett wrote of "such lunatical madmen as Emerson, Lowell, Parker *et id omne genus . . .*" Altogether it was a curious spectacle to see the liberal Mr. Greeley refusing to have anything to do with a Tom Paine birthday, and the reactionary Mr. Bennett opening the pages of his newspaper for a full and objective account of this celebration.

The same James Gordon Bennett who printed Ernestine's entire Tom Paine speech in his *New York Herald* a few months later reverted to character when he incited the mob to break up a meeting at which she attempted to speak as an abolitionist. That was in May, 1850, when the American Anti-Slavery Society met in New York to mark the sixteenth anniversary of its existence. "These abolitionists shall not be allowed to represent New York," he wrote in his paper, and exhorted the mob to "go on Tuesday morning May 7th to the Tabernacle and there look at the black and white brethren and sisters fraternizing, slobbering over each other . . . blaspheming and cursing the Constitution of our glorious Union . . ."

The mob, several hundred ruffians under the command of the notorious Captain Rynders, obliged and came ready for action. Isaiah Rynders, a big wheel in Tammany Hall politics, was an underworld figure with the right upperworld connections. His Empire Club was a favorite rendezvous for Democratic bigwigs as well as a headquarters for his organization of mobsters. Like Bennett he aligned himself with the pro-slavery forces and assumed the role of savior of the Union and protector of society against infidels and abolitionists. On the mayor's orders the police were conveniently absent that morning from the Tabernacle Hall, giving Captain Rynders and his hoodlums complete freedom to take the law into their own hands.

That afternoon Garrison, who had come from Massachusetts to deliver the main address at the Tabernacle meeting, dashed off a letter to his wife, in which he wrote,

> Well, we have had our meeting, and thus far, thank God, all goes well, even triumphantly with us, notwithstanding the desperate efforts of the New York papers to get up a ferocious mob against us. Not that we have not had a very tumultuous, nay, even stormy time; the ocean of feeling has been lashed into a fury, but the proud waves were stayed, and a song of deliverance is in our mouth . . .

From the Tabernacle the mob followed the abolitionists to the Society Library where they were to continue their three-day session. Here the mob spirit triumphed completely when speaker after speaker was compelled to leave the platform amidst bedlam and confusion without delivering his talk. At one point Ernestine, who had faced many a hostile audience in her day, mounted the platform and attempted to speak but the hisses and the jeers drowned out her voice. She stood there for a full quarter of an hour while all around her the clamor continued unabated. Finally she gave up and returned to her seat. At another session, when she was not on the platform, the same mob shouted, "Rose! Where's that sweet Rose?"

At the end of the second day the proprietors of the Library Hall became apprehensive about their property. Garrison realized that it would be folly to continue so he stepped forward for the last time and, addressing himself to the mob, said, "Gentlemen, we shall no longer cast pearls before swine! This meeting is finally adjourned."

The next day newspapers like the *Herald* and the *Globe* hailed the mob violence as an expression of patriotism. The

Tribune concluded its unbaised report on a note of irony: "Thus closed Anti-Slavery free discussion in New York for 1850."

In late October Ernestine was off on another journey, this time to Worcester, Mass., to attend the first National Woman's Rights Convention. This important event came in one of the most crucial periods in American history! Clearly, the burning question before the nation in 1850 was not woman's rights but slavery. Her recent experience with the Rynders' mob was but one of many examples of how explosive the slavery issue was in mid-nineteenth-century America. Not since the days of 1776 had the country been more tragically divided. Cries of "secession" and "disunion" rang out passionately from both sides of the camp, and the storm that was to break over the nation eleven years later was already gathering its menacing clouds. The Compromise proposed by Clay, supported by Webster, passed by Congress and signed by President Fillmore did not bring the "peace, concord and harmony of the Union," that some had hoped it would bring. It turned out to be more of an irritant than a solution to the aggravated problem. And the Fugitive Slave Law, regarded as the most important component of the Compromise, led to actual violence and bloodshed and helped swell the ranks of the abolitionists.

Yet, even at that critical juncture in the history of the country, the leading abolitionists of the day agreed with her, Lucretia Mott, Elizabeth Cady Stanton, Paulina Wright Davis and others that there was still another kind of slavery abroad in America that demanded their urgent attention—the slavery of woman, white as well as black. And so when Garrison was invited to endorse the call to the first national woman's rights convention he not only signed the call but replied, "I doubt whether a more important movement has ever been launched, touching the destiny of the race, than this in regard to the equality of the sexes."

Yes, she thought, a new day was dawning for half of the

country's population; indeed, for half of mankind. Significantly, the first rays of that dawn appeared on the horizon of New England, the home of our Pilgrim Fathers.

October 23 was a fine autumn day. Every tree in Worcester proclaimed the end of New England's Indian summer with a riot of colors, and the air was alive with a sharp, invigorating tang that only an early fall breeze can provide. But the atmosphere that morning was also charged with an element that had nothing to do with the weather—the excitement preceding an unusual event. For by the morning of the twenty-third all of Worcester knew that something very unusual was to happen in the city that day. That was why a huge crowd had collected in front of Brinley Hall long before ten in the morning to catch a glimpse of the strange women, local as well as out-of-town, who came here to attend the first national woman's rights convention.

Ernestine wore a russet gown and a gold guard chain around her neck. As she entered the rapidly filling hall her eyes shone with pleasure at the sight of so many of her old friends and fellow social reformers. There was Lucretia Mott whom Emerson, another signer of the Call, once described as the "flower of Quakerism." She was dressed in her modest Quaker gown, adorned by a muslin cap and scarf and a white silk shawl. At the age of fifty-seven this veteran reformer was the most venerated and respected figure in the hall.

And there was tall, fair-complexioned, Paulina Wright Davis, whose handsomely striking face was framed by a mass of auburn ringlets. Ernestine's association with her dated back to the early days of the petition campaign for the married woman's property bill.

There was a stir in the hall and all eyes turned toward the door. Someone important had just walked in. It was Frederick Douglass, broad-shouldered, lion-like, advancing with firm, vigorous step. And there, off in a corner of the hall, stood a cluster of women and towering above them was tall Sojourner

Truth, the ex-slave and itinerant preacher, resembling some biblical figure come to life.

In another part of the hall stood William Lloyd Garrison, his close friend and co-worker, Wendell Phillips, Abby Kelly Foster and Lucy Stone, both fiery abolitionists and veteran fighters for equal rights for women.

A face she missed in this gathering, dazzling with social reformers, was that of Elizabeth Cady Stanton. Elizabeth could not attend because of family obligations but she sent her greetings in the form of a letter to be read at the convention.

Suddenly it grew quiet in the hall. Sarah Earle, wife of the editor of the *Worcester Spy*, mounted the rostrum and called the assembly to order. She introduced Paulina Wright Davis as the president of the first national woman's rights convention. For Ernestine this was an unforgettable moment.

While the president delivered the opening address, an unfortunate incident occurred which marred somewhat the solemnity of the occasion. In an adjoining part of the building the American fat girl of the year, aged sixteen and weighing four hundred pounds, was on public display to the accompaniment of hand-organ music. The melodies that wafted into the main hall were clearly out of tune with Mrs. Davis's speech. The reporter for Bennett's *New York Herald* commented sneeringly that the fat girl was "a specimen of what woman would be if she had her rights. She ought by all means to have been made president of the convention."

Unfortunately the arrangements committee had failed to engage a professional stenographer (he was called phonographer in those days) to record the speeches. Ernestine, who was an extemporaneous speaker, spoke several times at this convention but her speeches went unrecorded. The published proceedings of the convention contain a footnote commenting on this regrettable fact: "The rich gems of thought and the thrilling eloquence of the extempore speeches are lost to those who were not present to listen . . . Ernestine L. Rose of New

York, gave utterance to her clear, strong thoughts in her own peculiarly graceful style of eloquence." However, thanks to the presence of newspaper reporters who quoted from her speeches there are a few brief samples of her "style of eloquence."

> "We have heard a great deal of our Pilgrim Fathers," she said, "but who has heard of the Pilgrim Mothers? Did they not endure as many perils, encounter as many hardships, and do as much to form and fashion the institutions of New England as the Pilgrim Fathers? And were not their trials, and is not their glory equally great? Yet they are hardly remembered."

> "I shall not use the language of censor and blame. So far as there is blame both sexes are entitled to their share of it. Man is as much the victim of his despotism as is woman."

> "I trust that if ever woman touched the sword it would be to sheath it in its scabbard forever."

The leaders of this new movement made it clear at the very outset that their claim for equality was not limited to the white-skinned woman alone. In a resolution, which was passed unanimously, they stated:

> *Resolved*, That the cause we are met to advocate—the claim for woman of all her natural and civil rights—bids us remember the million and a half of slave women at the South, the most grossly wronged and foully outraged of all women; and in every effort for an improvement of our civilization, we will bear in our heart of hearts the memory of the trampled womanhood of the plantation, and omit no effort to raise it to a share in the rights we claim for ourselves.

Ernestine carried this principle to an even higher level when she said, "We are not contending here for the rights of the women of New England, or of old England, but of the world." This view was shared by the entire leadership.

Among the many other resolutions passed was one drafted by Ernestine which pledged that woman would not rest until she achieved "political, legal and social equality with man." By and large these resolutions were an extension and elaboration of the principles expressed in the Declaration of Sentiments which had been adopted two years earlier at Seneca Falls.

Over a thousand people had crowded into Brinley Hall to attend the convention, and hundreds were turned away for lack of space. During some sessions many were standing in the aisle and around the platform "in a solid phalanx." At the end of the two-day session delegates went home as part of committees that were to carry on the work for the entire year until the next convention which, they decided, would again be held in Worcester. Ernestine was nominated to the Central

---

WOMAN'S RIGHTS CONVENTION.

AWFUL COMBINATION
OF
SOCIALISM, ABOLITIONISM, AND INFIDELITY.

The Pantalettes Striking for the Pantaloons.

Bible and Constitution Repudiated.

WORCESTER, Mass., Oct. 23, 1850.
That motley mingling of abolitionists, socialists, and infidels, of all sexes and colors, called the Woman's Rights Convention, assembled in this city, to-day, and an account of their proceedings we have the honor herewith to communicate to the *New York Herald.*
New York Public Library

Headline from New York Herald on first National Woman's Rights Convention Worcester, Mass—October 23, 1850

Committee and to serve as chairman of the Committee on Civil and Political Functions. Among others on this committee were Lucy Stone, Wendell Phillips, Abby Kelly Foster, William Lloyd Garrison and Elizabeth Cady Stanton.

Thus a new movement was born and the delegates departed in high spirits and with the elevating feeling that they had participated in the making of history. But the press, with notable exceptions, attacked this historic event even more vehemently than its predecessor at Seneca Falls. In New York the *Daily Tribune* was the only large metropolitan newspaper to report the proceedings fairly and accurately. Its reporter was so outraged by the false accounts he read in other papers that he added a postscript to his own report, warning his readers, "Do not be deceived by the reports in some of the Boston papers. Some of them had sent reporters here to caricature the proceedings. Shame on a corrupt and venal press."

But his warning was applicable with even greater force to his own city. The *New York Herald* concluded its vicious attack on the Worcester convention in the following words:

> There is not a lunatic asylum in the country wherein, if the inmates were called together to sit in convention, they would not exhibit more sense, reason, decency and delicacy, and less lunacy, blasphemy and horrible sentiment, than this hybrid, mongrel, piebald, crackbrained, pitiful, disgusting and ridiculous assemblage. And there we drop them, and may God have mercy on their miserable souls. Amen.

Had James Gordon Bennett really lived up to his promise and dropped them the women would have been delighted. But he continued to attack the movement at every opportunity. With respect to woman's rights his penchant for calumny was never sated, his fund of invectives never exhausted.

To the woman's rights women, Bennett's *Herald* personified what they called the "satanic press," but the more implacable enemy of their cause was not the man in the editor's chair but the man in the pulpit. The hostile press would spoof at them, lampoon them, call them crackpots fit for the lunatic asylum. But the hostile clergy would train their theological guns at them, invoke the authority of the church and the wrath of God against them. Compared to so formidable a foe as the clergy a spoofing editorial seemed almost harmless.

The clergy's most effective weapon was the Sunday sermon but it did not overlook the power of the printed word. A few days after the Worcester convention *The Orthodox Puritan Recorder* wrote that the entire affair brought to mind a saying the wise Arabs had, namely, "when a hen crows like a cock it is time to cut her head off." The orthodox editors did admit, mercifully, that this saying had "too strong a tone of orientalism," and so they improved on it with a proverb from Solomon: "As a jewel of gold in a swine's mouth, so is a fair woman who is without discretion."

This, then, was how the first National Woman's Rights Convention was received by a hostile press and by an even more hostile clergy. And as the rumble of this reception reverberated throughout the nation the two opposing camps came clearly into view. On the one side stood the spokesmen of America's womanhood with a handful of principled and courageous men at their side; their battle cry—equal rights for women! And on the other side was a formidable adversary combining the strength of a feudal law, a bigoted press and a powerful church. The battle lines were drawn. The struggle was on in earnest.

Chapter XIV

"WIT, PHILOSOPHY AND SATIRE"

COMPARED TO ERNESTINE's active public life, William lived a life of relative obscurity. But there is no evidence that he resented having to live in the shadow of his wife's glory. On the contrary, he gloried in Ernestine's achievements, sought out every newspaper item about her, clipped it and pasted it lovingly into a scrap book. His main contribution to the reform movement was to make it possible for Ernestine to do her work. His own participation in a public activity was usually of a Jimmy Higgins' nature—serving on arrangements committees, raising money, selling tickets.

Once he had the great satisfaction of seeing his talents as a silversmith linked directly to the cause of woman's rights. This happened in May, 1851, not in his own New York but in far-off Indiana. That year a group of Indiana women honored their legislative representative, Robert Dale Owen, son of Robert Owen, for "his true and noble advocacy of their independent rights to property . . ." by presenting him with a silver pitcher from the workshop of William E. Rose. The pitcher was described as having been executed in classical style and reflected the high quality of Mr. Rose's artistry and workmanship.

But why would the women of Indiana have to import a silver pitcher all the way from New York when they could easily have found a competent silversmith in their own state to make one for them? Based on the facts at hand we may assume that this was no ordinary business transaction. Ernestine and William Rose were devoted friends of Owen, the father, and that friendship had no doubt extended to Owen, the son, who was also a vigorous social reformer. Robert Dale Owen became a member of the Indiana State Legislature in the winter of 1836-37, the very time when Ernestine launched her petition campaign for a married woman's property bill in New York. It may even be that it was Ernestine who had inspired Owen to emulate Judge Thomas Herttell and introduce a similar bill for the married women of his own state. And so when the women of Indiana decided to honor Owen, it was only natural for those close to him to think of William Rose as the most suitable silversmith to create such a pitcher.

At the time of the testimonial Owen had not yet succeeded in his legislative efforts for a married woman's property bill. The lawmakers of Indiana had opposed such a measure as stubbornly as had their colleagues of New York. They even advanced the same arguments against the bill. "Woman's power," said one, "comes through a self-sacrificing spirit ready to offer up all her hopes upon the shrine of her husband's wishes." Another legislator insisted that the existing common law was an embodiment of the "divine law," and to change it would be tantamount to being against the "great fundamental principles of the Christian religion." Some even repeated the time-worn canard that the married women of France were living a life of sin and debauchery precisely because they enjoyed the independence that came with ownership of their own property.

Once Owen came within an inch of success but lost. This happened at a State Constitutional Convention where he had introduced a clause into the revised constitution that would grant married women the right to own their property. Owen had managed to get the clause passed. Then a clergyman arose to oppose it and, throwing at the clause the full weight of the Bible, succeeded in having the convention reverse itself. Altogether it took fifteen years of persistent struggle before the women of Indiana won a married woman's property bill similar to the one Ernestine had campaigned for in the state of New York.

But in 1851, while Ernestine followed with keen interest the developments in Indiana, she was already deeply involved in a petition campaign of her own in New York. Upon her return from Worcester she drew up a petition to the State Legislature, which stressed, among other things, the key demand of the new movement: ". . . the elective franchise with all the privileges of holding office, etc., the same as man . . ." People were startled at the mere sound of this radical demand; signatures were hard to obtain and some even slammed the door in her face, but 1851 was a far cry from 1836. Now when she knocked on a door she knew that others with similar petitions in hand were knocking on other doors; and at the bottom of each petition was a list of addresses where more could be obtained: at the office of the *New York Tribune;* at the Anti-Slavery office; the publishers Fowler & Wells had them; and, of course, one could get a plentiful supply at the home of Mrs. Rose, 37 Reade Street, New York.

That summer Ernestine traveled through some small communities in western New York, about 13 miles south of Rochester. She started out on a leisurely vacation but ended up on the lecture platform. Everywhere she arrived she caused a great stir of excitement and was beseiged with requests to speak. She did not have to be coaxed. As she herself explained, ". . . it ever gives me the greatest pleasure to contribute my mite toward the general stock of knowledge and happiness."

In the course of a short time she gave seven lectures in that area, five of them in churches. In some villages she spoke twice in the same church. Her topics were: "The Formation of Character," "The Present Social Evils," and "Woman's Rights." All of the lectures were well attended and enthusiastically received.

Why would a known and outspoken "infidel" be allowed to speak in churches? One can venture a guess. In such small communities as Rush, Honeoye or Smithtown, the church was the only large meeting hall available, and the ministers had to accede to the wish of their parishioners and grant them the use of the church. The fact was that after she had left some ministers set about to repair the damage. They delivered sermons calculated to offset the effect of her heresies. When Ernestine was informed that the minister of Rush delivered a series of sermons that were critical of her lectures, she commented, "I am glad he did so; it will do good, for as gold is purified and refined in the fiery furnace, so does Truth come out clearer and more beautiful from under severe criticism."

The last two weeks of that journey she spent with friends in Dutchess County, and there too she gave talks in Dover and Washington Hollow. She had little time for recreation but for Ernestine this was a full and gratifying summer.

But the big event that year came in the fall when she made another trip to Worcester, Mass., to attend the second National Woman's Rights Convention on October 15 and 16. She found that despite the hostile reception which the first convention had received from the clergy and most of the press the forces of the new movement had increased during the past year rather than diminished. Brinley Hall could no longer accommodate the overflow attendance; hundreds had to be turned away from each session and on the second day the entire convention had to be moved to the larger auditorium at City Hall. Messages of greeting were received from such luminaries as Ralph Waldo Emerson, Henry Ward Beecher, Horace Mann and Harriet Martineau. Paulina Wright Davis was again nominated permanent president of the convention but this time she did not have to vie for attention with the American fat girl whose absence from Brinley Hall no one seemed to regret. Generally things were running more smoothly this year, and thanks to the presence of a professional phonographer Ernestine's speech on woman's rights was not lost for those who were not there to hear it. It was a brilliant speech and its effect on that large audience was so profound that twenty years later when Paulina Wright Davis recalled that event she wrote, "In this convention Mrs. Ernestine L. Rose made an address of an hour in length, which has never been surpassed." *

Another high point at the convention was a message from France. It came in the form of a letter written in a prison cell in Paris by two women, Jeanne Deroine and Pauline Roland, both incarcerated for advocating the elective franchise for French women. "Dear Sisters," they wrote, "Your courageous declaration of woman's rights has resounded even to our prison, and has filled our souls with inexplicable joy." The letter, read by Rev. W. H. Channing, ended with these moving words: ". . . from the depth of the jail which still imprisons our bodies without reaching our hearts, we cry to you, Faith, Love, Hope, and send to you our sisterly salutations."

Ernestine, who had a first-hand knowledge of European despotism and woman's condition abroad, opened her speech with these words: "After having heard the letter read from our poor incarcerated sisters of France, well might we exclaim, Alas, poor France! where is thy glory? Where the glory of the Revolution of 1848 . . . ?"

A woman's rights convention was a unique and flexible instrument. There ideas flowed freely to as well as from the platform, and leaders of the movement debated not only with opponents but also with each other. Wrongs against woman had a long history. They were "hoary-headed with age" as Ernestine Rose said in her speech. But rights for woman was a relatively new and revolutionary concept. For a reform movement to succeed, its program must have not only a practical appeal but also a sound theoretical basis. While the leadership was in general agreement as to what woman's demands should be, there arose ideological differences from time to time. These they aired, not in the caucus room but on the open platform of the public convention.

---

* For text of speech see Appendix pp. 281-84.

In these debates Ernestine emerged as a passionate fighter for her point of view. Even those who disagreed with her could not help but admire her for the bold and forthright manner in which she defended her position. Equivocation and fuzzy thinking were alien to her. She had the happy faculty of being able to illuminate a subject with the bright light of logic without sacrificing the quality of human emotion.

At this convention Abby Kelly Foster raised the question of duty versus right. ". . . When woman shall feel her duty," she said, "she will get her rights. We who are young on this question of woman's rights should entitle our next book 'Woman's Duties.'" Mrs. Foster felt so strongly about this thought that she even presented it in the form of a resolution: "*Resolved*, That woman lacks her rights because she does not feel the full weight of her responsibilities . . ." Ernestine disagreed.

"We are told that if woman would only do her duty she would have her rights," she said, "implying that our rights spring from our duties. If we reflect a moment on the subject we will find this an error, a very prevalent error, and therefore the more necessary to be corrected. Our duties spring from our rights, our rights from our wants. The child, when it comes into existence, possesses rights arising from its necessities, but as yet it owes no duty to anyone; while the parents, having exercised certain rights and privileges, they owe certain duties to the child which when grown up to understand the relation it sustains to its parents and to society then owes in return duties in accordance with the rights and privileges it enjoys. The more rights we enjoy the greater the duties we owe. And he who enjoys most rights, owes in return the most duties. And therefore we say to society, you who enjoy all the rights, are in duty bound to protect every individual member in his rights. But as it is, while man enjoys all the rights, he preaches all the duties to woman. And hence we say to man—not in the spirit of censure, but charity and kindness, yet firmly do we say to him that instead of writing and preaching so much about the duties of woman, it is high time, as the elder brother, to set us the example in the performance of your duties. And in no way can you evince your earnest desire to do so than by giving woman her rights. And depend upon it she will not fail in the performance of her duties, not only as wife and mother, but also as a free, enlightened, rational member of the great family of man, highly conducive to the elevation and happiness of all."

As was usual after a woman's rights convention, no sooner was it adjourned than the brickbats came flying from editorial offices and pulpits. But this time the women had the satisfaction of knowing that their convention had won for them at least one convert to their cause from the ranks of the clergy, a group least likely to yield such converts. For Ernestine this was a double triumph for she had tilted verbal swords with the gentleman in question and he felt the sting of her sarcasm.

A year earlier Rev. Henry Bellows, editor of the Unitarian paper, the *New York Christian Inquirer*, had joined in the general attack on the first Worcester convention. He then wrote in an editorial: "Place woman unbonneted and unshawled before the public gaze, and what becomes of her modesty and virtue?" At this, the second Worcester convention, Ernestine replied to the clergyman's question as follows:

In his benighted mind the modesty and virtue of woman is of so fragile a nature that when it is in contact with the atmosphere it evaporates like chloroform. But I refrain to comment on such a sentiment. It carries with it its own deep condemnation. When I read the article I earnestly wished I had the ladies of the writer's congregation before me, to see whether they could realize the estimation their pastor held them in. Yet I hardly know which sentiment was strongest in me, contempt for such foolish opinions, or pity for a man that has so degrading an opinion of woman—of the being that gave him life, that sustained his helpless infancy with her ever-watchful care, and laid the very foundation for the little mind he may possess—of the being he took to his bosom as the partner of his joys and sorrows—the one whom, when he strove to win her affection, he courted, as all such men court woman, like some divinity. Such a man deserves our pity; for I cannot realize that a man purposely and willfully degrades his mother, sister, wife, and daughter. No! my better nature, my best knowledge and conviction, forbid me to believe it.

Upon reading the proceedings of the second Worcester convention, which contained Ernestine's address, Rev. Bellows had some second thoughts on the subject of woman's rights and he aired them in a long editorial in his paper. Admitting frankly that he had "regarded this movement with decided distrust and distaste," he now wrote, "At any rate, we confess our surprise at the weight of reasoning brought forward by the recent convention, and shall endeavor henceforth to keep our masculine mind—full doubtless of conventional prejudices—open to the light which is shed upon the theme."

The *New York Herald* reported Ernestine's speech at the convention as follows: "Mrs. Rose spun a very long yarn composed of wit, philosophy and satire." Like Balaam, the reporter came to curse but remained to praise. For what greater tribute can one pay a speaker than to say that her speech contained "wit, philosophy and satire"?

Chapter XV

CHAPTER AND VERSE

IT WAS A RARE EVENT in 1852 for a woman to speak in New York and be heard in Ohio. Yet this was what happened when Ernestine spoke in January of that year. Her speech at the one hundred and fifteenth anniversary of Thomas Paine's birthday was widely noted in other parts of the country. It was a foreign-policy speech which would have aroused much comment had it been made by a statesman; the fact that it was made by a woman and still received serious attention speaks eloquently for the woman.

The social ferment set in motion by the revolutions of 1848 had not yet subsided. With the aid of the Czar's military might the Austrian authorities had succeeded in toppling the new Hungarian government and compelled President Kossuth to flee his native land. Mazzini became an exile in Switzerland. Other patriots met a similar fate. But resistance to tyranny continued in various parts of the continent, and the embattled revolutionaries looked to America for aid and encouragement. But the American government had adopted a policy of non-intervention. It was against that policy that Ernestine lashed out sharply in her address, which the *New York Herald* of January 31, printed in its entirety.*

The *Cincinnati Nonpareil* wrote, "Her speech is truly forcible and eloquent; we cannot extract a passage without quoting nearly the whole speech." The *Ohio Democrat* devoted two columns to the address and introduced it as ". . . an

---

* For text of speech see Appendix p. 284.

off-hand, able, and spirited speech of a lady, Mrs. Ernestine L. Rose, the equal of which few men are competent. We give copious extracts to show what an honest, earnest, woman can do, when she tries." The *Ohio Times* also had much praise for the speech and quoted from it liberally. The *Boston Olive Branch*, a religious publication, found the speech "absolutely disgusting."

It was indeed a sign of the times when, in 1852, the editors of *Godey's Lady's Book* introduced in the magazine a new feature entitled, "Employment of Women." It informed its female readers of the newest openings for women in the field of business and industry. In 1836 such a feature would have been unthinkable. At that time *Godey's* wrote that "home is the empire of woman." That concept had not been abandoned, but in 1852 the magazine could no longer cling to it with the same tenacity without the risk of alienating some of its readers. On the one hand the rapid industrial development of the country created new areas of employment for women; and on the other the recent woman's rights convention at Worcester had stirred up a lively controversy on the woman question in the nation's press, the pulpits and the homes, and aroused the interest of many women, throughout the land, in the infant woman's rights movement. In the winter of 1852 the liberal-minded educator, Horace Mann, joined the discussion when he toured the country with two lectures entitled, "Hints To A Young Woman." *

The leaders of the woman's rights movement found the lectures disappointing. Up to that time they had regarded Mann as a friend of the movement, but after hearing his latest views on the subject they felt as though one from their own midst had turned traitor to the cause. The arguments he advanced as to why woman should not demand the right to

---

* In their published version, in book form, these lectures appeared under the title, *A Few Thoughts on the Powers and Duties of Women.* Syracuse, 1853.

vote, hold a public office or enter the world of politics were not new. They were the stock-in-trade arguments of every opponent of the movement from the day the women took to the convention platform at Seneca Falls. The advocates of woman's rights had ready and logical replies to these arguments. But in this instance logic was of small comfort when it had to compete with the enormous influence and prestige of Horace Mann, the well-known educator and legislator, soon to be appointed President of Antioch College.

When Mann delivered his two lectures in New York (February 17 and 29) Ernestine attended both. She asked for an opportunity to reply to the speaker's arguments right then and there, but her request was denied. And so she wrote Mr. Mann a letter in which she said in part, "But while listening to your lecture I was almost forced to exclaim with one of old, 'Can any good come out of Nazareth?'—can a politician be true to any subject that is not popular, when the Honorable gentleman before me can so easily stoop to pamper the vitiated taste of an already prejudiced public opinion, by giving the unthinking multitude the slang and ridicule they admire, instead of the arguments, truth and common sense they so much need?"

But the matter did not end there. Ernestine felt that there was the need of a public refutation of Mann's arguments and she undertook to do just that. She subjected his views on the woman question to searching and scathing analysis which she published privately in pamphlet form under the title, *Review of Horace Mann's Two Lectures.**

Perhaps it was just as well that Ernestine did not get the opportunity to refute Horace Mann's arguments on the spot. She was a master of the impromptu speech and what she had to say would no doubt have amused and instructed her audience, but the matter would have ended right there, in the lecture hall. Now, more than a century later, we too can "sit

---

* For excerpts from this pamphlet see Appendix pp. 284-87.

in" on this debate. And although many of the issues raised are, by now, academic, we still find the debate, historically speaking, instructive and Ernestine, certainly amusing.

The first two national woman's rights conventions went by without any disturbing incidents. They were orderly assemblies where proper decorum was observed not only by the speakers but by the audience as well. But the third national convention held in Syracuse September 8, 9, 10, 1852, marked the beginning of stormy woman's rights assemblies that frequently bordered on physical violence. The primary reason for this change was a change in tactics in the ranks of the opposition. As the woman's rights movement expanded both in strength and influence, the gentlemen of the cloth moved to counter this development with correspondingly aggressive means. They no longer confined the area of battle to the pulpit and the religious periodical; they took the good fight straight to the "infidel's" den—the convention hall. With Bible in hand they would invade the woman's rights assemblies, listen to some of the speeches and, at the strategic moment, ask for the floor and commence the attack, using the following quotations from the Scriptures as their most basic weapons.

In the third chapter of Genesis it is said:
". . . and thy desire shall be to thy husband and he shall rule over thee."

Saint Paul said:

". . . the head of every man is Christ; and the head of every woman is man; . . ."
(Corinthians I, 11:3)

"Let your women be silent in the churches; for it is not permitted unto them to speak, but they are commanded to be under obedience, as also saith the law."
(Corinthians I, 14:34)

"And if they will learn anything, let them ask their husbands at home; for it is a shame for women to speak in the church."
(Corinthians I, 14:35)

". . . but I suffer not a woman to teach, nor to usurp authority over the man but to be in silence; for Adam was first formed, then Eve; and Adam was not deceived, but the woman being deceived, was in the transgression."

(Timothy I, 2:12-14)

Saint Peter said:

"Likewise, ye wives, be in subjection to your own husbands . . ."
(Peter I, 3:1)

In 1852, in Syracuse, the religious question nearly wrecked the convention and threatened to split the young movement in two. Oddly enough, this time it was not a clergyman who precipitated the crisis but a clergywoman, Rev. Antoinette Brown. Young, handsome and eloquent, Miss Brown was somewhat of a sensation in those days. She was the first ordained woman minister in America and at the same time a dedicated fighter for woman's rights. She claimed to have derived her woman's rights ideas from the Bible and undertook to prove that there was no conflict between the two. Very early in the convention Rev. Brown introduced a lengthy resolution purporting to reconcile religion with woman's demand for equality.

To Ernestine this move portended a grave danger to the young movement. Were the convention to adopt such a resolution it would have meant that the movement itself had reached out for the explosive religious issue and by official sanction incorporated it into its program. Such a development was unthinkable from a tactical standpoint, and indefensible from the standpoint of principle. It would invite endless theological quibbling and thus side-track the movement from its vital issues at hand, and it would blur the clear and sound premise of the movement with the fog of religious speculation. Clearly, this resolution had to be blocked at all cost and Ernestine wasted no time in doing so. No sooner had Antoinette Brown finished than Ernestine was on the platform opposing the resolution with all the vigor at her command.

"For my part," she said, "I see no need to appeal to any written authority, particularly when it is so obscure and indefinite as to admit of different interpretations. When the inhabitants of Boston converted their harbor into a teapot rather than submit to unjust taxes, they did not go to the Bible for their authority; for if they had, they would have been told from the same authority to 'give unto Caesar what belonged to Caesar.' Had the people, when they rose in the might of their right to throw off the British yoke, appealed to the Bible for authority, it would have answered them, 'Submit to the powers that be, for they are from God.' No! on human rights and freedom, on a subject that is as self-evident as two and two make four, there is no need of any written authority." At this point she introduced a resolution which began, "*Resolved:* That we ask not for our rights as a gift of charity, but as an act of justice."

The resolution was followed by a speech which did not lack the standard ingredients of Ernestine's speeches—wit and humor. To illustrate how statesmen lacked the moral courage to face the issue of woman's rights squarely and honestly she told a story about Mr. Roebuck, member of the British Parliament. This statesman had gone on record favoring the granting of the elective franchise to all men who could afford to live in five-pound tenements. He was asked by the electors of Sheffield whether he would extend the same privilege to women who were able to pay the same amount. "But what was the honorable gentleman's reply?" asked Ernestine and added, ". . . I hope the ladies will pay particular attention, for the greater part of the reply contains the draught poor, deluded woman has been accustomed to swallow—Flattery:

" 'There is no man who owes more than I do to woman,' " said Mr. Roebuck. " '. . . There is nothing which for the honor of the sex, I would not do; the happiness of my life is bound up with it; mother, wife, daughter, woman, to me have been the oasis of the desert of life, and I have to ask myself, would it conduce to the happiness of society to bring woman more distinctly than she is now brought, into the arena of politics? Honestly, I confess to you, I believe not. I will tell you why. All their influences, if I may so term it, are gentle influences. In the rude battle and business of life, we come home to find a nook and shelter of quiet comfort after the hard and severe, and, I may say, the sharp ire and disputes of the House of Commons. I hie me home knowing that I shall there find personal solicitude and anxiety. My head rests upon a bosom throbbing with emotion for me and our child; and I feel a more hearty man in the cause of my country, the next day, because of the perfect, soothing, gentle peace which a mind sullied by politics is unable to feel. Oh! I can not rob myself of that inexpressible benefit, and therefore I say, No.' "

"Well," said Ernestine, "this is certainly a nice little romantic bit of parliamentary declamation. What a pity that he should give up all these enjoyments to give woman a vote! Poor man! his happiness must be balanced on the very verge of a precipice, when the simple act of depositing a vote by the hand of woman, would overthrow and destroy it forever . . . like a true politician he commenced very patriotically, for the happiness of society, and finished by describing his own individual interests."

The two opposing resolutions touched off a long and bitter debate which lasted for almost two days. Once again Ernestine took to the platform. "I can not object," she said, "to any one's interpreting the Bible as he or she thinks best; but I do object that such interpretations go forth as the doctrine of this convention, because it is a mere interpretation and not even the authority of the Book. It is the view of Miss Brown only which is as good as that of any other minister, but that is all. For my part I reject both interpretations. Here we claim human rights and freedom based upon the laws of humanity, and we require no written authority from Moses or Paul, because the laws of our claim are prior even to these two great men."

Lucretia Mott, the president of the convention, supported Ernestine's position. She cited the slavery question as an example of how the Bible was being quoted for and against this evil; and while the two opposing camps were hurling at each other quotations from the Scriptures the emancipation of the Negro was neglected. Herself a Quaker preacher, and one who never let a clergyman's argument go unchallenged, Lucretia would say, "It is not Christianity but priestcraft that has subjected woman as we find her."

When the two resolutions were finally presented for a vote the convention upheld Ernestine's. The soundness of her position was amply demonstrated right then and there by the scandalous behavior of Rev. Junius Hatch, a Congregational minister who had come to the convention with the obvious intent of disrupting it. Antoinette Brown found herself in the unenviable position of having to defend her interpretations of the Bible with regard to woman's rights against those of Rev. Hatch; and at the same time she had to argue against Ernestine's insistence that the Bible had no place at a woman's rights convention. But once the inflammable issue was tossed into the assembly there was no telling how far the conflagration would spread. The clergyman took full advantage of this situation. The fact that there was a division of opinion on this question within the ranks of the leadership itself only encouraged him to greater arrogance. His position was that held by the clergy generally; namely, that according to the Bible there should be no such conventions at all. Therefore he did everything to disrupt this one. He repeatedly interrupted other speakers and made coarse and vulgar remarks about women. Lucretia Mott tried to silence him but did not succeed; the men in the audience shouted, "Sit down!" and "Shut up!" but to no avail. It took a thirty-two-year old school teacher, plain in appearance and almost timid in manner, to succeed where others had failed. This young Quaker was so shocked by the minister's outrageous behavior that she rose in the middle of one of his harangues and called him a clergyman of the "pincushion" variety; the kind, she explained, that receive their religious training with the aid of women's sewing societies and who usually turn out to be the most bigoted and narrow-minded in their attitude to women. This description not only fitted Rev. Hatch very well, but it also had the desired effect; it finally silenced him. The name of that school teacher was Susan B. Anthony, who was then attending her first woman's rights convention.

Even James Gordon Bennett of the *New York Herald*, himself no mere amateur in the art of stirring up rowdyism, found the clergyman's remarks in poor taste. In his vitriolic attack on the convention Bennett also gave Rev. Hatch a verbal spanking for having resorted to "coarse jests" and "indecent language."

With the controversial Bible question at last out of the way the convention settled down to other business. A question that came in for considerable discussion was whether to organize the young movement into a more formal and tightly-knit organization, or whether to continue with the present loose arrangement of the annual convention and the various committees functioning between conventions. Contrary to what might have been expected from so clear-minded a realist as Ernestine, she came out strongly against organization. Her argument was that "organizations were like Chinese bandages. In political, moral and religious bodies, they had hindered the growth of man. They were the incubus of our nature. The moment a man has intellectual life enough to strike out for a new idea he is branded as a heretic." She admitted that there were times when organization was necessary to the achievement of certain goals, but in principle she was against it. Others at that convention shared Ernestine's view on this subject. At the end of the debate that view prevailed.

At the close of the convention an incident occurred which sheds additional light on Ernestine's character, particularly her scrupulous sense of fairness. Someone introduced a resolution which read as follows: *Resolved*, That the young women of our land be warned against the fallacies contained in Horace Mann's lectures delivered at various times and places for their especial benefit; and that they be very cautious how they accept such sophistries for the truth.

One would expect Ernestine to urge the passage of that resolution, but she did not. "I am glad that such a resolution has been offered . . . ," she said. "His sentiments were unworthy of a Man—much more of Horace Mann. But as probably few here have heard or read these lectures, I will not urge the acceptance of the resolution but move to lay it on the table." The resolution was not passed.

When the convention was over Ernestine was invited to remain in Syracuse a while longer and lecture. The announcement of her talk on "Human Culture and the Formation of Character" added that, "Mrs. Rose has been in the habit of paying for halls and all her expenses, and lecturing for nothing. This privilege has been denied her here and gentlemen have determined that the tickets shall be 12½ cents each." This determination on the part of the gentlemen had apparently not hurt the attendance in the slightest. A large audience came to City Hall to hear her, including the editor of the *Syracuse Daily Standard* who later commented editorially that although he found himself in disagreement with much of Ernestine's philosophy, "It is not saying too much to call it one of the most logically arranged and eloquently delivered lectures it has been our pleasure to listen to for a long time . . ."

Chapter XVI

MOBS, MEETINGS AND
MINISTERS

By 1853 ERNESTINE had stood on public platforms in this country for nearly seventeen years; she had faced audiences of various sizes, moods and tempers, including Captain Rynders' mob in New York. But the supreme test came in June of that year at Hartford, Connecticut, when the lights at Melodeon Hall were suddenly turned off in the middle of her speech, and she found herself standing on the platform in total darkness while a hostile, frenzied mob of close to two thousand was stamping, shouting and hissing all around her. To a speaker of lesser courage this could be a terrifying experience, enough to leave one speechless for the rest of the evening. Ernestine waited out the ordeal calmly, and her first remark, as soon as the lights came on again, earned for her applause even from those who came to hiss her.

The occasion for this unusual event was a Bible convention. Not a Bible convention called together by preachers and ministers, but one organized and presided over by social reformers, including abolitionists, freethinkers, infidels and advocates of woman's rights, "for the purpose of freely and fully canvassing the authority and influence of the Jewish and Christian Scriptures." A combination of such a subject with such speakers guaranteed to produce a riotous meeting, and it did. Hartford had never before witnessed anything like it. During the last session of the four-day convention, soon after Ernestine had finished her second address, the assembly broke up in a state of uncontrollable chaos, with the mayor of Hartford in the hall, surveying the scene.

It was Garrison, the man who opened every anti-slavery meeting by reading a portion from the Scriptures, who masterminded the Bible convention. Because Hartford was the home of Yale's Trinity College and a citadel of orthodoxy, it was regarded as a place that would benefit most from such a gathering. This was not the first time that Garrison had digressed from abolitionism to become a spokesman for religious reform. Much to the displeasure of some of his colleagues who felt that the abolitionist movement was embattled enough as it was without getting embroiled with the organized church, Garrison was largely responsible in 1840, and again in 1848, for the anti-Sabbath conventions in Boston; and now he was to subject the Bible itself to the test of a critical examination. As the Call to the convention stated, "We invite, therefore, all who feel an interest in this question, without distinction of sex, color, sect, or party to come together, that we may sit down like brethren in a communion before the altar of intellectual and spiritual freedom."

It would have been unthinkable for Ernestine not to answer such a Call. As an Owenite she believed that man was the victim of error and superstition and that the Bible fostered both; and as a woman's rights advocate she knew from personal experience how obstinately the clergy, using the Bible as their authority, opposed woman's demands for equal rights. She came to Hartford not only to give her views of the Bible but also to represent her sex. She was the only woman speaker at the convention.

About seven hundred divinity students descended upon Melodeon Hall to lend support to the several clergymen who had undertaken to defend the Bible against the infidel heretics. They stamped their feet, hooted and shouted. At times the speakers' voices were completely drowned out by the deafening noise. The reporter for the *New York Herald* wrote that once, when Ernestine spoke in rebuttal, ". . . the storm which had been brewing burst like an avalanche upon her head. Groaning, hissing, stamping, barking, crowing, and every token of disapprobation were most liberally lavished upon her, but she bore it bravely."

Being a woman, a fighter for woman's rights and a free-thinker, the frenzied mob lashed out at her with particular fury. One of the rioters found the gas-meter and turned off the gas in the middle of her speech. To Garrison they appeared at that moment "like a troop of demons let loose from the pit." When the lights went on again Ernestine said, "When the lights were extinguished it reminded me of one of the true things we find in the Bible, that some there are 'who love darkness better than light.'" For a moment the hissing and the stamping gave way to laughter and applause.

Always the Owenite, always mindful of the fact that man is the product of his environment, Ernestine never lost her temper when facing an unruly mob. At the first interruption in her speech she paused and calmly said, "My conviction is that man always acts as well as he can; and if I see my poor, unfortunate fellow-being act as it appears to me inconsistent and irrational, I can but pity him for it."

At the third interruption she lifted her eyes to the gallery, where most of the troublemakers were concentrated, and said, "My friends, there was once a time when I had a voice strong enough to speak against all opposition, and be heard, but that time is past. My constitution has been somewhat broken, and mainly broken in the great conflict against error. I had hoped that whatever our opponents might think of my opinions, they would behave like gentlemen, though believers and defenders of the Bible." There were cries of "Hear! Hear!" and one lady in the audience called out to her, "If you have a heart to speak, speak on." Ernestine smiled and said, "I thank my sister for saying so. I have a heart to speak, and I will speak."

She did speak on for a full hour, and again the next day for an hour and a half. Much of what she said was drowned out by the tumult but thanks to the presence of a professional stenographer in the hall her speeches were preserved in the published proceedings of the convention.

The end of the convention was greeted with a flood of vituperous editorial comment in newspapers from various parts of the country denouncing the meeting as a gathering of infidel and abolitionist fanatics whose aim it was to destroy Christian civilization. Garrison and the other speakers were roundly attacked, but Ernestine was singled out as a special target for the editors' fury. The *Hartford Courant*, referring to Ernestine, wrote, "Shame then to the woman who will so unsex herself . . . amid an assembly of male Infidels and scoffers . . ." And the *Boston Bee* found that ". . . worse and more melancholy than all, was Mrs. Ernestine L. Rose of New York, her heart saturated with the fiery liquid of infidelity, and her tongue uttering sentiments too shockingly wicked to repeat."

If Ernestine increased the number of her enemies among the clergy as a result of her speeches at the Bible convention she gained the friendship of an ex-clergyman, whom she greatly admired and respected. His name was Joseph Barker, an Englishman who came to America in 1851 and settled in Ohio. His reputation as a fighter for freedom preceded him to this country. In England he had been a leader of the Chartist movement. During the turbulent days of 1848 the British authorities arrested him. While he was in prison his followers elected him to Parliament. He had hardly settled in his new homeland when he made contact with reform and anti-slavery circles. Ernestine had heard much about him but had not met him until she came to the Hartford convention of which he was president. It marked the beginning of a warm friendship. The more she saw of him the more she admired him. To the readers of the *Boston Investigator* she described him as a "faithful and fearless reformer," and the possessor of "an uncommonly strong, decided, firm, clear and intelligent mind..." In August, 1855, they both attended a reform convention at Waverly, Tioga County, N.Y., where Barker delivered at least six major addresses during the convention's nine sessions. Ernestine was so impressed with his outstanding performance that she wrote in her account, "I have never heard a lecture so replete with facts, truth and arguments as every one of those given by Mr. Barker . . . he is so fearless, so powerful, so perfectly invincible that you listen to him with wonder and amazement. . . . Such a man is invaluable."

The admiration was not one-sided. In 1854 Mr. Barker revisited England and delivered a series of lectures in Sheffield on American social reformers. In one of them he said this about his friend: "Ernestine L. Rose is the most perfect specimen of intellectual and moral excellence I have had the happiness to know . . . Her powers of mind, her powers of speech, her purse, her health, her life, are one continual sacrifice to humanity . . . Her eloquence is irresistible. It shakes, it awes, it thrills . . . To hear her reason you might fancy she was all intelligence; to hear her plead you would think her an incarnation of benevolence." This, from the man she so greatly respected, was a most thrilling tribute.

Some years later Mr. Barker made an about face and returned to the fold of the church and the pulpit. In 1874, one year before his death, he published his autobiography under the title, *Modern Skepticism: A Journey Through the Land of Doubt and Back Again.* His second apostasy created quite a stir in free thought and infidel circles. The *Boston Investigator*, always a hotbed of theological dispute, bristled with criticism of his defection. As far as is known Ernestine did not join in this public denunciation of him. But one could well imagine how painful her disappointment must have been.

On a cloudy August morning about two hundred men and women, Negro and white, gathered at the Fulton Street pier in New York to board the steamer *Island City*, for an excursion trip to Flushing, L.I. They were brave souls every one of them. It had rained heavily the night before and part of the morning; and even now the overcast sky threatened a downpour momentarily. It was hardly the weather for an all-day picnic. But this was no ordinary pleasure trip. It was a trip with a purpose, and for these passengers the importance of the purpose had, apparently, outweighed considerations about the weather.

Their destination was St. Ronan's Well, an enchantingly beautiful grove overlooking the entire Sound, where, under the open sky, they would celebrate the nineteenth anniversary of the British West Indian Emancipation, which took place in 1834. William Lloyd Garrison and Ernestine Rose were among the speakers to address them and, being abolitionists, they understood the significance of attending such a celebration in New York, in the year 1853.

For the past several years the pro-slavery forces in the North had been increasingly more vocal and aggressive due largely to the fact that the threat of secession emanating from the South frightened the Northern manufacturers into believing that they might lose the Southern market. Abolitionists like Garrison and Ernestine Rose knew that it was an empty threat and warned against being taken in by it. But the Northern merchant class would not take any risks; for them the issue of slavery was reduced to the practical choice between profit and principle and profit won. Under the guise of the patriotic slogan that the Union must be saved at all costs they supported the evil Fugitive Slave Law; and when James Gordon Bennett incited the mob to break up anti-slavery meetings he did so with the blessing of the genteel merchant class. New York abolitionists well remembered the stormy Tabernacle meeting in May of 1850 when the mayor and the chief of police left them to the tender mercies of Captain Rynders' Tammany hoodlums.

Under these circumstances the American Anti-Slavery Society had suffered reverses, but rallied again in 1853 and its revitalized New York branch felt itself strong enough to organize this out-door celebration.

At exactly 9 A.M. the *Island City* tooted its horn and sailed. In the meantime the clouds had lifted and the sun had come out bringing several hundred more people to the pier, ready to join in the celebration. But they had missed the boat and the most they could do was to wave enviously to the departing passengers. The trip lasted an hour and a half. Around 1 P.M. a heavy downpour descended on the audience and the celebration, already in progress, was continued indoors in a building prepared for just such an emergency.

Ernestine spoke right after Garrison, who delivered the main address. In introducing her, Lauren Wetmore, president of the New York City Anti-Slavery Society said, "I have the pleasure to announce to you a speaker from that portion of mankind who are not always represented on occasions like this, by their own orators." Her speech was frequently punctuated by laughter and applause as she related her experiences in Columbia, South Carolina, in the winter of 1847.

"What is it to be a slave?" she asked. And she answered:

"Not to be your own, bodily, mentally, or morally—that is to be a slave. Ay, even if the slaveholders treated their slaves with the utmost kindness and charity; if I were told they kept them sitting on a sofa all day, and fed them with the best of the land, it is none the less slavery. For what does slavery mean? To work hard, to fare ill, to suffer hardship, that is not slavery; for many of us white men and women have to work hard, have to fare ill, have to suffer hardship and yet we are not slaves. Slavery is, not to belong to yourself—to be robbed of yourself . . . This is the great abomination of slavery, that it deprives a man of the common rights of humanity, stamped upon him by his maker . . .

"But the great act of emancipation of 800,000 human beings has shown to the world that the African race are not only capable of taking care of themselves, but are capable of enjoying peacefully as much liberty and as much freedom as the white man . . ."

No speech of Ernestine's was complete without her touching on the woman question, and this one was no exception.

She saved that subject for the very end of her address, and concluded with the following words: "Emancipation from every kind of bondage is my principle. I go for the recognition of human rights, without distinction of sect, party, sex, or color."

Considering the bad weather the celebration was a huge success, but the pro-slavery *New York Herald* called it "a contemptible failure." As for Ernestine, the *Herald* reported that "she had the same four cork-screw ringlets on each side of her face, the same white teeth, and the same disposition to show them, as usual. Time deals gently with Mrs. Rose and it would be gratifying if she would do the same with the English language."

In its reports about Ernestine the *Herald* applied a peculiarly double standard. When she delivered an address at a Thomas Paine birthday celebration she was the charming, witty and eloquent Mrs. Rose, whose speech was worthy of being printed in its entirety; but when she spoke at an anti-slavery rally she was unattractive and needed tutoring in English.

During the first week of September, 1853, so many public events took place in New York City that New Yorkers and visiting out-of-towners were at a loss as to what to attend first —the World Temperance Convention, the Whole World Temperance Convention, the Anti-Slavery Convention, the Woman's Rights Convention, or the first World's Fair ever held in the United States.

For those seeking excitement, convention is a drab word presaging a dull time. But it is safe to assume that those who went to any one of the four conventions had a more exciting time than those who chose to go to the Fair, although it was the latter that provided the incentive for the three reform movements to converge upon New York all at once, on the theory that out-of-towners who came to the Fair might also wander in to one of the conventions and get some food for thought as well.

Since the woman's rights meeting came at the very tail end of all the others it inherited a floating frenzied mob whose urge for violence had been whipped up to a high pitch by the *Daily Herald* and the clergy, with the result that this convention, held at the Broadway Tabernacle on September 6 and 7, was the stormiest in the history of the woman's rights movement. So loud and frequent were the interruptions from the gallery that the official stenographer and the newspaper reporters sitting close to the platform could not hear much of what the speakers were saying; even less was heard by the large audience that filled every available seat in the hall.

Ernestine Rose, who had a reputation for keeping her composure under any situation and for winning the attention even of ruffians, found herself helpless in the face of this unruly mob. And William Lloyd Garrison, brimming over with anger, turned toward the gallery and cried out, "Where is the man who presents himself decently and proffers a word of reasonable argument against our cause? I have yet to see that man. Instead we have blackguardism, defamation, rowdyism, profanity; . . ." He was interrupted by a burst of hisses. "Hiss, ye serpents!" he shouted back. "Ye have nothing else to offer. There is not one of you to whom God has given a brain to fathom an argument."

Present in the audience was the distinguished Horace Greeley. The woman's rights movement had been wooing Mr. Greeley ardently, and for good reason. "When he speaks," Lucy Stone once said of him, "the nation listens." But Mr. Greeley was always more generous with the pages of his *Tribune* than with his personal endorsement of the movement. His sympathy with the cause, though genuine, was limited and hedged with reservations. He actually believed that woman was not man's intellectual equal, and said so. But he also believed that if woman wanted the right to vote she was entitled to it and he, as a man, would not object. He maintained that it was woman's duty to achieve that right by her own efforts. It was therefore somewhat of a minor triumph for the movement that Mr. Greeley consented to come to this convention, although he was there as a guest and not as a speaker. But before the first evening session was over he found himself embroiled in more than he had bargained for, and emerged the hero of the evening.

This happened when Ernestine stepped forward to deliver her major address. She had hardly opened her mouth when she was greeted with a burst of boos and hisses. It took some time before she was allowed to begin her speech, but the interruptions from the gallery were so loud and persistent that it was impossible for her to continue. At that point Horace Greeley strode off the platform, walked up to the gallery and, according to the *New York Herald*, got himself tangled up in what was then called a "mugs." He and a ruffian had an exchange of words which led to an exchange of blows. The commotion in the hall was now at its height. The entire convention was on its feet. The noise was deafening.

"Friends, be seated," Ernestine pleaded from the platform, "be seated and I will continue my remarks." But the audience would not listen. Finally and with the aid of a policeman Greeley succeeded in stilling the uproar and was cheered for restoring to the convention a semblance of order. In this atmosphere, crackling with tension and violence, Ernestine tried to explain the laws of New York State as they applied to married women, pointing out some of the legal pitfalls they must guard against. She cited the newly won married woman's property bill as an example of how deceptive the law could be with regard to woman's rights. That bill granted a married woman ownership of the real estate she had brought with her into marriage, or which she inherited after marriage. But if she asked her husband to sell it for her the money he received was legally his as soon as it came into his hand.

And there were things a woman had to learn about wills and testaments. In the first place, only the husband could make out a will, the wife had no such right. If she had made out a will prior to marriage the husband could nullify it. In New

York State, Ernestine reminded her audience, "wills may be made out by all persons, except idiots, persons of unsound mind, married women and infants. Male infants ought to consider it quite an insult to be placed in the same category with married women. No, a married woman has no right to bequeath a dollar of the property, no matter how much she may have brought into marriage, or accumulated in it. Not a dollar to a friend, a relative, or even to her own child to keep him from starving. And this is the law in the nineteenth century, in the enlightened United States, under a Republic that declares all men to be free and equal."

If the husband died without leaving a will the law permitted the widow to live in the house for forty days rent free. Beyond this she was entitled to an interest in one third of the real estate for the rest of her life. Ernestine figured out that if the real estate was worth a thousand dollars the widow's share would amount to twenty dollars and two cents!

The situation was entirely different when the wife died. Then "all that is left is her husband's; there is no interference of the law, no change is made, no stranger intrudes on his home and his affliction; no one dares to ask a question concerning the things which she, whom he loved, has left behind her. But it is otherwise when the husband dies . . . strangers assume authority denied to the wife and mother; the sanctuary of affliction and sorrow must be desecrated, everything ransacked and assessed by the agents of the law."

Until these discriminatory laws were abolished women had to be taught how best to protect themselves under the existing legal framework. For this reason a will expert named Joseph A. Dugdale was invited, from time to time, to address a woman's rights convention on the fine legal points pertaining to wills. Dugdale was not an inspired speaker, and the subject of last wills and testaments was hardly a cheerful one for an audience consisting largely of young women, many of whom were still unmarried. But the prospect of remaining penniless was even less cheerful. For the potential widow the fine print in her husband's last will and testament was literally a matter of survival. And so Mr. Dugdale had to be listened to with urgent, if not rapt, attention.

The rowdyism that marked the first day of the Tabernacle convention continued unabated on the second day. When Sojourner Truth rose to speak a deafening roar of shouts and hisses filled the auditorium. For the ruffians beheld on the platform not only a woman but a Negro and the mob that came to break up a woman's rights convention was also pro-slavery. But the tall, sixty-year old ex-slave was a veteran of many storms and braved this one as well. Dressed in a blue gown and wearing a white kerchief around her head she stood there calmly surveying the audience, waiting for the tumult to subside. "Is it not good for me to come and draw forth a spirit," she began, "to see what kind of spirit people are of? I see that some of you have got the spirit of a goose, and some have got the spirit of a snake. . . . I've been lookin' round and watchin' things, and I know a little mite 'bout woman's rights too. I come forth to speak 'bout woman's rights and want to throw in my little might, to keep the scales a-movin'. I know that it feels a kind o' hissin' and ticklin' like to see a colored woman get up and tell you about things, and woman's rights. We have all been thrown down so low that nobody thought we'd ever get up again; but we have been long enough trodden down now; we will come up again, and now I am here. . . . I am sittin' among you to watch; and every once and awhile I will come out and tell you what time of night it is."

At the last evening session Lucretia Mott, who presided, introduced a guest to address the convention. She was Madame Mathilde Francesca Anneke, a German lady with a handsome round face, and a social reformer with a colorful revolutionary background. Born in Westphalia and raised a Catholic, she became an author, editor and educator, and had traveled the arduous road from religion to free thought. Her husband, a Prussian artillery officer, had been arrested and tried for treason for having joined the revolutionary forces in the 1848 uprising. While he was in jail she published two newspapers; one of them was *Die Frauenzeitung* with which she pioneered in woman's rights. Both papers were suppressed by the police. Upon his release from prison her husband rejoined the revolutionary forces, with Carl Schurz as his aide-de-camp and Madame Anneke as his mounted orderly. In 1849 they were compelled to flee Germany and, like so many other revolutionaries of that period, found a haven in the United States. At the time of the convention she was living in Newark, N. J., where she once again was publishing *Die Frauenzeitung.*

As Madame Anneke stepped up to the dais, Ernestine stood by her side ready to translate her speech from German into English. But the mob would not even let her begin. "I wish to say only a few words," Madame Anneke said, trying to make herself heard above the tumult. "On the other side of the Atlantic there is no freedom of any kind, and we have not even the right to claim freedom of speech. But can it be that here too there are tyrants who violate the individual right to express opinions on any subject? And do you call yourselves republicans? No, there is no republic without freedom of speech." But she could not continue. Having left the sickbed to greet the convention, she was too weak to outshout the mob.

Wendell Phillips rose and tried to still the tumult. "Allow me to say one word," he pleaded with the rowdies, "purely as a matter of the self-respect which you owe to yourselves . . . this New York audience is now looking upon a noble woman . . . one who has faced the cannon of Francis Joseph of Austria, for the rights of the people. Is this the welcome you give her to the shores of republican America?"

For a moment it appeared as though Phillips' plea had an effect on the mob. But this was an illusion. Madame Anneke was forced to withdraw from the rostrum amidst a roaring noise. When another intervention by Phillips had failed, it was clear that the situation was beyond control. It was decided that the police be called upon to restore order, but since it was

against the principles of a Quaker to resort to the use of force
Mrs. Mott relinquished the president's chair to Ernestine Rose,
who immediately stepped forward and said, "As presiding officer for this evening I call upon the police. The mayor, too,
promised to see that our meetings shall not be disturbed, and I
now call upon him to preserve order. As citizens of New York
we have a right to this protection, for we pay our money for
it." Her voice, loud and clear, rose above the babel but the
police did not intercede. Encouraged by the indifference of
the law the mob became even more arrogant. At this point
Ernestine called out, "I regret that I have to call upon the police to keep order; and if they are not able to do it, I call upon
the meeting to help them." The meeting's response was pandemonium. Phillips leaped to his feet and, looking up to the
gallery, shouted, "I warn you that the truth has often floated
further on the shouts of a mob than from the lips of the most
eloquent speaker." A fine thought by a great orator, but the
mob was unimpressed. The official stenographer gave the following description of these last moments of the convention:
"The confusion now reached its climax; a terrific uproar,
shouting, yelling, screaming, bellowing, laughing, stamping
. . . prevented anything orderly being heard, and the convention, on the motion of Mrs. Rose, was adjourned *sine
die* . . ."

Commenting on the end of the convention, Horace Greeley's *Tribune* and William Cullen Bryant's *Evening Post*
sharply condemned the mob spirit that invaded the assembly;
but Bennett's *Herald* gloated editorially, hailing the last day
as "a great day for New York, a day to be long remembered
in its annals."

It is important to note that even at this stormy New York
convention the leadership continued to forge the bond of solidarity between themselves and their sisters abroad. Amidst
the noise and tumult of the mob the following resolution was
unanimously adopted, "*Resolved*, That inasmuch as this great
movement is intended to meet the wants not of America only,

but of the whole world, a committee be appointed to prepare an address from this convention to the women of Great Britain and the Continent of Europe setting forth our objects and inviting their cooperation in the same." Ernestine Rose was nominated to serve on this committee.

One month after the riotous Tabernacle meeting Ernestine was in Cleveland attending the fourth National Woman's Rights Convention. The Cleveland assembly was not as tumultuous as was the one in New York, but neither was it all peace and harmony. Voices were raised, tempers flared up and feelings ran high; but on the whole the clash was one of ideas and not of fists, and the three thousand people who occupied every available inch of space at Melodeon Hall were treated to a refreshing experience in democracy; not the caucus room but the entire convention became the ideological laboratory for the growing woman's rights movement. Leaders aired their sharply divergent views on basic issues of principle pertaining to the movement on the public platform and invited the audience to participate in the debate. In this open and democratic process of forging and crystallizing the ideology of the movement Ernestine played a leading role. The *Cleveland Plain Dealer* was quick to recognize this and wrote that Mrs. Rose was "decidedly the master spirit of the convention."

When Joseph Barker advanced the argument that "Woman can safely be trusted with her rights," and pleaded with the men not to fear that women will some day use their rights against them, Ernestine rejected this line of reasoning. "I promise not how we shall use our rights," she said. "I will no more promise how we shall use our rights than man has promised before he obtained them how he would use his rights." There was one argument, she pointed out, why woman should obtain her rights, and this she regarded as "the argument of arguments . . ." namely, "on the broad ground of *human rights*." And, as was customary at those conventions, she concluded her remarks with presenting a resolution: "*Resolved,*

That by human rights we mean natural rights, in contradis-
tinction from conventional usages . . ."

She clashed with other speakers on yet another question of
principle. Someone had stated that man was fully conscious of
his tyranny over woman and therefore must be held responsible for it. Once again Ernestine disagreed. ". . . I will repeat it
as one of my views and principles," she said, "and I presume
it will not be too presumptuous to say, it is the principle of all
the friends who advocate this cause; we do not fight with man
himself, but only with bad principles. Man is inconsistent, and
he has been made through that inconsistency, tyrannical. Man
has been unjust because bad laws always will make bad men.
We have bad laws hence man has been bad; but so thoroughly
good is human nature that in spite of bad laws man is not as
bad as he might be under them. . . . You will say these laws
were made by man. True! But they were framed in ignorance
of the ultimate end or aim of the human being, man or woman,
and ignorance of the relations of the sexes . . . This is an additional reason why we wish all these laws altered, for it can be
no otherwise than inconsistent when one half of the race
frame laws for the other half. Man is not now, in the full
sense, man, any more than woman is, in the full sense, woman.
It requires both to enact rational and proper laws for the
rational government of both; and this is the reason why we
claim our rights fully, fearlessly and entirely."

On this point William Lloyd Garrison was in sharp disagreement with Ernestine. He said, ". . . our eloquent friend,
Mrs. Rose, who stood on this platform and pleaded with such
marked ability, as she always does plead in any cause she un-
dertakes to speak upon, told us her creed. . . . For my part, I
am not prepared to respect that philosophy. I believe in sin,
therefore in a sinner; in theft, therefore in a thief; in slavery,
therefore in a slave-holder; in wrong, therefore in a wrong-
doer; and unless the men of this nation are made by woman to
see that they have been guilty of usurpation, and cruel usurpation, I believe very little progress will be made. . . ."

These disagreements over fundamental questions could not be resolved in one debate, or even in ten; but the debates were, in themselves, vital to achieving ideological clarity. They helped crystallize views and opinions and define positions of individual leaders, thus underlining more clearly the areas of agreement and clearing the way for a more harmonious working together. In this respect a woman's rights convention was, in the fullest sense of the word, a market place of ideas.

In Syracuse it was Rev. Hatch who created a disturbance and in Cleveland it was Rev. Dr. Nevin who succeeded in turning an orderly assembly into a scene of confusion. He so outraged the good taste of the audience with his insensitive attacks on people that at one point Garrison could control himself no longer and called out in anger, "It is utterly useless to attempt to correct the individual. He is manifestly here in the spirit of a blackguard and a rowdy."

In fairness to Rev. Nevin it should be said that he was not the only one to inject the religious question at this convention; he merely sought to make the most of it by foul means or fair. It was also introduced by Rev. Antoinette Brown despite the fact that only a year ago, at Syracuse, her attempt to harmonize woman's rights with the Bible had nearly wrecked that convention. Now, in Cleveland, a three-cornered debate developed between Rev. Brown, Rev. Nevin and ex-Rev. Barker which threatened to wreck this convention. And while this heated theological battle raged, wrote the *Cleveland Plain Dealer*, "The cause of woman was all this while in the background."

In Cleveland, as in Syracuse, Ernestine did her utmost to lift the convention from the theological quagmire and restore it to its proper level. "I want to make a suggestion to the meeting," she said. "This is the afternoon of the last day of our convention. We have now heard here the Bible arguments on both sides, and I may say to them that I agree with neither . . . 'There is a time and a season for everything,' and this is no time to discuss the Bible. I appeal to the universal experience of men to sustain me in asking whether the introduction of theological quibbles has not been a firebrand wherever they have been thrown. We have a political question under discussion; let us take that question and argue it with reference to right and wrong, and let us argue it in the same way that your fathers and mothers did when they wanted to throw off the British yoke." Finally, common sense prevailed and the last session of the convention proceeded in an orderly fashion.

Ernestine, too, had her tilt with Rev. Nevin but not on the subject of religion; she would not be drawn into that. But when he resorted to the favorite argument of some legislators and clergymen that granting American women their rights would make them as licentious and immoral as were the women of France, Ernestine leaped to the defense of French womanhood. "I throw back the slander he uttered in regard to French women," she said with emotion. "I am not a French woman, but if there is no other here to vindicate them, *I* will do it. The French women are as moral as any other people in any country; and when they have not been as moral, it has been because they have been priest-ridden. I love to vindicate the rights of those who are not present to defend themselves."

At the end of that stormy afternoon session, when Garrison and Rev. Nevin had clashed sharply, the two men had suddenly met face to face in the vestibule of the hall, whereupon the clergyman, still bitter over Garrison's remarks, demanded an apology. When Garrison refused to apologize, Rev. Nevin, in a fit of violence, seized the other's nose, wrenching it hard; but Garrison, true to his principle of non-violence, did not retaliate. He merely said to the clergyman, "Do you feel better, my friend? Do you hope thus to break the force of my argument?" Soon friends of Dr. Nevin appeared on the scene and separated them.

A somewhat different, and probably more authentic, version of this episode appeared in the *True Democrat*, which described the incident as follows: "After the meeting adjourned,

D. R. Nevin, a brother of the parson, met Garrison at the
street entrance, and demanded from him an apology for the
gross insult to his brother. Garrison, of course, refused to
render the required satisfaction, whereupon the young man
took him by the proboscis, and gave it a considerable tweak,
remarking that he would take the liberty of pulling an apology
from his face. The affair created considerable excitement."

Dr. Nevin's friends did their utmost to hush up this incident and even pleaded with the ladies in charge of the convention report to omit it from the record. But history de-
creed otherwise; and whether it was Nevin himself or his
brother who committed the foul deed, the world may now
know that for his staunch advocacy of woman's rights the
gallant Garrison even had his "proboscis" tweaked.

On the way home from Cleveland Ernestine and Lucretia
Mott stopped off in Buffalo to address a woman's rights meeting held in Townsend Hall. The reporter for the *Buffalo
Commercial Advertiser* referred to the two women as the
"Old Girls from New York." Ernestine was described as "a
female filibuster," who "went off like an overloaded musket
and was evidently disposed to kick." The meeting was attended by about three hundred people but judging from the
account in the *Advertiser* one would think that they had come
to witness the performance of two circus clowns rather than
to hear two of America's outstanding women reformers on
an important subject. The most objective part of the account
is a description of the speakers' apparel. Ernestine was reported as wearing "a black satin dress, open in the front, with
a lace stomacher, lace undersleeves and black lace mittens.
A brooch, a watch and chain, and some sparkling rings."

She had been home little more than a month when she was
off again on another trip, this time to Rochester, N. Y. to
attend a two-day state convention on woman's rights. The
movement had already made sufficient inroads into various
parts of the State for the leaders to consider a bold thrust in

the direction of the legislature. This may well explain the concentration of so many national figures at a state gathering. The speakers' list glittered with such names as Frederick Douglass, Susan B. Anthony, Antoinette Brown, Amelia Bloomer, Matilda Joslyn Gage, William Henry Channing and Rev. Samuel J. May of Syracuse. Ernestine could very well have been spared the arduous trip from New York. But this was more than an ordinary state convention; it was also a meeting of the high command to lay out the plans and map the strategy for a move on the State capital in the winter of 1854. Ernestine was elected to a committee whose task it was "to prepare and to present an address to the Legislature of New York . . ." But if these speeches were to have any effect at all on the hard-bitten legislators they would have to have the visible support of their constituents. And so, at the close of the convention, an appeal was issued to the women *and men* of the state to "instantly and energetically circulate the petitions in their respective neighborhoods." In two months time thirteen thousand signatures were collected from thirty counties.

Sallie Holley, a well known anti-slavery orator, also attended the Rochester convention and later was introduced to Ernestine. Several days later she noted her impression of Ernestine in a letter dated December 6: ". . . Ernestine L. Rose is a charming woman and at times playful . . . She is far before any woman speaker I ever heard. She is splendidly clear and logical . . . But, oh! I cannot give any idea of the power and beauty of her speech. I can only stammer about it a little."

Chapter XVII

QUEEN OF THE PLATFORM

IN THE WINTER OF 1854 the woman's rights movement made its first grand entrance into Albany, N. Y., by holding a state convention in that city. The event was scheduled to last only two days, February 14-15, but the population's interest in the controversial subject of woman's rights and in the personalities of its leading advocates was so great that the two days stretched to fourteen, and for two full weeks the State capital was in a whirl of excitement. In the evenings the women lectured to crowded halls; in the daytime they were in the Legislature, arguing their cause before Assembly and Senate committees; newspapers opened their columns to the subject; readers wrote irate letters to the editor; the principals involved dashed off replies. Albany had not seen anything like it before, and did not regain its composure for weeks afterwards.

Unlike previous woman's rights conventions, this one was aimed directly at the hearts and minds of the lawmakers, and the lawmakers were not taken by surprise. The convention Call which was printed in practically every newspaper in the state declared in the very opening sentence that a batch of petitions demanding changes in the law "will be presented to the Legislature around the middle of February." Their curiosity aroused, some legislators even came to the convention. The *Albany Transcript*, describing one session, wrote, "The meeting last evening was attended by the largest and most brilliant audience of the series. A large number of members of the Legislature were there, and a full representation of our most influential citizens . . . Mrs. Rose was the sole speaker, owing to the necessity which had called the others away . . . She was listened to with the most profound attention, and encouraged by frequent and prolonged applause." After paying tribute to other convention speakers the *Transcript* went on to say, "But Mrs. Rose is the queen of the company. On the educational question in particular she rises to a high standard of oratorical power. When speaking of Hungary and her own crushed Poland, she is full of eloquence and pathos, and she has as great a power to chain an audience as any of our best male speakers."

After Ernestine had appeared before a Senate Select Committee, the *Albany Register*, which did not share the *Transcript's* high opinion of her, was somewhat annoyed with the senators for being timorous in her presence. "They were calm," wrote the *Register*, "but evidently felt themselves in great peril . . . The Honorable Senators quailed beneath the trial."

A high moment in Ernestine's visit to the Legislature came when she addressed a Committee of the Assembly. The large audience, composed mainly of women, filled every available seat in the chamber and the galleries and some crowded into the lobbies, while the legislators sat around the desks usually occupied by the clerks. Ernestine spoke at some length. At one point, looking squarely at the lawmakers, she said, "Gentlemen . . . these are not the demands of the moment or the few; they are the demands of the age; of the second half of the nineteenth century. The world will endure after us, and future generations may look back to this meeting to acknowledge that a great onward step was here taken in the cause of human progress." When she had finished the chamber echoed with applause.

As Ernestine turned her gaze from the somber faces of the legislators to those of her vast and spirited audience she may well have indulged in a moment of retrospection. Eighteen years ago she had sent off to Albany her first petition, containing five signatures, the fruit of five months' work in behalf of a Married Woman's Property Bill. She had stood alone then, and her five signatures had no doubt landed in some legislator's waste basket. But today, as she spoke, she had the mandate not only of those present in the chamber, and of the thousands who signed the petitions; she was the spokesman of a young and vigorous movement that was daily bringing the concept of woman's rights into ever wider areas of the American population. No wonder some legislators, as they listened to her, "quailed beneath the trial."

And so did the *Albany Register*, but it did more than quail; it fumed and raged, and bemoaned the fact that "there should be any who are willing to follow the lead of such foreign propagandists as the ringleted, glove-handed, exotic, Ernestine Rose . . . This Mrs. Ernestine L. Rose, with a train of followers, like a great kite with a very long tail, has, for a week been amusing Senatorial and Assembly Committees, with her woman's rights performances free of charge . . . Those committees have sat for hours, grave and solemn as owls, listening to the outpourings of fanaticism and folly of this Polish propagandist . . ." In its zeal to paint her in the blackest colors, the *Register* even stooped to falsifying facts. It wrote that Ernestine came to America because "she was compelled to fly in pursuit of freedom." Ernestine promptly replied, and her letter to the editor which the *Register* printed, read in part:

"Every one who ever advanced a new idea, no matter how great and noble, has been subjected to criticism and therefore we too must expect it . . . But there is one thing which I think even editors have no right to do, namely: to state a positive falsehood, or even to imply one, for the purpose of injuring another . . .

"In the article alluded to, you say: 'Ernestine L. Rose came to this country, as she says, from Poland, whence she was compelled to fly in pursuit of freedom.' It is true that I came from Poland; but it is false that I was compelled to fly from my country, except by the compulsion, or dictates of the same spirit of 'propagandism,' that induced so many of my noble countrymen to shed their blood in the defence of the rights of this country, and the rights of man, wherever he struggles for freedom.

"But I have no desire to claim martyrdom which does not belong to me. I left my country, not flying, but deliberately. I chose to make this country my home in preference to any other, because if you carried out the theories you profess, it would indeed be the noblest country on the earth. And as my countrymen so nobly aided in the physical struggle for Freedom and Independence, I felt, and still feel it equally my duty to use my humble abilities to the uttermost in my power to aid in the great moral struggle for human rights and human freedom."

What the women wanted from the Legislature was an extension of the rights they had gained six years earlier with the passage of the Married Woman's Property Bill. They asked that a married woman be allowed to own in her own name not only the property she inherited but also the money and property she obtained through her own efforts during her marriage. What was the good of owning property, they argued, if you could not buy, sell, sign a contract, or in any way engage in business activities of your own? Giving her ownership of her own earnings would prevent a husband from coming to his wife's employer at the end of the week to claim her pay.

Another law the women asked for was one that would grant mothers the custody of their children. According to existing statutes a father could, without the mother's consent, and even in the face of her protests, apprentice his children to any trade of his choosing, or for the purpose of working off his debts. And if he so desired, the father could will away his children to a guardian of his own choice and thus deprive them of their mother altogether.

The women also petitioned for the right to sue, the right to be sued, to be tried by a jury and to have women on the jury whenever a woman was on trial. And finally they demanded what they regarded the most important right of all, the right to vote and to be voted for.

The legislators, having heard the oral arguments for these demands, and having before them thousands of petitions, now pondered what to do next. Some were of the opinion that the petitions should go to a Select Committee for consideration, but Assemblyman Burnett, of Essex, argued against it. As far as he was concerned these women did not deserve any consideration whatsoever because, he said, "they do not appear to be satisfied with having unsexed themselves, but they desire to unsex every female in the land, and to set the whole community ablaze with unhallowed fire. I trust, sir, the House may deliberate before we suffer them to cast this firebrand into our midst." In his eagerness to defame them the gentleman from Essex even resorted to the self-contradictory charge that what these "unsexed women" really wanted was to replace the sacred institution of matrimony with "species of legal adultery." And finally he invoked the familiar Bible argument: "We know that God created man as the representative of the race; that after his creation, his Creator took from his side the material for woman's creation; and that, by the institution of matrimony, woman was restored to the side of man and became one flesh and one being."

The Assembly decided to refer the petitions, with an accompanying address by Elizabeth Cady Stanton, to a Select Committee of seven. But Mr. Burnett's defeat was as momentary as it was inconsequential. Five weeks later, when the Committee brought in its report, he emerged victorious. The report was a long and sanctimonious apology for denying the petitioners' requests. "A higher power than that from which emanates legislative enactments," the lawmakers intoned piously, "has given forth the mandate that man and woman shall not be equal . . . and civil power must, in its enactments, recognize this inequality. We can not obliterate it if we would, and legal inequalities must follow." The Committee did make two recommendations. One, that existing laws be so amended as to give a mother a say in the selection of a guardian for her children, or in the choice of their apprenticeship; and, two, when a wife had to go to work to support herself and the children she was entitled to her own earnings. But even these concessions were ignored by the Assembly and the net result was zero.

The women were disappointed but not disheartened. The twelve-year struggle for the married woman's property bill had taught them a valuable lesson: the Legislature might be stubborn, but it was not invincible; it would give way under pressure, provided the pressure was strong enough and persistent enough. They now aimed to make that pressure formidable. They sat down and planned their strategy for the years ahead. From now on they would hold a woman's rights meeting in every county of the state; step up the petitions campaign; increase the sale of literature and hold an annual state convention in Albany when the Legislature convened for its winter session.

Susan B. Anthony was made general agent in charge of the overall program. One of her most difficult problems was that of getting known speakers for these meetings. Ernestine Rose was one of the few women she could depend upon. That year woman's rights meetings were held in fifty-five different counties of the state; twenty thousand pieces of literature were sold and a new batch of petitions was filled with thousands of signatures. Ernestine was a featured speaker at many of these meetings. She traveled with Susan from place to place in all kinds of weather until her health broke down and she was compelled to go home. On a cold January day she spoke for two hours at Bath, Steuben County, N. Y., to a crowded hall, on the legal disabilities of woman. Afterwards the Bath newspaper commented editorially: "She [Ernestine Rose] is one of the best speakers we have ever heard, and we can only regret that a woman of such brilliant intellect should be wasting her energies in a cause for which there is not a shadow of hope."

But in Binghamton, Broome County, N. Y., where she spoke three months later, the editor of that town's paper took a more optimistic view of the movement. "The 'Reform' is sweeping on and cannot fail, with such advocates as Mrs. Rose and Miss Anthony, greatly to promote the *rights* and redress the *wrongs* of Woman."

While the legislators in Albany had been debating what to do with the petitions and thinking up reasons why they should not do anything about them, Susan B. Anthony and Ernestine went on an exploratory trip to Washington, D. C., to see how the nation's capital would react to the question of woman's rights. Susan assumed the role of organizer and general manager of the enterprise, and Ernestine was the main attraction as the speaker. In Washington they found little enthusiasm for the subject of woman's rights and a lot of prejudice against Ernestine Rose.

Even more than her unorthodox views on religion it was her abolitionism that made her suspect. This was especially true of Alexandria, Va. and Baltimore, Md., which were also part of their itinerary. From Baltimore Susan wrote to Garrison, "From the land of slavery I write. There is no mistaking the fact. The saddening, hateful evidences are on every side." One of the evidences was a general apathy to any kind of social reform. Their greatest fear, observed Susan, was "the fear that some word shall be uttered which shall endanger their 'pet institution.'"

When Susan tried to rent a hall for Ernestine's lecture the proprietor said to her, "You know we are a sensitive people, and don't like to allow persons to speak in our halls, who will introduce topics foreign to those they announce."

"I suppose you refer to the topic of slavery?" Susan came to the point.

"Yes," the man replied.

"Well, sir," said Susan, "I wish you to understand that Mrs.

Rose is an out and out abolitionist. She is here to speak on woman's rights, and wishes the hall for that purpose; but if she should feel disposed, as I hope she will, to give an anti-slavery lecture, she will duly inform all parties concerned of her intentions."

During their week's stay in Baltimore Ernestine gave four lectures, two of which were on the subject of woman's rights. Her last lecture given at the Maryland Institute drew a capacity crowd and many were turned away for lack of space.

Their difficulty in obtaining a suitable lecture hall began in Washington, where they were completely unsuccessful in that respect. In desperation Susan turned to the Representative Chamber as a likely place for Ernestine to speak on a Sunday, but Chaplain Milburn refused the use of that room on the ground that "Mrs. Rose was not a member of any church." To this Susan replied that "our country stands for religious as well as civil liberty." The chaplain admitted that this was so but remained adamant in his refusal just the same. She then sought permission from Professor Henry to use the hall of the Smithsonian Institute. But he, too, discouraged her, saying that "it was necessary to avoid discussion of any exciting questions there, and it would disturb the harmony of feeling for a woman to speak." Fortunately Congressman Gerrit Smith of Peterboro, N. Y., himself an abolitionist and sympathetic to the cause of woman's rights, was in Washington at the time. He welcomed them warmly at his home, and two of the three lectures Ernestine gave in the capital were either in his own drawing room or at another private residence obtained through his influence. Her last lecture, entitled the "Nebraska Question As Deduced From Human Rights," was delivered in a place called Carusi's Saloon.

The Kansas-Nebraska Bill was the most hotly debated political issue of the year because it had a direct bearing on the thorny slavery question. It aimed at carving up the territory of Nebraska into separate territories granting each the right to determine for itself whether to allow slavery within its territorial confines or to forbid it. Abolitionists were violently opposed to the bill on the ground that it would open up the free territories for an extension of slavery. Senator Stephen A. Douglas of Illinois, who introduced the bill, was burned in effigy; the Democratic party was split in two and the bill's final passage on May 26, as the Kansas-Nebraska Act, led to the formation of the Republican Party.

Ernestine, naturally, spoke against this bill and, in her severe criticism of Senator Douglas, said, ". . . no one can place confidence in a traitor to his own principles." But whether the bill was passed or not, she felt, the mere fact that it had stirred up so much debate in Congress was a gain for the anti-slavery forces. Until the introduction of the Nebraska Bill Ernestine was not a disunionist, and in this respect differed from Garrison and the Garrison abolitionists who would have no union with the slave states. But something very unusual happened to her in Washington. She had walked into Carusi's Saloon a unionist and came out a disunionist. In the course of her lecture she had literally talked herself over to Garrison's position. In May 1855, while addressing an anti-slavery convention, she described to a loudly cheering audience how this startling change had come about: "Not more than a year ago last March," she said, "I was in Washington, and while there I spoke on the Nebraska Bill. When I went to the lecture room I had no idea that I was a disunionist; I never knew it; I never suspected it. But while there, in speaking of the Nebraska Bill, I endeavored to find some reason to show why the Union need not be dissolved, and yet slavery be abolished—for I have been anti-slavery all my life-time. While I thus endeavored to find the reasons and suggest the means for abolishing slavery without dissolving the Union, I convinced myself of the impossibility of it, and I said so at the time; for, like a true Quaker, I always depend upon the 'moving of the Spirit' for the time being, and whatever comes into my mind, I give utterance to it; and when I went home from that lecture I said to a friend of mine, 'If I have not succeeded in convincing any one else, I have succeeded,—and I am very happy to know it,— in convincing myself.' "

In Alexandria Ernestine gave two lectures on woman's rights. Four years later she still remembered the experience. "I mentioned the word 'slave,' " she told a Vermont audience, "not in connection with slavery, but simply in connection with the subject of woman's rights; but it was enough. It aroused the whole audience. The papers came out the next day and said, 'Mrs. Rose spoke very well until she undertook to meddle with our institutions, and if she comes here again the people will have to protect themselves.' Courageous South! Chivalric South! A little woman utters the word 'slave' and their institutions are in danger!" But the *Alexandria Gazette* did credit her with being "good-looking," with having "a graceful voice, pleasant accent, just foreign enough to be interesting," and with being a strong-minded woman in the best sense of the term."

While they were still in Washington Ernestine suggested one day to Susan that they visit Anne Royall, editor and publisher of the *Huntress*, a publication that robbed the sleep of many a congressman and politician because they never knew what skeleton in their political closet "Godless Anne Royall" might dig up and expose to public scorn. They found her, at the age of eighty-five, working away on her next editorial, totally oblivious to the state of disarray of her apartment, and the neglect of her own appearance. Susan was a little shocked at this but said to her hostess, "What a wonderful woman you are." "I know it," replied the old lady, without the slightest pretext at modesty. They were saddened to learn about six months later that Anne Royall had died.

The last stop of their three-week tour was Philadelphia where they had no trouble getting a lecture hall for Ernestine, and where they both were warmly entertained by the Motts.

It was a pleasure to be back among friends, and in a city with a strong anti-slavery pulse-beat.

The leaders of the woman's rights movement were aware of the fact that, in the person of Ernestine Rose, they had in their midst a controversial figure. The opposition, especially the clergy, did not let them forget that. No other woman in that group was as open to the charge of "infidel" as was Ernestine; pointing a finger at her, the opposition would brand the entire movement with that stigma. Women like Elizabeth Cady Stanton, Lucretia Mott, Lucy Stone and Susan B. Anthony, often slandered themselves, were not easily intimidated by these charges and did not value Ernestine less because of them. If anything they admired her for having the courage to express her views publicly even if these views were not very popular. No one, not even the opposition, could say that Ernestine was sailing under false colors.

But there were also some who felt that Ernestine's position of leadership in the movement hindered rather than advanced the cause of woman's rights. Not that they found any fault with her qualities as a leader; it was her reputation as a radical that made them uncomfortable. Why provide the enemy with added ammunition to be used against us, they would argue. Is the task of making people accept the concept of woman's rights not difficult enough without having to fend off charges of infidelity? Would we not attract more supporters to our cause if a woman like Ernestine were not our leader?

This line of reasoning took on concrete expression in Philadelphia shortly before the fifth national convention opened in that city, on October 18, 1854. When Susan arrived in Philadelphia a day before the convention, she walked into a heated, behind-the-scenes conflict over Ernestine. The conflict evolved around the presidency of the convention. Ernestine had been proposed to preside over the meeting but sharp opposition arose to her taking the president's chair on the ground that placing her in this position of honor would render the movement even more vulnerable to the attacks of its enemies. Susan rejected this line of argument and vehemently fought against it. She defended Ernestine's right to be president as a matter of principle. The woman's rights platform, she argued, should have room for all religions or for none. Six months earlier, when she was with Ernestine in Washington, she defended her right to lecture at the Representative Chamber on the same principle. There she lost, but here she won.

Upon taking the president's chair Ernestine informed her audience that she was still in a weakened condition, having but recently recovered from an illness which she described as "a severe inflamation of the lungs." But despite this handicap she spoke several times during the proceedings, and showed great skill and tact in steering a long debate on the religious issue which occupied much of the convention's time. It was introduced by Rev. Henry Grew of Philadelphia, whom Garrison respected and admired as "a man of purity and charity," and who, in May, 1850, had participated in the stormy anti-slavery meeting held at the Broadway Tabernacle in New York, which Captain Rynders and his mob tried to break up. But for his views on woman's rights he went to the Scriptures and there he differed from other clergymen only in tone; in substance, he found that woman's subjection was authorized by the Bible itself.

Garrison, Lucretia Mott and other speakers gave him no quarter. "Mr. Grew goes to St. Paul to prove that woman is not equal to man," Garrison said, "Why go to the Bible . . . The human mind is greater than any book . . . If there be truth in the book, we take it; if error, we discard it . . . We must look at all things rationally." Ernestine, who rarely allowed herself to be drawn into a debate on the religious question at a woman's rights convention, must have smiled with satisfaction at hearing Garrison say that. These were her very own thoughts on the subject.

At the end of his argument Garrison did something which must no doubt have startled Rev. Grew, and perhaps even surprised the rest of the convention. He introduced the following two resolutions:

> *Resolved,* That while remembering and gladly acknowledging the exceptional cases which exist to the contrary, we feel it a duty to declare in regard to the sacred cause which has brought us together, that the most determined opposition it encounters is from the clergy generally, whose teachings of the Bible are intensely inimical to the equality of woman with man.

> *Resolved,* That whatever any book may teach, the rights of no human being are dependent upon or modified thereby, but are equal, absolute, essential, inalienable in the person of every member of the human family, without regard to sex, race or clime.

Both resolutions were unanimously adopted. Thus the woman's rights movement, for the first time in its existence, officially branded the clergy as its "most determined opposition," and disavowed the Bible's authority with regard to the question of woman's rights. That this happened at a convention at which Ernestine presided is not without its touch of irony, considering the fact that those who opposed her nomination for president did so on the ground of her reputation as an "infidel."

Another resolution was passed at the end of the convention, which William Rose may proudly have copied into his scrapbook. It read:

> *Resolved,* That the thanks of this convention are due, and are hereby conveyed, to Mrs. Ernestine L. Rose of New York, for the courtesy, impartiality, and dignity with which she has presided over its proceedings.

Chapter XVIII

THE BUSIEST YEAR
OF HER LIFE

IN FEBRUARY, 1855, the women returned to Albany to hold
their second state convention and present the new petitions to the legislators. Once again Ernestine was one of the
principal speakers before the various Senate and Assembly
committees. She became a familiar figure to the lawmakers.
And very soon she became familiar with their routine. They
would hear her out politely, go through with the motion of
referring the petitions to a Committee; and several weeks
later would come the report denying all the petitioner's requests.

The following year the chairman of the Judiciary Committee, Judge Samuel A. Foote of New York, decided to have a
little fun at the expense of the women. As he gave his report
on the petitions the chamber echoed with repeated bursts of
laughter. The women, he said, "have the best seat in the cars,
carriages, and sleighs; the warmest place in the winter, and the
coolest place in the summer. They have their choice on which
side of the bed they will lie, front or back. A lady's dress costs
three times as much as that of a gentleman; and, at the present
time, with prevailing fashion, one lady occupies three times as
much space in the world as a gentleman. It has thus appeared
to the married gentlemen of your Committee, being a majority
. . . that, if there is any inequality or oppression in the case,
the gentlemen are the sufferers. They, however, have presented no petitions for redress; having, doubtless, made up
their minds to yield to an inevitable destiny.

"On the whole, the Committee have concluded to recommend no measure, except that as they have observed several instances in which husband and wife have both signed the same petition. In such case, they would recommend the parties to apply for a law authorising them to change dresses, so that the husband may wear petticoats, and the wife the breeches, and thus indicate to their neighbors and the public the true relation in which they stand to each other."

The women described Judge Foote's behavior as "a piece of buffoonery worthy only of a mountebank in a circus." Although the majority of the legislators voted with him and many shared his contempt for the women who led this campaign, it should be pointed out that there were also some lawmakers, a minority to be sure, who were warm friends and supporters of the woman's rights movement. Notable among them was Judge William Hay of Saratoga. He was so outraged by his colleague's performance that he wrote a letter to Susan, saying, "I write this in the Assembly Chamber which has so recently been disgraced by an old fogy—Sam. A. Foote. He can not, however, prevent the agitation as to woman's rights . . . Next winter we may hope to be more successful—if not then, success is merely postponed. It has become a question of time only . . ."

Susan knew that the good judge was right; it was just a matter of time. But the length of time depended upon the labors that she and the others would put in. And so she went back to the counties of the state, the hamlets and the villages. Some days Ernestine was by her side; at other times it was another speaker. And there were times when she was all alone. But when February came around the women were back in Albany holding another convention, and presenting the legislators with a new batch of petitions.

By 1856, the women of New York State had not had a single legislative victory since the passage of the married woman's property bill eight years earlier. But the crack in the legal armor which that bill made was growing wider with each new petition campaign. The laughter which Judge Foote evoked from his colleagues in the legislative chamber, at the expense of the women, was more akin to whistling in the dark than to laughing in broad daylight.

1855 was probably the busiest year in Ernestine's life, the year in which she lectured the most, traveled the most and was most in demand. It was also the year in which her health was so undermined that she was compelled the next year to suspend all social reform activities for a period of six months. It is enough to glance at her speaking schedule and itinerary, keeping in mind the difficult travel conditions of the fifties and her general poor state of health, to wonder how she survived that year altogether. The first week in January she was already on the road, traveling in the western part of New York State. Between the second and twenty-seventh of that month she addressed fifteen meetings in fifteen different places as part of the intensive petition campaign prior to the second Albany convention, only a month away.

A group in Taunton, Mass., had been negotiating with her for a lecture since December 1854, and after an extensive correspondence and changes in dates she was finally able to settle on a date in February 1855. In one of her letters to Taunton, written from Canandaigua and dated January 12, 1855, she wrote:

Dear Sir:
> I just received yours of the 8th and am very glad you were able to postpone me till Feb. the 7 for I have lectured so many evenings in succession that I feel quite sick and worn out and will have to return home to recuperate. I will endeavor to be with you on the sixth in the evening or seventh in the morning, as I do not exactly know how long it takes to go there not having been there before.
>
> Yours respectfully,
> Ernestine L. Rose.

At an earlier stage of the negotiations she wrote:

"I am glad you prefer the subject of Woman's Rights, as I think it is a very good one . . . Should you know anyone in a neighboring town who would interest himself in getting up a meeting while I am there I should be glad to speak on the same or any other subject . . ."

And when all was finally settled she wrote from New York, on January 29th:

Dear Sir:

    I send you a few scraps my husband took from some papers of Washington, Baltimore, and Alexandria, Albany, and also from a Buffalo paper, please preserve them as he would not wish to have them destroyed . . .

Ten days after her Taunton lecture she was already in Albany addressing various legislative committees. In March and again in May she lectured in Boston. In May she addressed the anti-slavery convention in New York and later attended the convention of the New England Anti-Slavery Society where she shared the speakers' platform with the leaders of the abolitionist movement. When she was through speaking Wendell Phillips, who followed her to the rostrum, said, "The speech, ladies and gentlemen, to which we have just listened, has Waldo Emerson's attribute of eloquence—it has *a life behind it*. What we have to do at the North is, to feel our souls our own—to dare to think independently of institutions and majorities, and the old associations about us. The friend who has just taken her seat has taught us that lesson by a life that, before some of us had awakened to the duty of being free, was exerting its influence upon those about her. I am glad when she comes to the anti-slavery platform to give us the benefit of her clear insight, and her long example. They are the veteran troops of reform and free thought, that form the basis of every movement for the bettering of the race." With these remarks Phillips went to the very core of Ernestine's personality. No higher or more genuine tribute could be paid her than to call attention to her independence of mind.

In the middle of August Ernestine was in the summer resort of Saratoga, N. Y., not as a vacationer but as a lecturer on woman's rights. With her were Susan B. Anthony and Rev. Antoinette Brown. Since summer was never a time for woman's rights conventions what did these three national leaders do in Saratoga? The answer is that they were very enterprising and resourceful reformers who would not miss an opportunity to advance their cause. Saratoga was a fashionable spa which attracted vacationers from various parts of the state and country, including the South. Many of them were of the upper social stratum who were not likely to wander into a woman's rights convention in their own city, or of their own accord seek information about the subject, yet they were in a far better position to give financial support to the movement than some who attended conventions. For both these reasons it was important to reach them; it was a matter of Mohammed going to the mountain.

From Saratoga Ernestine did not go directly home. Instead she went to Waverly, Tioga County, N.Y., where a group that called itself Friends of Progress had issued a Call to a social reform convention to be held under its sponsorship. None of the names that appeared on the Call was familiar to her, and she already knew that other reformers who had received it refused to attend on the grounds that they did not know with whom they would share the platform. Ernestine, however, did not have the heart to say no and so she went. When she got there she was vastly relieved to learn that she was not the only one to respond; Joseph Barker had also answered the Call.

One would think that in an out-of-the-way place like Tioga County a social reform convention might be a novel experience to the native population but hardly exciting to such a veteran reformer and widely traveled cosmopolitan as Ernestine Rose. Not so. It turned out to be quite an adventure. In addition to the immense satisfaction of breaking new ground she had two unusual experiences.

During the last evening session of the convention, while Joseph Barker was speaking, Ernestine noticed, from her seat on the platform, that several young boys had entered the hall and, under instructions from two grown-ups, were beginning to set off firecrackers beneath the stairs. Their aim was to create a panic in the hall by shouting fire. They almost succeeded. The audience was already on its feet, ready to flee. But Ernestine, who had watched the plotters all the while, stepped forward and pleaded with the people not to be alarmed. She allayed their anxieties and in a few minutes order was restored and Mr. Barker continued with his speech for another half hour.

Later on, while she herself was speaking, a woman from the audience came up to the platform, carrying a baby girl. She placed the infant in Ernestine's arms and said, "Will you please give her a name." Ernestine studied the child's face while the audience looked on in amazement. "It was the most lovely little creature," she later recalled, "sound asleep, with a sweet smile playing around its little mouth, highly suggestive of innocence, purity and happiness . . ." With the child still in her arms she made a little speech about the responsibilities of parents and society to children. Then she turned to the woman and asked, "What is the little one's surname?"

"Lyons," the woman replied.

"Then I name her Ernestine Frances Lyons," she said, and handed the baby back to the woman. There was a burst of applause from the audience.

She had been home hardly more than three weeks when she was already off on her longest trip of the year, a two-month lecture tour out West that included speaking engagements in Salem, Winchester, Mansfield, Dayton and Cincinnati, in Ohio, and in Adrian, Battle Creek, Ypsilanti, Ann Arbor and Detroit, in Michigan. In Battle Creek she spoke at a convention of the Michigan Anti-Slavery Society, and in Cincinnati at the sixth National Woman's Rights Convention. During her brief stay in Cincinnati she attended several of Dr. Buchanan's classes in anthropology, each class lasting two hours. She found his lectures on the "science of man" most engrossing and regretted that she could not remain for the entire course. Before she left that city she visited, in the company of Joseph Barker, the final resting place of her friend Frances Wright who had passed away a year ago. The solemn occasion evoked a flood of memories, "deep thoughts, earnest feelings and a stronger devotion to the cause of freedom and of right for which she [Frances Wright] had to suffer so much."

In the last week of October she went to Indianapolis to speak at a state woman's rights convention together with Lucretia Mott, Frances D. Gage of St. Louis and Joseph Barker. The *Indianapolis Daily State Sentinel*, after voicing its disagreement with her "peculiar doctrines," went on to say about Ernestine that "she is in every sense a true orator, her voice being full and melodious and not, in the least, marred by a slight foreign accent. Her gestures were in themselves eloquent . . ."

Late in November she returned to New York after a two-month absence from home, very much exhausted from the trip and looking forward to an interval of peace and rest before she filled one more out-of-town lecture date on her calendar, the last of the year. This, it turned out, was wishful thinking. She had hardly unpacked her travel bags when she found herself embroiled in a controversy that demanded her immediate attention. It concerned that last lecture of the season which was to be given at Bangor, Maine, in the latter part of December.

Several months earlier she had been invited by a committee of highly respected Bangor citizens to participate in the "Independent Course," a series of anti-slavery lectures. Among the other invited speakers were Wendell Phillips and Frederick Douglass. On November 3, while she was still on her tour through the West, the *Bangor Mercury* launched a scurrilous attack on her with the first of a series of three articles. Behind this attack were two clergymen one of whom preferred to remain anonymous; the other, who was very much in the open, was Rev. G. D. Little, an orthodox minister. Through the pages of the *Mercury* one of these gentlemen allowed himself to say that "it would be shameful to listen to this woman, a thousand times below a prostitute." She was accused of being a president of an infidel club in New York; of making speeches at Tom Paine birthday celebrations "at which Christ is uniformly treated with the choicest blasphemies . . ." She was referred to as "a *female Atheist*"; and such a one is so bad that "we hold the vilest strumpet from the stews to be by comparison respectable." Next to such vicious vilifications even the factually correct statement that she was "a *female* born of Jewish parents in Poland" smacked of anti-woman, anti-Semitic and anti-foreigner prejudices.

She had been blissfully unaware of all this until she returned to New York and William showed her an item he had clipped from the *New York Tribune* containing a reference to the *Mercury's* attack on her. As soon as she was able to procure the three *Mercury* articles she wrote a letter to the *Tribune* answering the attack and branding the charges as falsehoods. The letter reads in part:

> "From the tenor of those articles it is evident that the writer meant others who were invited to lecture in the course as well as me; but being too cowardly to attack any of them personally, he concentrated his whole malice upon me, feeling himself quite safe, as I am only a woman, a foreigner, and (as the sectarian world calls me) an 'Infidel' at that . . . I stand before the world as I am, unprotected and unsupported by sect or party . . . My opinions are publicly given, and I fear no investigation of them.

> "In principle I know no compromise, I expect no reward, I fear no opposition, and can therefore afford to pass by in silence the outpourings of a bitter spirit, and only pity him who possesses it.

> "But I think it my duty to point out at least *some* of the false statements . . . and not wishing to send it to the editor of the *Mercury*—for a man who evidently takes pleasure to calumniate and slander a person of whom he is utterly ignorant, cannot possess manliness, justice and honor enough for me to reply to

him personally—I therefore ask it of you as a favor, as some remarks including my name in reply to some of his articles have appeared in the *Tribune*, to give this a place in your paper, and greatly oblige

Yours, very truly,

Ernestine L. Rose."

In the meantime another Bangor newspaper, the *Daily Journal*, reprinted some excerpts from the *Mercury* articles. When Ernestine learned about this she wrote a letter to the editor of the *Journal*, which he printed under the heading, "Mrs. Rose In Her Own Defense." This led to an open feud between the two papers and Ernestine, sitting in New York, was the subject of a most heated controversy in the community of Bangor. But there was more to come. Rev. G. D. Little, who was violently opposed to Ernestine's speaking in Bangor and did everything possible to prevent it, wrote a letter to Rev. Amory Battles, a Universalist minister and member of the committee that had invited Ernestine to speak at the "Independent Course," urging him to withdraw the invitation to Ernestine and cancel her proposed lecture. This Rev. Battles refused to do and a private correspondence developed between the two ministers on the subject. Unsuccessful in his efforts, Rev. Little now suggested that they make their correspondence public. Rev. Battles, having no taste for a public controversy with Rev. Little, refused. The latter, now doubly frustrated, printed a letter in the *Mercury* which grossly misrepresented Rev. Battles' views, leaving him no choice but to make public the genuine version of his reply to Little. He published his letter in the *Whig and Courier*, and if the controversy, now in its fifth week, had produced nothing else but this letter, it would have been worth while. For here Rev. Battles lifts the entire dispute above the level of bitter acrimony and personal recrimination, and comes to grips with the fundamental principles of the Bill of Rights.*

Mrs. Rose did appear in the "Independent Course" but by

---

* For the text of Rev. Battles' letter see Appendix pp. 287-88.

the time she stepped off the train she had become the central character of a drama that was played out with ever-mounting intensity in the newspaper pages, the pulpits, the kitchens and the parlors of Bangor, with the community split between the hissers and applauders, depending on which side of the controversy one took. One Bangor resident who ranged himself on the side of Ernestine wrote to the *Boston Investigator*, "You cannot conceive nor can I describe the intense excitement caused here by the constant and unremitting attacks upon Mrs. Rose." The excitement was greatly heightened by the arrival of Wendell Phillips, another featured speaker in the "Independent Course," a week before Ernestine. Phillips flayed her attackers mercilessly from the platform, and expressed admiration and respect for Ernestine.

The forces of bigotry in Bangor were thoroughly routed and Ernestine who, in this dragged-out controversy, became the symbol of free speech, emerged victorious. She was welcomed at the station by three members of the committee and escorted to her hotel. The hall which could seat at the most two thousand never had such a big turnout. She lectured twice in two successive evenings to large and enthusiastic audiences. After her second lecture the *Bangor Daily Journal* commented: "We understand Mrs. Rose disposed of her adversaries last evening. Returns of the dead and wounded have not come in." And the *Bangor Jeffersonian* summed up the entire episode in a sober editorial entitled: "The Crisis Passed" which reads in part:

"Mrs. Ernestine L. Rose, whose coming here was sought to be prevented by the most gloomy forebodings of disaster and moral ruin, arrived in this city on Monday week, delivered two lectures in the 'Independent Course' and has departed, leaving the city safe! The conflict was terrible, the danger most imminent, but the crisis has passed and the city breathes freer. The smoke of the unparalleled conflict having cleared up from the field, a census of the dead and wounded discloses none but members of the assailing party. Happy termination of a fearful crisis!

"Mrs. Rose appeared very much like other women. She is of medium size, dresses 'neat but not gaudy,' not *en bloomer,* is graceful in manner, and a rather effective speaker. She speaks without notes, and gesticulates in speaking somewhat more than Lucy Stone. Her marked foreign dialect is the only thing that detracts from an agreeable elocution . . .

"Whatever others may say, we do not believe that Mrs. Rose's appearance in the 'Independent Course' has in the least degree unfavorably affected the moral sense of this community, hindered the onward progress of healthy social reform, or weakened any man's or woman's faith in the divine inspiration of Holy Writ. The public attack upon her was, in our judgment, wholly unprovoked, wanton and malicious. The only damaged party are the assailants, who, we trust, will, from this bit of experience, hereafter manifest better manners and a more tolerant spirit towards those persons who may be invited to this city by an association of respectable citizens."

Ernestine's triumph was not limited to Bangor alone. Some citizens of Portland, Maine, became interested in her as a result of the controversy and invited her to speak in their city as well. She accepted the invitation and her two lectures in Portland were a great success.

It was late in December and the Maine experience, coming at the end of a crowded and arduous year, left her physically spent. But there was the victory to consider, a most gratifying way of rounding out the busy year of '55.

Chapter XIX

A TRIP ABROAD

B Y THE END OF 1855 Ernestine had reached the limit of her
physical resources and depleted her phenomenal recuperative powers. Even a Bangor victory, exhilarating as it was,
could no longer sustain her. She had had one lecture, one
meeting, one convention too many; and if she was to continue
to be of use as a social reformer she had better heed the danger
signal. She talked the matter over with William and they decided to go abroad for a long vacation. A sea voyage; a change
of climate; new sights, new people, and, above all, a safe distance from the lecture platform, was what she needed; was
what they *both* needed. In the past several years she had been
away from home far too many times, and though he realized
the importance of these frequent trips, understanding her
absence could hardly compensate for the need to be close to
her. With each trip the notices in her scrapbook grew larger
in number, but so also did his hours of loneliness. At last, they
would have a complete holiday together for six months! The
mere thought of it was enough to raise their spirits.

On April 30, 1856, in the midst of preparations for the
journey, Ernestine wrote a letter to the *Boston Investigator*,
publicly saying good-by to her many friends and readers.
She described herself as "a volunteer soldier in the cause of
Truth," and hastened to assure them that she was leaving her
post "not as a deserter, but on furlough to gather fresh
strength for the glorious battle of freedom." That furlough
was to take them to England, France, Germany and Italy.

"Whether I shall be able once more to see my own poor native land, Poland, I know not." She was looking forward with great anticipation to meeting again "our dear venerable friend, Robert Owen," who was soon to celebrate his eighty-sixth birthday.

The impending trip abroad, her first in twenty years, provided the occasion for some reminiscing. She recalled that her lectures and social reform work had taken her to twenty-three states, and that she had been the object of much slander, abuse and persecution. But the thing that stood out in her mind, above all else, was the fact that "by the mass of people I have always been treated with civility and kindness . . ."

On May 5, twenty years, almost to the day, since she and William had arrived in this country, they boarded the packet ship *Northumberland* for their first return trip to Europe. Ernestine was forty-six now and William forty-three. Twenty years ago they had brought to their adopted land their youth, their zeal and their ideals. Their youth, in terms of years, they no longer had, but the youthfulness of their ideals time could not take from them, nor could it diminish the ardor of their zeal. They were both, each in their own way, soldiers on furlough from the "glorious battle of freedom."

When the ship began to sail they stood close to each other at the railing, watching the New York skyline recede slowly, into the background, just as twenty years earlier they had watched it coming slowly into view. They were happy then; they were even happier now.

The ocean crossing took five weeks during most of which time Ernestine was seasick. Three weeks after their arrival in London this unpleasant memory of the journey was still sharply edged in her mind. In her first letter to the *Investigator* she wrote, "Sea sickness! has that unutterable and inexplicable misery ever been defined? If so, I have never read it, and I am sure I will not attempt to describe it." She attributed both the duration of the journey and the almost unrelieved illness to the kind of vessel they traveled on. The packet ship depended entirely on favorable winds for speed and was easily buffeted about in a storm. Compared to the steamer she found the packet wanting. But with it all there were some pleasant, sunny days when the breezes were mild and refreshing and the vast expanse of the ocean had a soothing effect on her.

In her letters she revealed a keen eye for detail, a sensitiveness to nature's many moods and faces and the poetic means with which to describe them. But even in her most lyrical moments she was not too far removed from reality. One of the most noteworthy qualities of her descriptions is the skill with which she combined observations of natural phenomena with reflections on life and society. "The ocean," she observed, "is a vast theatre for contemplation, and is highly suggestive of thought." When she abandoned herself to that theatre she was able to write:

> The ocean in a calm, looks to me like a nation which by long and unsuccessful attempts to free itself from the iron yoke of despotism, has subsided into apathy and inaction which is like the calm of death, and which will require the raging of a tempest to call it again into life. I prefer the breezes to blow, and the sea to be in motion. To me it seems more natural, truthful and real. I like to see the waves rise and dash against the sides of the vessel, as at an intruder and an obstacle to their progressive motion; and although the billows in their anger look dark and threatening, yet they soon rise to the surface crowned with the beautiful silver-crested foam which, like moral greatness in man, can be obtained only by contact with each other . . . Anything but a dead calm, physical, mental or moral. It is conservative, anti-progressive. In it there is no health, no hope, no life.

They found London as so many others have found it—in a fog; and the fog rarely lifted. Her comment on the weather was summed up succinctly in the following sentence: "England boasts that the sun never sets on her dominions; we might with equal justice say that the sun never rises clear on London." But for Ernestine the weather was something one commented upon and then promptly ignored. It had not the slightest effect on her crowded itinerary.

At the first opportunity they took a trip to Seven Oakes, 27 miles out of London, to see Robert Owen. They found him remarkably well for his age, and there was perhaps more truth than boastfulness when he told his visitors, "Since I saw you, nine years ago, I have not spent an hour without laboring for the cause of humanity." As they strolled leisurely in the beautiful gardens that surrounded Owen's residence the subject of spiritualism came into the conversation, most likely introduced by Owen himself, who for many years had been an ardent believer in the powers and benefits of spiritualism. He saw no contradiction between his utopian socialist philosophy and this mystical new faith. Ernestine never fell under the spell of the spiritualist rappers even though some of her associates in the abolitionist and woman's rights movements had succumbed to them at one time or another. She regarded Owen's fanatic devotion to spiritualism as the aberration of a brilliant mind and it in no way detracted from her veneration of him. But neither would she because of her great respect for him compromise on this or on any other issue on which they disagreed. "It is needless to say," she wrote, "that his endeavors to convince me *into* it, and mine to convince him *out* of it, met with equal success."

The short visit with Owen, it seems, was the most leisurely part of their London stay; the rest of the time was spent in a whirlwind of activity. They went to all the art galleries and all the museums. At Madame Tussaud's Exhibition, where 378 wax figures of the leading European monarchs and statesmen were on display, Ernestine climbed into Napoleon's Waterloo carriage and then sat in his St. Helena garden chair, "but I could feel none of the glory!" she reported. She even took in the "Chamber of Horrors," and the dungeons of the White Tower where she was overcome by serious and painful reflections on the human suffering that people lived through within these dark and damp enclosures. "The place is filled with reminiscences of barbarism," she wrote, "which sicken the heart and crush the spirit even to behold."

After that depressing experience it was a relief to visit the zoological and botanical gardens; the mint where one could watch with fascination the process of gold being melted into currency, ready for use; and that "wonderful piece of workmanship," the tunnel under the Thames. One could almost sense the weariness in her words as she wrote, "Sightseeing is the hardest labor that can be performed." But she performed it with gusto and enjoyed every minute of it.

She would not have regarded her visit in London complete had she not attended at least one debate in the House of Commons. But this was something more easily achieved by a man than a woman. All a man had to do was obtain a permit from a member of Parliament. A woman's permit came from the Sergeant-at-Arms, through the good offices of an M.P.; she had to apply in writing, wait about two weeks and even then was lucky if she got it. In short, every possible obstacle was placed in a woman's path to discourage her from even applying. Ernestine resented this rank discrimination against her sex and would not be a party to it. ". . . Let silly men do all they can to keep woman out," she wrote, "she can always outwit them! If she only wished to enter into the Garden of Eden, not even the cherubims with fiery swords could keep her out; and as I had a desire to hear the debate in the House of Commons, I went in, and without any permit." She failed to tell us how she accomplished this feat.

In her last letter from London, dated July 15, 1856, and written several days before they left for Paris, Ernestine made some comments on the social composition and habits of the English people. "In reality there is no middle class," she observed. "There are many castes and grades; each grade looks down with contempt on all those beneath, and with slavish subserviency on those above it. There is no more sympathy between any two of these grades than between the highest and the lowest. The people have not much energy or spirit."

Naturally she was most interested in the status of social reform in England. She found that reform movements in England were "sound asleep," and that if a reform was to have any kind of success, it had to be initiated by someone in the upper strata of society.

She summed up her general impressions of England in the following way: "Everything here is slow and heavy; it requires time, long, long time to move anything, (except the weather). The buildings are massive; the animals strong; the people heavy and dull, and as long as they have enough beer to drink, they are quite content to be taxed heavily to support a most extravagant aristocracy, who despise them for it."

But she had a totally different impression of France and their four-week stay in Paris was easily the highlight of their European tour. London was not lacking in external beauty, but it was a beauty lacking in warmth. Not so Paris. "The bold and massive of London is in Paris softened down by artistic taste, elegance and refinement." But more than that Paris to her spoke the "language of universal brotherhood . . . its inmost heart vibrates for all times, nations and grades . . . oppressed as it is *at present* by political tyranny, there still is life . . . it lives; it may be wrong but still it lives . . ."

If sightseeing imposed a physical strain in London, it was not less tiring in Paris; but here it was twice as pleasurable because of her feeling for the city and its people. Beginning with the Louvre they saw everything that was of artistic or historical significance. At the *Manufacture Imperiale des Gobelins*, a government-directed tapestry establishment, she spoke to some of the workers about their conditions. She learned that though highly skilled in their craft, their salary was pitifully low—five hundred dollars a year. Some of the carpets they made sold for as high as thirty thousand dollars.

Paris thrilled her with its beauty, elegance and aesthetic treasures, but she also felt the heavy hand of oppression that lay on the city. Everywhere one turned there were soldiers in uniform, as though all of Paris were a military barrack. But even more depressing was the vast, ubiquitous army of spies which the despotic regime of Louis Napoleon, now Emperor Napoleon III, engaged to sniff out the words freedom and liberty wherever they might be uttered. Dressed in civilian clothes, these shadowy figures were not readily identifiable to the visitor, but the French had a nose for them and knew the prudence of silence. ". . . Paris is still as the grave," Ernestine observed. But that was so only on the surface; beneath this facade of silence the pulse of liberty beat ever so strongly in the literary and reformatory circles which she described as "the head and heart of France." She and William had the good fortune of being introduced into one such circle and were able to observe at first hand how they functioned under prevailing oppressive conditions. "Even in their own houses," she reported, "they first have to lock the doors and windows before they dare unlock their hearts." They could not publish their thoughts without running the risk of imprisonment. But they found a way out. They would send the manuscripts of their pamphlets to the free state of Sardinia, Italy, and have them printed there, and then smuggle them back into France and distribute them secretly by the thousands. At one such secret meeting Ernestine and William heard read a poem by Victor Hugo from his work, the "Judgment." Somehow a copy of it had appeared in Paris, in manuscript form. It was duplicated in hundreds of manuscripts, circulated and read at secret gatherings. "It is a sublime thing," Ernestine wrote of the poem, "and as bold and strong as beautiful."

They were especially fortunate in having met Mme. Jenny P. d'Hericourt, a French physician and writer, whom Ernestine described as "a woman of noble character, great energy and talents . . . a thorough reformer, particularly for woman's rights. . . ." Mme. Hericourt introduced them to some of the leading French reformers and later wrote a biographic sketch of Ernestine.

Not only were people spied on but their mail too was scrutinized. Her friend Holyoake from London wrote her a letter advising caution in her correspondence. She heeded his advice. All her letters about Paris carry the dateline Berlin (Prussia). The last one was a hymn to the French people: "They combine the finest elements in human nature. The Frenchman is frivolous on trifles, but he is the philosopher on any subject of importance . . . Even the most ignorant man, he who cannot write his name, visits and examines the various museums and inquires into the nature and meaning of things; he looks with rapture at a beautiful piece of sculpture, or painting of a philosopher or a patriot, and listens with delight to the elevating strains of Beethoven, or Mozart . . . In taste, natural grace, and a certain refinement, all Frenchmen are alike."

She wrote only one letter about her impression of Italy, but not a word about Germany; and there is no indication that she visited her native Poland.

On their way home they stopped in England again because the steamer *Europa* which took them to New York sailed from Liverpool. They spent their last day in London with Robert Owen who had come in especially from Seven Oakes to see them. So far the trip had been all holiday. In her six months of travel Ernestine did not address a single public meeting. That record was almost spoiled in the last few days of her vacation when demands came for her to speak in various places, including London, Glasgow and Liverpool. Time did not permit it and she was probably as much disappointed as were her friends who had extended the invitations.

But the record was not entirely unbroken. The speaker's platform she had managed to avoid on land caught up with her on the ocean. On the last evening of their journey the passengers were treated to a program of entertainment. Two noted English actors read from Shakespeare, others sang and recited, and Ernestine, by request, delivered a talk on the subject: "The Rights of Man as the Basis of the Rights of Woman."

The *Europa* crossed the Atlantic in twelve days and two hours, proving beyond a doubt the superiority of the steamer over the packet. Henceforth she was to travel only by steamer.

In the midst of unpacking she dashed off a short letter to the *Boston Investigator* informing her friends and readers of their return. "Mr. Rose is very well, and has been so all summer . . . I have suffered some from fatigue, having traversed over a great distance in a comparatively short time, which did not allow us much repose, but I hope that after I get rested I shall feel the benefit of it." She had little time to get rested. The seventh National Woman's Rights Convention was only four days away.

After six months of constant travel Ernestine appreciated the fact that the convention took place within walking distance of her home, at the Broadway Tabernacle. The convention opened on a note of cheer and optimism, and for good reason. For the first time in seven years the movement could glance back at its short history and smile. "Never before has any reformatory movement gained so much in so short a time . . . ," said Lucy Stone in her opening remarks as president. "Now almost every Northern State has more or less modified its laws." She was referring, in the main, to laws governing the property rights of married women. And Ernestine followed in the same optimistic vein. "Compare the first convention held seven years ago with this," she said. "Compare public opinion at that time with public opinion now." When progress was reported from the State of Michigan Ernestine was especially attentive. In 1846 she was the first to sow the seed of woman's rights on Michigan soil. Now the Legislature of that state had seriously debated a bill to grant mothers the custody of their own children (a right which even the mothers of New York State had not yet attained in 1856) and were it not for the strong opposition of a Mormon member, a disciple of Brigham Young, Michigan might have been the first state in the Union to have passed such a law. Although the law varied from state to state, in none of them had the mother equal control of the children with the father. In New York State, for instance, a mother's legal control of her child lasted until it was eighteen months old. After that age the father's claim on the child was complete.

Ernestine gave a first-hand account of the woman's rights movement abroad. In Great Britain, she reported, where even the male population did not fully enjoy the right to vote and where the principle of universal suffrage was extended only to the wealthy and propertied classes, the woman's rights movement was slowly making progress in the face of tremendous odds. She spoke with great warmth and admiration of the French women, their courage and ingenuity.

Late in the last evening session of the convention, when both delegates and guests had been thoroughly saturated with speeches on woman's rights, including two brilliant orations by Rev. Thomas Wentworth Higginson and Wendell Phillips, Ernestine stepped forward to deliver her principal address. One would think that not a single fresh thought could be expressed any more on the subject, and even if it could no one would listen anyway. But this self-educated daughter of a Polish ghetto spoke so movingly on the subject of education and the mother's role in the rearing of the child that the entire audience listened with rapt attention. "The wisest in all ages have acknowledged," she said, "that the most important period in human education is in childhood—that period when the plastic mind may be moulded into exquisite beauty that no unfavorable influences shall be able entirely to destroy it—or into such hideous deformity, that it shall cling to it like a thick rust eaten into a highly-polished surface, which no after-scouring shall ever be able entirely to efface. This most important part of education is left entirely in the hands of the mother. She prepares the soil for future culture; she lays the foundation upon which a superstructure shall be erected that shall stand as firm as a rock, or shall pass away like the baseless fabric of a vision, and leave not a wreck behind. But the mother can not give what she does not possess; weakness can not impart strength. With an imperfect education—dependent position—made from the cradle to the grave to look to man for strength, support and protection; can she develop the powers, call out the energies, and impart a spirit of independence in her sons? Can a weak, timid, cowardly mother, call out in her sons courage, fortitude and heroism? Brought up ever to look up to man as her only oracle of right can she inspire her sons with a love of truth and an adherence to right, which not even the fear of death shall be able to shake? No; the stream can not run higher than the source that feeds it. The mother must possess these high and noble qualities, or she never can impart them to her offspring."

From time to time the plight of the "fallen sister" would be touched upon at a woman's rights assembly and usually in realistic terms. The widely spread phenomenon of prostitution in many American cities was traced directly to its economic roots. In New York alone there were between fifteen and forty thousand seamstresses whose weekly earnings amounted to $1.87½. From this sum $1.50 would be deducted for board. A seamstress making fine shirts received 12½ cents per shirt. She could not produce more than nine shirts a week. If a woman turned to teaching in New York her salary was fifty dollars a year; and for every vacancy there were five hundred applicants. At the same time it was estimated that in 1856 there were about ten thousand women in New York whose main source of income was prostitution, on a regular basis. These vital statistics were not entirely unrelated.

The *New York Daily Times*, in an editorial printed on the eve of the convention, warned the women that ". . . if they insist on a political equality with men, they will forfeit that legal right to protection which they now enjoy." In her speech Ernestine made her reply to the *Times*. "Man protecting woman!" she said, with all the sarcasm at her command. "Go into the streets at night—look at the wretched beings who wander them, in many cases the only home they possess—and you will have the practical evidence of his protection. What a bitter mockery it is to make a being helpless,

to tie hand, heart and head, and tell him that it is from pure
affection, so as to have the pleasure of protecting him! . . .
Man's protection brought them there! He has brought her up
so helpless as to be unable to protect herself, to look to him,
her only assailant, as her natural protector; and then he has
taken advantage of her ignorance, inexperience and depend-
ence . . . to attract, ensnare, betray . . . Say not the accusation
is hard—the fact is harder; and yet I lay it not to man's wilful-
ness, but his ignorance, for he is as greatly the sufferer as
woman is."

Compared to the *Times* editorial which drew much fire
from some speakers, the article in Bennett's *Herald* was a
model of restraint. After tossing a few mild sneers and snick-
ers at the women, the *Herald* asked, with tongue-in-cheek,
"We beg respectfully to inquire the precise difference between Woman's Rights and Free Love; or where one com-
mences and the other ends?" It was as though now that the
Times was there to take pot shots at the woman's rights
movement Bennett could afford to relax.

Chapter XX

"FREE LOVE," TRUE LOVE
AND OTHER MATTERS

IF ERNESTINE HAD kept a diary the entry for February 9, 1857, would probably read as follows: Had unusual experience today . . . met with poet Walt Whitman . . . tall, bushy-bearded, striking . . . alive to the world . . . talked about many things, but mainly about Frances Wright . . . told me that his father, a carpenter, was a great admirer of Fanny's and a subscriber to her *Free Enquirer* . . . father would take young Walt, then a mere boy, to hear Fanny lecture . . . he was completely enchanted by her . . . the impression was lasting . . . he was curious to know all about her life . . . talked about my favorite book—*A Few Days In Athens* . . . Whitman was impressed with the fact that Fanny was only twenty when she wrote this brilliant exposition of the principles of Grecian philosophy . . . of all the photographs he had seen of her he likes best the portrait engraving where she is shown seated . . . Must re-read the *Leaves* now that I met the poet . . . one of my favorite lines . . . "I am the poet of the woman the same as the man. . . ."

Whether Ernestine kept a diary or not is a matter of conjecture; but it is a fact that Walt Whitman kept a notebook, and thanks to that fact we know that the two met on that day and talked about Frances Wright. Whitman captured the essence of their talk in about 140 words of penciled notes which he had jotted down either during or after his conversation with Ernestine.

It is not known under what circumstances the two met; whether by chance at some literary party, or whether Whitman had deliberately sought out Ernestine for the purpose of talking to her about Frances Wright. In Whitman's life Frances Wright was more than a childhood idol; intertwined with the image of a beautiful woman with a spellbinding voice was the symbol of rebellion against tyranny and oppression. Both had etched themselves deeply on the young impressionable mind of the future bard and became part of the social leaven which later lent strength and fiber to his own democratic song. Whitman looked upon his *Leaves of Grass* as ". . . an attempt . . . to put a Person, a human being (myself, in the latter half of the Nineteenth Century, in America) freely, fully and truly on record." At the age of 38, with the second edition of the *Leaves* already out, he may still have been etching in the details of that personal record of which Frances Wright was a vital part. If so he could not have come to a better person for information about her than to her friend and admirer Ernestine Rose, the Frances Wright of the fifties.

In 1858 the *New York Times* had not yet matured to the motto of "All the news that's fit to print," and so on June 29 of that year it indulged in a bit of sensationalism that was worthy of the journalistic level of the *Herald*. It devoted its entire front page to a story calculated to excite the curiosity of its readers with such titillating headings as "Free Lovers . . . Spiritualists . . . Trance Mediums . . . Abolitionists . . . and all sorts of Queer People . . . A Spicy Time On Free Love . . ." Ironically enough, the *New York Herald*, for some inexplicable reason, did not print a word of this story; but in fairness to the *Times* it should be stated that the staid and respectable *Tribune* outdid its rival by at least a column and a half. The *Tribune* did however display a modicum of restraint by not splashing it on the front page as though it were the most important news of the day.

All this to-do was about a report of the Rutland Free Convention held in Rutland, Vt. on June 25-26-27. Reform conventions were an integral part of the American social scene in the fifties. Almost any day a reader could expect to find in his newspaper an account of a temperance, anti-slavery, woman's rights or some other social reform convention that took place in his town or in some other part of the country. What distinguished the Rutland convention from all others was that while most conventions concentrated on a single subject the Rutland gathering covered the waterfront. On its agenda it listed such subjects for discussion as Government, Free Trade, Slavery, Woman's Rights, Marriage, The Sabbath, Spiritualism, Land Reform, Maternity, The Bible, Immortality, Shakerism and, just in case anything might have been omitted by oversight, there was also an "etcetera." This, plus the fact that the convention was held in a huge canvass tent put up especially for that purpose on the outskirts of Rutland and designed to accommodate about twenty-five hundred people, gave it a kind of carnival quality which aroused the curiosity of many, who were more interested in excitement than in enlightenment. The Call, signed by four prominent citizens of Rutland and about 150 from other parts of Vermont, left no doubt in anyone's mind that the invitation was as all-embracing as the scope of the agenda, "Come, then, friends of Freethought, Come one, come all. Men of all religious creeds, and men of no creed, shall find equal welcome . . . The only common ground on which we seek to meet is, that of *fearless discussion* . . ." George William Curtis, editor of *Harper's Weekly*, also endorsed the convention but apparently had second thoughts about it and did not attend. Perhaps he had yielded to the pressures of his more "respectable" friends. One such friend, George Templeton Strong, expressed his disapproval in his diary. On June 24, 1858, on the very eve of the convention, he wrote: "George . . . is getting deplorably mixed up with the Lucy Stones and Mrs. Roses . . . and has just united with the craziest of them in

PROCEEDINGS

OF THE

FREE CONVENTION

HELD AT

RUTLAND, VT., JUNE 25TH, 26TH, 27TH, 1858.

SUBJECTS DISCUSSED:

GOVERNMENT,	MARRIAGE,	MATERNITY,
FREE TRADE,	THE SABBATH,	THE BIBLE,
SLAVERY,	SPIRITUALISM,	IMMORTALITY,
WOMAN'S RIGHTS,	LAND REFORM,	SHAKERISM, &c.

SPEAKERS:

ANDREW JACKSON DAVIS,	MRS. MARY F. DAVIS,
MRS. JULIA BRANCH,	PARKER PILLSBURY,
MRS. ERNESTINE L. ROSE,	STEPHEN S. FOSTER,
WILLIAM ROBSON,	S. B. BRITTAN,
GEORGE SENNOTT,	HENRY C. WRIGHT,
REV. A. D. MAYO,	ELDER MILES GRANT,
MRS. FRANCES D. GAGE,	WILLIAM GOODELL,
ELDER F. W. EVANS,	MRS. ELIZA W. FARNHAM,
AND OTHERS.	

PHONOGRAPHIC REPORT BY J. M. W. YERRINTON.

NEW YORK:

S. T. MUNSON, 5 GREAT JONES STREET.

1858.

signing a call for a grand convention at Rutland, Vt., . . . It's a pity, for George is a nice fellow. . . ."

Yet it is doubtful whether the Rutland convention would have achieved all that notoriety were it not for the fact that it attracted into its large tent a certain Mrs. Julia Branch from New York whom the *Times* described as being ". . . petite and on the sunny side of thirty," a woman of literary inclinations, a poetess, writer for the New York Sunday papers, and quite pleasing to the eye. Mrs. Branch introduced the following resolution which set off the verbal fireworks around the Rutland convention:

> *Resolved,* That the slavery and degradation of woman proceed from the institution of marriage; that by the marriage contract she loses control of her name, her person, her property, her labor, her affections, her children, and her freedom.

When Mrs. Branch was through elaborating on her resolution some in the audience were of the impression that she was advocating free love as an alternative to marriage. A Mr. Tiffany thereupon proceeded, with equal eloquence, to defend the institution of marriage based on genuine love. At this point Ernestine stepped forward to make her position clear on this matter. Alluding to Mrs. Branch she said, "The lady is a stranger to me, I have never seen her. I do not know what her views are about the remedy, and not knowing them, I cannot say whether I agree or disagree. I did not understand, as Mr. Tiffany did, that she meant to let loose the untamed passions either of men or women; *if she meant that, I totally and utterly disagree*" (italics added). Here Mrs. Branch interjected: "I did not mean it in that light."

Mrs. Rose: "That is right."

The resolution which Ernestine supported and voted for was quite different from the one proposed by Mrs. Branch. It read as follows:

> *Resolved,* That the only true and natural marriage is an exclusive conjugal love based on perfect equality between one

man and one woman; the only true home is the isolated home based on this exclusive love.

Yet, despite Ernestine's clear and unmistaken position on this question, the *Times* in its full-page report stated: "Mrs. Ernestine Rose is active; so is Mrs. Julia Branch. Both these ladies go for free love on principle." On the very same day that this report appeared Ernestine wrote a letter to the *Times* refuting the charge that she was an advocate of free love. "This I most emphatically deny," she said. "I have never advocated these sentiments from the simple reason that I do not believe in them." She then restated what she had really said on this subject at the convention. The *Times* printed her letter, but the damage had been done. The *Paterson (N.J.) Weekly Journal* and other publications had repeated the slander and given it wide currency. In 1861, three years after the Rutland convention, when she lectured at Milford, Mass., there were still echoes of this accusation. The *Milford Journal* attacked her as a disciple and advocate of "free love."

"All kinds of odd subjects were up for discussion," reported the *Times*, "but through the whole ran an undercurrent of Free Love." The stenographic report of the Rutland convention fails to substantiate this charge. It shows that all kinds of subjects were indeed discussed, including the one introduced by Mrs. Branch, but "free love" was not the dominant theme of the convention. Ernestine, who was a vice-president of this unusual assembly, spoke several times, touching on a variety of subjects, including slavery and woman's rights. One speech stands out in particular as a tour de force of oratorical skill since it was a speech of rebuttal for which she had no time to prepare. It was a reply to Mr. S. B. Brittan of New York, an exponent of spiritualism, who delivered a discourse on the subject: The Natural Evidences of Immortality. In the course of his talk Mr. Brittan said, "When such men as Robert Owen who have resisted all the efforts of the church for three-quarters of a century . . . are forced to accept the truth they so stoutly denied, it is meet that common skeptics should investigate the claims of the subject or be silent."

As soon as Mr. Brittan sat down Ernestine stepped forward and said:

"I never hear the name of Robert Owen, but I feel rising within me a sentiment amounting almost to reverence for that noble man. I have had the unspeakable pleasure of being intimately acquainted with him for years, and on matters of fact, such as can be demonstrated—on any point concerning the general intercourse between man and man, I would most implicitly take his word. But if Robert Owen should tell me that he had seen a mouse draw a three-decker through the streets of New York, I would say, 'I cannot believe it.' 'But am I not Robert Owen?' 'Why, certainly; and I believe that you believe you have seen it; but that can be no authority for me.' . . . [Hear! hear!]

"But I will tell you what does make a difference. Suppose your child falls into a well, and while it is struggling in the water, a man comes up to help you take him out,—will you stand to convince him of the immortality of the soul before you pull the child out? I tell you, men are overboard; the slave groans in his chains; woman groans in her supposed inferiority and in her oppression; man groans in his ignorance; men and women groan in poverty; society groans in dishonesty, in falsehood, in dissipation, in vice, in crime, in misery. Shall we leave this out of sight, and argue the question whether a man lives after he is dead or not? If there were nothing else to do but to spend our time in mere speculation, I should have no objection; but the time is not ours."

On November 17, 1858, Robert Owen died. He was 87 years old. Ernestine was deeply shaken by his death. Soon after she learned of the sad news she wrote a letter to the *Investigator* in which she said, ". . . my heart is too full to write more at the present, for to the regret at the loss of the world's benefactor, is added the pang of losing an inexpressibly dear friend . . ." But he was more than a dear friend. The two men who had the most profound influence on her life were her father, the rabbi of Piotrkow, and Robert Owen, one of the fathers of utopian socialism. From her father she inherited the quality of total dedication to a faith; from Owen she inherited that social faith which she found worthy of her total dedication.

When the news of Owen's death became known in New York some of his friends and disciples met at Ernestine's home, 72 White Street, and made plans to hold a memorial meeting in his honor at Stuyvesant Institute, 659 Broadway, on December 27, 1858. At that meeting Ernestine delivered the main address, which the *New York Herald* called "historical."

For reasons beyond the movement's control no national woman's rights convention was held in 1857. That year many of the female principals were either having babies of their own, or attending to the births of their children's babies. Ernestine was home sick. The only available leader who was ready to go into action was Susan B. Anthony. But even the indefatigable Susan could not perform the miracle of running a national convention all by herself. And so the event had to be postponed till next year. All other activities throughout the state over which she had charge continued without interruption.

Beginning with 1858 the movement was definitely on the ascendancy. Not only were there new faces in the convention hall but there were also new faces on the speakers' platform. That was the year when George William Curtis, the editor of *Harper's Weekly* and a leading literary figure, made his first appearance at a woman's rights convention. Another newcomer to the ranks was Mrs. Eliza W. Farnham, author and prominent leader in prison reform. The famous Hutchinsons who frequently sang at anti-slavery rallies made their debut at a woman's rights meeting in Mozart Hall.

But perhaps the biggest catch of all was Rev. Henry Ward Beecher who, in terms of reputation and prestige, was the most influential minister of his day. In the winter of 1859 Rev. Beecher delivered his first lecture on woman's rights at Cooper Institute, in which he came out squarely for woman suffrage, a step even his own wife was reluctant to take. His fee for the lecture was a hundred dollars and he insisted on getting it in advance. Susan was able to meet this request without difficulty because financially, too, the movement was in the black that year. In 1858 Francis Jackson, a wealthy Bostonian, had donated $5,000 to the cause of woman's rights. A year later another Bostonian, Charles F. Hovey, willed an annual grant of $8,000 to be divided among various social reforms, including woman's rights.

No one could appreciate these gifts more than the much-harried Susan B. Anthony who was constantly harassed by financial pressures. Now she was able to print pamphlets, hire halls, engage a battery of speakers at the magnificent salary of 12 dollars a week, and generally intensify the educational campaign in New York State to an unprecedented degree. In 1859 alone woman's rights conventions were held in forty different counties, lectures given in about a hundred and fifty towns and villages, and the entire state was blanketed with woman's rights literature.

Early in 1859 George William Curtis, himself a recent recruit to the movement, offered the following bit of advice to Susan B. Anthony: "Rather than have a radical thinker like Mrs. Rose at your suffrage conventions, you would better give them up. With such speakers as Phillips, Theodore Parker, Chapin, Tilton and myself advocating woman's cause, it cannot fail." Needless to say neither Susan nor the other leaders heeded Mr. Curtis's advice. They continued to hold conventions with Ernestine as a featured speaker.

That year she spoke most eloquently in a crowded Mozart Hall of the great change in public opinion which the movement had helped to bring about on the question of woman's education. Her remarks were frequently interrupted not only by the rowdies in the gallery, but also by the spontaneous laughter of an appreciative audience. "Formerly," she said, "all that was deemed requisite in the education of woman was that she should be able to sign her name to the marriage con-

THE EIGHTH
National Woman's-Rights Convention

WILL BE HELD IN

NEW YORK CITY,

AT MOZART HALL, 668 BROADWAY,

On Thursday and Friday, May 13 and 14, 1858,

Commencing at 10 o'clock Thursday A. M.

Lucy Stone, Ernestine L. Rose, Wendell Phillips, Wm. Lloyd Garrison, C. Lenox Remond, Mary F. Davis, Caroline H. Dahl, Rev. T. W. Higginson, Aaron M. Powell, Frances D. Gage, and others,

will address the several sessions of the Convention.

We regret that so many of the noble men and women, who, in spirit, are fully with us, should have so long withheld from us, kind words of recognition and encouragement.

We earnestly ask all those who believe our claims are just, who hope and look for a higher type of womanhood in the coming generations, to assert, now, their faith in the everlasting principles of justice, that have no respect for age, sex, color, or condition. Is it too much to ask that the BRADYS, the CURTIS', the CHAPINS, the BEECHERS, and the STOWES shall cheer us by their presence at our coming Convention, or by letter make known their position in regard to this movement? Feeling assured that our cause is just, that our positions are tenable, our platform is FREE for all fair discussion.

Communications for the Convention may be addressed to SUSAN B. ANTHONY, ANTI-SLAVERY OFFICE, 138 NASSAU STREET, NEW YORK.

American Antiquarian Society

Handbill distributed to advertise the Eighth National Woman's Rights Convention, 1858 tract, and even that could be dispensed with for she could use her 'x' mark. Arithmetic was deemed entirely superfluous for, what, indeed, had woman to count? Her children she could count on her fingers!! But that time is passed and the fact is that the Press, as often the led as the leader, the Bar, still oftener led than leading, and the Pulpit, always in the rear of public opinion, are all together, at last, pleading for the education of woman." Now, she said, the agitation must be concentrated on the next phase, "the *kind* and the *quality*" of woman's education.

This was progress, progress of a movement which, in less than a decade, had changed the thinking of a nation. One year later came an even greater triumph.

On March 20, 1860, after six years of persistent and stubborn agitation, the movement won a major victory. On that date the New York State Legislature passed an *Act Concerning the Rights and Liabilities of Husband and Wife*, which granted the women nearly everything they had asked for in their petitions, except suffrage. From now on a married woman was the sole owner not only of the property she had inherited prior to marriage but also of the properties and earnings she had acquired during marriage; and she could dispose of them as she pleased without her husband's interference. She could make investments, engage in business enterprises, sign contracts. In the eyes of the law she was no longer a minor or an idiot; she could sue and be sued. Also, at long last, she achieved an equal control of her own children. This right was granted her by clause nine of the Act, which read as follows:

> Every married woman is hereby constituted as the joint guardian of her children, with her husband, with equal powers, rights, and duties in regard to them, with the husband.

On May 12, 1860, when the leaders ascended the platform of Cooper Institute, N. Y., to commence the tenth national convention the glow of victory was still upon them. To this, the tenth anniversary of the movement, they brought a rich harvest of woman's rights, the fruit of ten years of labor. Indeed, so high was their elation over what they had won that what they still had to win seemed just around the corner. Even practical Ernestine said with sweeping confidence: "But whatever remains to be acquired will be easily obtained, compared with that which has been already secured." She could not have been more wrong. What had yet to be obtained was the movement's main objective, the elective franchise, and that was still more than half a century away from them.

But who would deny them now their moment of unrestrained optimism; the satisfaction of savoring the sweet wine of victory in public? We were scoffed at, they said, we were maligned, ridiculed, mocked and misrepresented by the opponents of our cause. But look what we accomplished against all these odds!

Susan B. Anthony chose this occasion to chide the cautious literati of her own sex who would not associate themselves with the movement. "Who of our literary women," she asked, "has yet ventured one word of praise or recognition of the heroic enunciators of the great idea of woman's equality—of Mary Wollstonecraft, Frances Wright, Ernestine L. Rose, Lucretia Mott, Elizabeth Cady Stanton?" There was good reason for Susan's bitter tone. The leading literary women of the day put their careers ahead of woman's rights. They had made their mark in the world and would not jeopardize it by being stigmatized as "strong-minded women."

Ernestine was fifty years old then. Her mass of black ringlets showed streaks of gray; her face, the rounded fullness that comes with age. When she rose to speak she gazed long and appreciatively into the faces of her two-thousandfold audience. The applause she received was generous and well deserved, a tribute to a veteran of many battles, to a Queen of the Platform at the peak of her career. In a voice full and resonant she painted a vivid word picture of her first winter in America; of how she had collected five signatures in five months, an episode that had become legend in the woman's rights movement. But before she spoke of her own efforts she paid warm tribute to her illustrious predecessor and friend, Frances Wright, the ". . . first woman in this country who spoke on the equality of the sexes . . . She was subjected to public odium, slander and persecution. But these were not the only things that she received. Oh, she had her reward! . . . the reward springing from the consciousness of right, of endeavoring to benefit unborn generations. How delightful to see the moulding of the minds around you, the infusing of your thoughts and aspirations into others, until one by one they stand by your side, without knowing how they came there! That reward she had."

Thinking ahead and considering the various government offices that woman might fill with honor if she had the vote, Ernestine said, "She [woman] could do in Congress, too. Go there and see how your representatives occupy their time, with their feet on the top of their desks, a paper before them, and a thing that ought to be exiled from civilized life (you know what I mean) [spittoon] at their side, but, which must be there if the floor is to be kept clean!"

The hall rocked with laughter. Ernestine was in exceptionally fine form that evening. Congressmen were not the only ones to receive the sting of her sarcasm. She also had something to say about "some ladies who think a great deal can be done in the Legislature without petitions, without conventions, without lectures, without public claim, in fact, without anything but a little lobbying. . . . I, as a woman, being conscious of the evil that is done by these lobby loafers in our Legislature and in the halls of Congress, object to it," she said. "I will wait five years longer to have a right given to me legitimately, from the sense of justice, rather than buy it in an underhand way by lobbying. I am one who acts above board. Whatever my sentiments may be, good, bad or indifferent. I express them and they are known. . . . But what has induced them, what has enabled them to do that work? The woman's rights movement, although they are afraid, or ashamed even of the name 'woman's rights.' "

At one point in the evening's proceedings a high dramatic moment occurred which thrilled the entire convention. Present in the hall was Judge Erastus D. Culver of Brooklyn. Someone in the audience recognized him and called for him to speak. The judge obliged. He told his listeners that on this very day several cases had come before his court involving female litigants and in each case he had invoked the new law to the advantage of the woman. In one instance when the lawyer for a woman said, "I will offer the lady as a witness," the lawyer for the opposite side leaped to his feet, protesting, "She is a party out of sight in law; in law, she is one of the invisibles." Whereupon the attorney for the lady put his hand in his pocket and brought out a newspaper clipping containing the new law which granted woman the right to institute legal action in her own behalf. As he cited the new statute his colleague, who had not kept up with the times, listened with disbelief. He was handed the clipping and upon reading the new law with his own eyes, turned to the judge and said, "If your honor please it is so; they have emancipated the women from all obligations to their husbands."

When the laughter and the applause subsided the judge cited another instance—that of a wife who complained that her husband, a drunkard, wanted to take away their two children from her. Ignorant of the new law, the lawyer for the husband cried out, "Well, we claim our paramount rights—that the father shall have custody of the children." He, too, was surprised to learn that on March 20, 1860, these "paramount rights" were relegated to the past, and that henceforth a mother was entitled to equal guardianship of her children with her husband. "In view of that law," I said, "I can not take the children away from the mother; she has just as much right to them as her husband, and if she says she must have them, I will let her have them."

The judge's decisions were hailed with loud and long

cheers. He remained standing until it grew quiet. He still had something to say. "Now, ladies and gentlemen," he said, "I have never been identified with this woman's rights movement, but I tell you what it is, we have got to admit some things. We have got to admit that these indefatigable laborers, amid obloquy and reproach, in Church and State, by buffoons and by men, have at last set the undercurrent in motion. The statute-book is their vindication tonight."

Ernestine Rose, recalling perhaps another time and another judge, the Hon. Thomas Herttell, who was the first New York State legislator to set this "undercurrent in motion," was so moved by Judge Culver's words that she stepped up to the rostrum and said, "I have been most happy to hear the remarks of Judge Culver. Who can doubt our success when judges, and noble ones, too . . . come forward to endorse our movement! . . . Freedom, my friends, does not come from the clouds, like a meteor; it does not bloom in one night; it does not come without great efforts and great sacrifices; all who love liberty have to labor for it." Who in that crowded hall knew the truth of these simple words better than she?

With a major legislative victory already won, one might have expected this convention to end on the same note of cheer, optimism and harmony with which it had begun. It did not. By the time the president had said: "The convention stands adjourned," tempers were ruffled, harmony was gone, and the leadership sharply divided on a fundamental question of policy.

Elizabeth Cady Stanton chose this occasion to come to grips with a controversial issue which had been hanging fire in the movement for some time—the question of divorce. She introduced ten resolutions aimed at liberalizing the existing divorce laws and then devoted her entire speech to an elaboration of this subject. The instant she sat down it was apparent that she had thrown a bombshell into the convention.

Rev. Antoinette Brown Blackwell rose at once and introduced thirteen resolutions opposing Elizabeth Cady Stanton's ten. The gist of all of them was that she was against divorce. Marriage, she said, "must be, from the nature of things, as permanent as the life of the parties."

Wendell Phillips objected most strenuously to the introduction of this issue at a woman's rights convention. He was even against printing the two sets of resolutions in the convention report. Garrison rose to say that in the main he agreed with his friend, Phillips, but was opposed to the move to strike the resolutions from the convention journal.

The only two leaders at the convention who unequivocally supported Elizabeth Cady Stanton were Susan B. Anthony and Ernestine Rose. Both argued that the question of divorce did come within the scope of this movement. Susan made a strong plea for the inclusion of the resolutions in the convention report. Phillip's motion was put to a vote and was defeated.

Ernestine's speech, being primarily one of rebuttal, was of necessity composed on the spot.

"Mrs. President:" she began, "The question of a divorce law seems to me one of the greatest importance to all parties . . .

"It were indeed well if woman could be what she ought to be, man what he ought to be, and marriage what it ought to be . . . But, alas! it is not yet; and I fear that sermons, however well meant, will not produce that desired end; and as long as the evil is here, we must look it in the face without shrinking, grapple with it manfully, and the more complicated it is the more courageously must it be analyzed, combatted and destroyed.

"I therefore ask for a divorce law . . . I ask that personal cruelty to a wife, whom he swore to 'love, cherish, and protect,' may be made a heinous crime . . . for which divorce shall be granted . . . I ask for a law of Divorce, so as to secure the real objects and blessings of married life, to prevent the crimes and immoralities now practiced, to prevent 'Free Love,' in its most hideous form, such as is now carried on but too often under the name of marriage, where hypocrisy is added to the crime of legalized prostitution. 'Free Love,' in its degraded sense, asks for

no Divorce law. It acknowledges no marriage, and therefore requires no divorce. I believe in true marriages, and therefore I
ask for a law to free men and women from false ones."

The correspondent of the *New York Saturday Press* reported that this was the first woman's rights convention he
enjoyed. He conceded that the female speakers were all "able
women," but complained that they were a bit too repetitious
for his taste. "I was infinitely relieved," he wrote, "when Mrs.
Ernestine L. Rose took the floor. A good delivery, a forcible
voice, the most uncommon good sense, a delightful terseness
of style, and a rare talent for humor, are the qualifications
which so well fit this lady for a public speaker. In about two
minutes she managed to infect her two-thousand fold audience
with a spirit of interest . . ."

The divorce debate touched off on the convention platform
did not end there; it continued to reverberate throughout the
nation, in the press, the public lyceums and the homes. This in
itself was an indication that the issue was of vital interest to
many people.

But the negative reactions that came from without the
movement did not depress the exponents of a new divorce law
as much as did the rift which this question caused within the
movement. They were especially disappointed in the stand
taken by Wendell Phillips, whom they held in great esteem.
Lucy Stone who prior to the convention fully supported
Elizabeth Cady Stanton on this issue now changed her mind
and went over to Phillips' position; while Lucretia Mott
joined ranks with Ernestine Rose, Susan B. Anthony and
Elizabeth Cady Stanton. In a letter to Susan, Parker Pillsbury
summed it all up neatly in one sentence: "What a pretty kettle
of hot water you tumbled into at New York!" But Elizabeth
Cady Stanton steadfastly held to her position. "We are right,"
she wrote to Susan. "My reason, my experience, my soul proclaim it . . . The men know we have struck a blow at their
greatest stronghold. Come what will, my whole soul rejoices
at the truth I have uttered. One word of thanks from a suffer-

ing woman outweighs with me the howls of Christendom."

In time the family rift within the movement was healed and even Wendell Phillips came to realize that divorce was a legitimate issue at a woman's rights convention. But a new and far more serious rift now loomed on the horizon. The nation was speeding headlong to the rift of secession. The legalistic patchwork devised to retain both the wholeness of the Union and the institution of slavery within it had grown too thin to withstand the moral conflicts and contradictions inherent in the Compromise. The shot fired at Harpers Ferry was but a tragic prelude to the shot fired at Fort Sumter; the former startled the nation, the latter split it asunder. The convention of 1860 was already meeting in the shadow of an impending disaster, but none of the leaders suspected that five years would have to go by before they would hold another national convention. When calamity struck the nation they abandoned, temporarily, the battle for woman's rights, and joined the battle for the preservation of the Union and the liberation of the slave.

After the intensive campaign that preceded the legislative victory of 1860 Ernestine found herself physically spent and sorely in need of a rest. Now that the tenth national convention was over there was nothing to stand in the way of a long summer vacation. She chose Queens, L.I., as the ideal place for it. In a letter to the *Investigator* dated August 14, 1860, she wrote, "For several weeks past I have been residing on the Long Island Flats, and have felt nearly as flat as the soil." But the reason for her letter was not so much to report on her health as to tell of an incident which, to many of her readers, must have had a a familiar ring by now, namely, that even on her vacation, and with the best of intentions not to get involved in any activities, Ernestine nearly always ended up on the lecture platform.

One day the family she boarded with invited her to a picnic given by the town schools, to be held in a grove in Flushing.

She went along and had a most enjoyable time. Everything about the outing seemed right. The grounds were beautiful, the weather perfect and the picnickers, about 1200 of them, were making the most of it, dancing, singing, swinging, in short, having themselves a picnic. And Ernestine, who did not know a soul there except the family that brought her along, followed the entire panorama from a distance with a great deal of pleasure. Suddenly she became aware of someone standing over her. She looked up and saw two gentlemen, both total strangers. She was therefore greatly surprised to hear one of them say, "Mrs. Rose, glad to see you here; we know you, and have come as the school committee to request you to address the children."

"I'll be very happy to," she said. She was helped up on a table and presently the picnickers were transformed into an audience. She spoke for about 15 minutes and addressed herself more to the parents than to the children. Her remarks so impressed her listeners that several days later another Queens gentleman called on her to invite her to speak on education in the "Republican Wigwam" in a nearby grove. She accepted. So far all went smoothly. Then someone had the idea to ask the minister of the church to announce her lecture from his pulpit next Sunday. The minister not only refused but launched an attack against Ernestine, and urged his parishioners to stay away from her lecture, saying, "I would never allow a daughter of mine to listen to *such* a woman."

But the clergyman's exhortations had little effect on his worshippers. He may have succeeded in keeping his own daughters from attending but many other daughters, and mothers, turned out in full force to hear Ernestine lecture and, incidentally, hear for the first time a woman speak in public in that part of the country. "One gentleman," Ernestine wrote in her letter, "a deacon who felt a little too warm, called his wife and sister to 'Come out! Come out!' But the disobedient daughters of Eve refused!" Speaking of the effects of the lecture she said, "It has caused quite a little stir, and given the people, if but for a few days, to think and talk about something else besides prayer meetings and potatoes. I have been requested to speak again as soon as they can make arrangements. Thus much for Long Island. A little tempest is better than none at all, where all has been oppressive stagnation."

In its account of the school picnic the *Long Island Farmer* wrote, "Several addresses were given, one by a lady who spoke with singular eloquence, but we could not learn her name." Ernestine's comment was, "Who will ask, 'What is in a name?'"

Chapter XXI

THE WAR YEARS

1860 WAS A YEAR of great historic moment in the life of this country. It marked the beginning of a new and bloody phase in the struggle between freedom and slavery. For the woman's rights movement it signified the end of a glorious decade of incessant growth and activity. The legislative triumph which the women had celebrated at their tenth national convention indicated how close were the victories that might have been theirs had not these revolutionary events thrust themselves so precipitously upon them.

Lincoln was elected on November 6, and on December 20, South Carolina seceded from the Union. Ernestine, though herself a Democrat, worked for Lincoln's election because the new Republican Party held out a greater promise for the liberation of the slave, but on the key issue of slavery the party did not go far enough to suit the Garrisonian abolitionists, and Ernestine was now a Garrisonian. So far Lincoln had committed himself only to preventing the further spread of slavery but not its destruction in the states where it already existed. The abolitionists saw a grave danger in this compromise. Their slogan was: "No Compromise with Slaveholders! Immediate and Unconditional Emancipation!" Ernestine subscribed fully to that slogan. The new party had to be steered away from the course of compromise to a policy of emancipation and only an aroused public could induce it to make that change. The abolitionists mobilized their forces for a series of anti-slavery meetings to be held in the larger cities and towns of New York State, with Susan B. Anthony in charge of the campaign.

They began with Buffalo on January 3, 1861, and were met by a hostile mob that rioted for two days and finally seized the platform and turned off the gas. The reception the abolitionists received in that city was indicative of what they could expect from the rest of their itinerary. Everywhere they were met by a mob bent on preventing the holding of an anti-slavery meeting and, for the most part, the mob succeeded.

Though in the main these riots were instigated by Democratic officials, Susan placed the blame squarely at the doorstep of the Republicans. After her experience at Rome she wrote, "The Republican paper called us pestiforous fanatics and infidels and advised every decent man to stay away." In Albany, their last city, the situation was different. There, too, the mob was out in full force but Mayor George H. Thacher, although a Democrat, was determined to let the abolitionists hold their meeting. He was guided in his decision by the principle that free speech must be upheld at all cost. He had about sixty policemen on hand with strict orders to quell any disturbance while he himself took a seat on the platform, placed his revolver across his knees and told Susan to proceed. Ernestine, who had come to Albany for the wind-up meeting of the campaign, also sat on that platform together with Lucretia Mott, William Lloyd Garrison, Gerrit Smith, Frederick Douglass and Elizabeth Cady Stanton. She spoke both in the afternoon and evening sessions. The *Albany Republican Statesman* reported that "Ernestine Rose who made a speech strongly denunciatory of the South, declared herself a Democrat, claimed to have helped elect Lincoln because she considered anti-slavery principles true democracy; called James Buchanan a miserable coward, gave Mr. Seward a sharp rub and prophesied that he would never be elected President if he was in favor of compromise with the South."

Before the evening session came to a close the Mayor said

to Susan, "If you insist upon holding your meetings tomorrow, I shall still protect you, but it will be a difficult thing to
hold this rabble in check much longer. If you will adjourn at
the close of this session I shall consider it a personal favor."
Susan agreed with the mayor that it would be best to adjourn
the meeting for good. The mob surged out into the street and
waited for the abolitionists. There was no telling what might
have happened had not the mayor and his sixty policemen
escorted the speakers to their hotel. Frustrated again, the
mob now burned the mayor in effigy.

As soon as the anti-slavery meeting was over some of the
same speakers held a State Woman's Rights Convention in
Albany, on February 7 and 8, and Ernestine, Lucretia Mott
and Elizabeth Cady Stanton appeared before a Judiciary Committee that held a hearing on the divorce bill currently pend-
ing before the legislature.

Events were moving at a rapid pace toward the climax of
Fort Sumter, now only two months away. Susan made an attempt to organize a national woman's rights convention to be
held in New York in May, but by that time the fatal shot had
been fired and the country was torn in two. At this critical
juncture in the nation's life, woman's rights seemed a secondary issue even to some of its most ardent advocates; the burning issue of the moment was the preservation of the Union. To
abolitionists this meant a Union entirely free from slavery.
Emancipation was now the dominant theme in Ernestine's
public addresses. At the one hundred and twenty-fourth anniversary of Thomas Paine's birthday, held at the City Assembly Rooms in January 1861, she said, "The question which
now distracts the country is no longer one of color—it is freedom or slavery, life or death of the North . . . whether we
shall barter away the rights, the progress and the civilization
of the free states for the inestimable blessing to belong to
South Carolina . . . let the watchword be, No more compromise! We expiate now the crime of having compromised so
often . . ." A year later, when illness prevented her from at-

tending a Paine celebration in Boston, she sent her toast by mail and here too the theme was one of no compromise: "The President, Cabinet, and Commander-in-Chief . . . May they soon awaken from the lethargy in which the opiate of slavery has so long kept them, to the consciousness of the facts—1st, that there is a war; 2nd, that it cannot be brought to a successful termination by the sugar-plums fired from Sherman's popgun on the 'hospitable shores' of South Carolina, but by bullets directed with a fearless and energetic hand; . . ." Several months later, at an infidel convention in Boston, she introduced a resolution urging the convention to go on record ". . . to aid in emancipating the slaves wherever found and of whatever color." There was debate and disagreement on this resolution but in the end it was adopted.

During those grave and perilous days Ernestine continued with her free thought activities. In April 1861 she delivered a lecture in Boston entitled, "A Defence of Atheism" in which she said: ". . . I consider no place too holy, no subject too sacred for man's earnest investigation . . ." An example of her talent to say much in few words is this epigrammatic sentence from her speech: "Hypocrisy is the prolific mother of a large family." In this address Ernestine revealed that she was conversant with both the subject of theology and the world of science. The views she expressed in this speech she maintained throughout her life. Soon after her death a friend of hers wrote: "Only about six weeks ago she gave me a copy of her 'Defence of Atheism,' and said she had nothing to alter."

In the spring of 1862 the woman's rights movement suffered a setback. While the women of New York State were busy helping in the war effort, caring for the sick and wounded, replacing their husbands and sons in the fields, knitting socks, scraping flint, making jellies, in short, doing everything possible to lighten the burden of the administration and comfort the men in uniform, their legislature in Albany perpetrated a sneak attack on their hard-won gains.

On April 10, 1862, the New York Legislature amended the *Act Concerning the Rights and Liabilities of Husband and Wife* which was passed on March 20, 1860. Two of the most important laws in the 1860 Act, the one granting the mother equal guardianship of her children, and the other, giving the widow the sole control of the property in case of the husband's death, for the support of her minor children, were repealed. The revised guardianship law read as follows:

> "No man shall bind his child to apprenticeship or service, or part with the control of such child or create any testamentary guardian therefore, unless the mother, if living, shall in writing signify her assent thereto."

On the surface it may appear that the change is one in wording only and not in substance, but upon closer examination of the law it becomes obvious that a very neat sleight of hand was committed here by the lawmakers. "Assent in writing" is a far cry from joint guardianship and from having "equal powers, rights, and duties . . . with the husband." How secure can a mother feel in the control of her children when that control rests on the slender thread of her signature beneath a document, which, if prepared by an unscrupulous husband a credulous and trusting wife could easily be deceived into signing? The change was made so quietly that the women were unaware of it until it became law. When Lydia Mott who lived in Albany wrote Susan the news, Susan replied, "Dear Lydia: Your startling letter is before me. I knew some weeks ago that that abominable thing was on the calender, with some six or eight hundred bills *before* it, and hence felt sure it would not come up this winter, and that in the meantime we should sound the alarm . . . But what can we do now when even the motion to retain the mother's joint guardianship is voted down? Twenty thousand petitions rolled up for that—a hard year's work!—the law secured!—the echoes of our words of gratitude in the capital have scarce died away, and now all is lost!"

Nineteen years later this hurt was still smouldering. In 1881, when Susan, Elizabeth Cady Stanton and Matilda Joslyn Gage were preparing the first volume of the *History of Woman Suffrage,* they referred to this event as the "cowardly act of the Legislature of 1862 . . ." and of the legislators they wrote with bitterness that "these dastardly lawmakers, filled with the spirit of slaveholders, were stealing the children and the property of the white mothers in the Empire State," while they were doing their utmost to win "the freedom of the black mothers of the South." This, they said, would never have happened if woman possessed the power of the ballot. Here then was additional proof that their demand for the elective francise was both valid and justified.

When in May 1863 the leaders of the woman's rights movement met again in a national convention it was not to discuss woman's rights but to deliberate how best to assist the government in the hour of its gravest need. The Emancipation Proclamation proclaimed by Lincoln with great reluctance had already been in effect for more than four months and had not yet wrought the desired miracle on the course of the war which had been deteriorating at an alarming pace. Henry B. Stanton, Elizabeth's husband, painted a most disturbing picture of the nation's state of affairs as he saw it from the vantage point of the capital. In a letter to Susan written from Washington in January of that year he said, "The country is rapidly going to destruction. The army is almost in a state of mutiny for want of its pay and for lack of a leader. Nothing can carry the North through but the Southern Negroes, and no one can marshal them into the struggle except the abolitionists . . . You have no idea how dark the cloud is which hangs over us . . . We must not lay the flattering unction to our souls that the Proclamation will be of any use if we are beaten and have a dissolution of the Union. Here then is work for you, Susan, put on your armour and go forth!"

The Proclamation which was hailed in many abolitionist quarters as a tremendous step forward on the part of the administration was, by the admission of these same abolitionists, a far cry from the ideal solution to the problem. Yet even this half-way measure was in danger of being torpedoed by Congress and of remaining no more than an empty promise by an harassed president. What was urgently needed here was a strong expression of the people that would strengthen Lincoln's wavering hand and let Congress know in no uncertain terms that the people would not stand for any more compromises in the name of preserving the Union. Indeed what was needed was a thirteenth amendment to the federal Constitution with teeth in it; one that would go to the heart of the slavery issue and grant unequivocal freedom to *all* the slaves, not only to those of the rebelling states.

Henry B. Stanton had knocked on the right door with his letter to Susan. If what was needed was a force to rouse the public from its apathy and educate it to the need of the hour who was better suited for this task than the women who had served their apprenticeship in the twin social reform movements of anti-slavery and woman's rights?

Out of this May convention, attended by delegates from various parts of the country, there emerged a new organization, the Women's National Loyal League with Elizabeth Cady Stanton as its president and Susan B. Anthony as its secretary. Ernestine served on the policy-forming Business Committee.

The birth of the League was not a smooth one. At its very first session the convention ran into a snag, ironically enough, over the word "women." Among the resolutions submitted by Susan there was one which read as follows:

> "*Resolved*, There never can be a true peace in this Republic until the civil and political rights of all citizens of African descent and all women are practically established."

The delegate from Wisconsin objected, saying, "I hope this resolution will not pass." She felt that this resolution would associate the League with the unpopular cause of woman's rights and thus harm the new organization. Another woman said, "The Negroes have suffered more than the women, and the women, perhaps, can afford to give them the preference. Let it stand as regards them, and blot out the word woman." We witness here a foreshadowing of a much larger struggle around the issue of woman versus the Negro with regard to the vote, which was to erupt a few years later but which no one at the convention could possibly have visualized at the moment. In the debate which this resolution had touched off Ernestine gave her reply to both women. "I for one object to the proposition to throw woman out of the race for freedom," she said. "And do you know why? Because she needs freedom for the freedom of man. Our ancestors made a great mistake in not recognizing woman in the rights of man. It has been justly stated that the Negro at present suffers more than woman, but it can do him no injury to place woman in the same category with him . . . It can do no injury, but must do good, for it is a painful fact that woman under the law has been in the same category with the slave . . ."

Angelina Grimké Weld followed Ernestine, saying, "I rejoice exceedingly that that resolution should combine us with the Negro." Susan took the floor and said, "I hope the discussion will no longer be continued as to the comparative rights or wrongs of one class or another. The question before us is . . . is it possible for this government to be a true democracy, a genuine republic, while one-sixth or one-half of the people are disfranchised?" But the woman from Wisconsin persisted in her objection and so Ernestine rose to speak a second time. "It is exceedingly amusing to hear persons talk about throwing out woman's rights," she said, "when, if it had not been for woman's rights that lady would not have had the courage to stand here and say what she did. Pray, what means 'loyal'? Loyal means to be true to one's highest conviction . . . It is because we are loyal to truth, loyal to justice, loyal to right, loyal to humanity, that woman is included in that resolution." When the resolution finally came up for a vote it was carried by a large majority.

At Cooper Institute where the League held its evening session Ernestine delivered a major address on the course of the war, which must have made some in the audience and even on the platform squirm uncomfortably in their seats. She was sharply critical of the administration's conduct of the war, of the Cabinet and of the President's wavering policies. Her tone was in marked contrast to the mild, almost conciliatory tone of the speakers that preceded her. In an address read by Susan from the "Loyal Women of the Country to Abraham Lincoln, President of the United States," and which was later sent to him, there were such phrases as, "We come not to criticise or complain," and "It is not our mission to criticise the past." True, the letter said that "so long as one slave breathes in this Republic, we drag the chain with him" and this was, after all, the key issue in the war. But as for the implementation of this principle it spoke in such general terms as, "let the men who wield the nation's power be wise, brave and magnanimous, and its women will be prompt to meet the duties of the hour with devotion and heroism."

Ernestine did not have implicit faith in the nation's leaders with regard to the conduct of the war. Their past performances did not warrant blind trust in them. She was in agreement with the League's main objective. That was why she was one of its founders and one of the shapers of its program, but she did not feel bound to adopt the League's conciliatory tone. "I speak for myself," she declared, "I do not wish any one else to be responsible for my opinions. I am loyal only to justice and humanity. Let the Administration give evidence that they, too, are for justice to all, without exception, without distinction, and I, for one, had I ten thousand lives, would gladly lay them down to secure this boon of freedom to humanity. (Applause) But without this certainty I am not

unconditionally loyal to the Administration . . . Then I say
to Abraham Lincoln 'Give us security for the future, for
really, when I look at the past, without a guarantee, I can
hardly trust you.' And then I would say to him 'Let nothing
stand in your way; let no man obstruct your path.' "

The chief obstructionist in her view, as far as the military
operations were concerned, was General McClellan and she
aimed her sharpest barbs at him, to the delight of the entire
audience. "Why, my friends," she said, "from July 1861, to
October, 1862—for sixteen long months—we have been electrified with the name of our great little Napoleon! And what has
the great little Napoleon done? Why, he has done just enough
to prevent anybody else from doing anything . . . Well, we
have disposed of him partially, but we *pay* him yet, and you
and I are taxed for it.

". . . It is a mockery to say that we emancipate the slaves
we cannot reach and pass by those we can reach. First free the
slaves that are under the flag of the Union. If that flag is the
symbol of freedom let it wave over free men only. The slaves
must be freed in the Border States. Consistency is a great
power."

When Garrison had been ready to burn the Constitution in
public as a document condoning slavery, and was ready, in
the name of moral consistency, to secede from the South,
Ernestine was a Unionist, until the Kansas-Nebraska Bill in
1854 led her to become a Garrisonian. Now, Garrison swung
behind Lincoln, eager to hold together the Union even at the
expense of some compromises, while Ernestine would not
yield an inch to the slaveholders. ". . . I would rather have a
small republic without the taint and without the stain of slavery in it," she said, "than to have the South brought back by
compromise. To avert such calamity, we must work. And
our work must mainly be to watch and criticise and urge the
Administration to do its whole duty to freedom and humanity."

It was, perhaps, the desire to mitigate the tenor of Ernes-

tine's criticism that led Elizabeth Cady Stanton to say soon
after Ernestine had spoken, "I suppose all the loyal women
will agree with me that we owe to the President and the Government in these hours of trial, whether they make mistakes or
whether they do not, words of cheer and encouragement;
and, as events occur one after another, our criticisms should
not be harshly made."

The Loyal League proclaimed as its immediate task the roll-
ing up of a giant petition with a million signatures from all
over the country. Nine months later they were able to present
to Senator Charles Sumner the first installment of a hundred
thousand signatures from about 23 states.

Now that the women were circulating Loyal League petitions instead of woman's rights petitions their former critics
changed their tune about them. The villains of yesterday became the heroines of today. Suddenly they were discovered to
possess such commendable qualities as wisdom, intelligence,
virtue, loyalty, devotion and patriotism. James Gordon Bennett, however, was consistent throughout. Commenting editorially on the Loyal League convention, the pro-slavery
Herald stated, "As to the women's convention, that which was
originally designed for a most patriotic and praiseworthy mo-
tive has been distorted into an atheistical revolutionary
woman's rights movement under the leadership of Lucy Stone,
Susan B. Anthony and Ernestine L. Rose."

In the midst of the war for the liberation of the Negro
slave Ernestine took time out to defend the honor of the
Jewish people. The battle arena in this instance was not the
lecture platform or the convention hall but the pages of the
Boston Investigator. One day, when the issue dated October
28, 1863, arrived, Ernestine was shocked to find in that free
thought paper an anti-Jewish diatribe written by none other
than her friend Horace Seaver, the editor himself! He began
with an attack on the ancient Jews, charging that "they were
about the worst people of whom we have any account . . ."

From there he went on to say that he thought it was a good thing that the Jews were scattered all over the earth because "they were a troublesome people to live in proximity with . . ." He then offered his views on modern Judaism, finding it "bigoted, narrow, exclusive, and totally unfit for a progressive people like the Americans, among whom we hope it may not spread . . ."

Ernestine, who had experienced anti-Semitism at first hand in Poland and Germany, knew that even democratic America was not entirely free from anti-Jewish bias. But to discover it in her own circle of freethinkers, and in the very paper to which she had been a contributor for over two decades, was a bitter pill to swallow. At the first opportunity she wrote Horace Seaver the following stinging reply:

". . . Mr. Editor, I almost smelt brimstone, genuine Christian brimstone, when I read in the *Investigator*—'Even the modern Jews are bigoted, narrow, exclusive, and totally unfit for progressive people like the Americans among whom we hope they may not spread . . .' Indeed! That hope smacks too much of the Puritan spirit that whipped and hung the Quaker women, to be found in the liberty-promoting, freedom-loving *Investigator*. You 'hope.' Now suppose, as we always desire to promote what we hope for, you had the power as well as the inclination, would you prevent their spreading? How? Would you drive them out of Boston—out of 'progressive America,' as they were once driven out of Spain?

"But where is the danger of their 'spreading?' In this city, Philadelphia, Cincinnati, and other places, they have synagogues, and have no doubt spread as much as they could, and no calamity has yet befallen any place in consequence of that fact; and wherever they are they act just about the same as other people. The nature of the Jew is governed by the same laws as human nature in general. In England, France, Germany, and in the rest of Europe (except Spain), in spite of the barbarous treatment and deadly persecution they suffered, they have lived and spread and outlived much of the poisonous rancor and prejudice against them, and Europe has been none the worse on their account.

"Of course, where they are still under the Christian lash, as in Rome, where for the glory of God, their children even are stolen from them, self-preservation forces them to be narrow and exclusive. In other countries more civilized and just, they are so too; they progress just as fast as the world they live in will permit them. In France there is hardly any difference between Jew and Christian. The Jews occupy some of the highest positions in the Army, the State, in literature, the arts and sciences; the same is the case, more or less, in Germany and other enlightened countries. Are then the Jews in Boston so much worse, that their spread is to be dreaded even by Infidels? If so, it would prove the pernicious example and influence of Puritanism."

Ernestine concluded her long letter by saying, ". . . let the subject be impartially investigated and it will be found that, take them all in all the Jews are as good as any other sect . . . Will you tell me they are cunning, sharp traders? Then I will point you to the renowned 'Yankee' who, it is admitted by all, excels the Jew in that art. . . . Then let us as Infidels . . . not add to the prejudice already existing towards the Jews, or any other sect.

Yours for justice,
Ernestine L. Rose."

As far as Ernestine was concerned she had answered the charges fully and considered the matter was closed. The editor printed her letter but, unfairly, gave it in two separate weekly installments, thus depriving the reader of the cumulative impact of Ernestine's argument. In addition, he tagged on to each installment a postscript of his own rebuttal, giving himself the benefit of meeting his adversary piecemeal. In his reply he stated that he found Ernestine's arguments far from convincing, that he had nothing against Jews personally but repeated that he did "not like Judaism well enough to see it spreading in this country . . . and if the Yankees, as a class, like money as well as the Jews, we question whether so many of the former would now be found in the ranks of the Union

Army. They would more likely stay at home to deal in 'old clothes,' at a profit of 'fifteen pershent.' "

Ernestine did not let his renewed slanders go unanswered. She wrote another long letter to the editor which was printed with an even longer reply by him. Now the controversy was on and it lasted for a full ten weeks. The editor would simply not retreat from his original position and the more he defended it the more he exposed his anti-Jewish bias. With each new reply Ernestine bore down on him with the full weight of her knowledge of the subject and her fierce and uncompromising sense of justice. As the controversy progressed its tone became increasingly more edgy and one could almost hear the gnashing of teeth beneath the facade of a "polite" discussion. At one point in the debate Seaver became so exasperating that Ernestine tossed politeness to the winds and wrote in her reply, "You make unwarrantable assertions which convict you out of your own mouth of as much folly as bigotry, for you have not had the candor fairly to answer one question; but without giving a simple reason continue your, to say the least, unwarrantable tirade against them [the Jews] . . . Now whatever you may say on the subject, pray keep Judaism and the Jews distinct, and don't compare January with May, but January with January, and May with May; for whatever you may know of the ancient, you evidently know nothing of the modern Jews, and don't accuse me of going to the moon or to some other wonderful thing simply because I don't like your prejudice against the Jews, nor against any other people; and above all, keep your temper in an argument."

She had written her first reply to the editor on January 29, 1864; two months later she brought the controversy to a halt and concluded her final letter with the following words: "But as you say, I have 'hit' you hard enough, and unless forced by further quibbles, insinuations, new issues and prevarications, I am quite content to let the subject rest, satisfied in having done my duty in defence of justice."

Some readers also got into the fray. A Mr. William P.

Wood from Washington, D.C., who came to Ernestine's defense, added this interesting bit of information, "I did not know her to be one of the 'chosen people' but was so well pleased with her progressive liberality of sentiment, and her independence in its expression, that some years since I named my only daughter Ernestine Rose Wood."

It is doubtful whether Ernestine succeeded in freeing the editor from his anti-Jewish bias since he maintained throughout that he did not have any such thing. But the readers must certainly have benefited from an extended discussion on Jews in which not only their religion but many other aspects of their life were presented by Ernestine in their proper historical perspective.

The editor of the *Jewish Record*, who followed the controversy from the sidelines with great interest, praised Ernestine for her fighting stand, saying that although she had abandoned her religion she still possessed "some of the old leaven of the Jewish spirit . . ."

Chapter XXII

CRISIS IN THE RANKS

AT THE AGE OF FIFTY-FIVE and in broken health Ernestine
found herself in the midst of a tempestuous ideological
battle that was raging within the ranks of the woman's rights
movement. This happened soon after the Civil War when the
people were rejoicing over the conclusion of four years of
bloody strife and looking forward to a period of peace and
reconstruction. At this particular time the captains of the
woman's rights movement hastily mobilized their forces for
a showdown with the Republican administration over the issue of woman suffrage. When their support of the war had
been needed the promise of suffrage had been held out to
them, but when the crisis was over the party said to them,
now is not the time to honor that promise; now is the "Negro's
hour"; woman's hour will come later. When their support
had been needed, Senator Charles Sumner of Massachusetts
had sent his greetings to the first anniversary of the Loyal
League: "I am grateful to your Association for what you have
done to arouse the country to insist on the extinction of slavery." Now that same Senator turned his back on their pleas
and regarded their petitions to Congress as "most inoppor-
tune."

The Administration argued that the enfranchisement of the
Negro was vital to the very existence of the Republican Party.
Without it the Thirteenth Amendment would be ineffectual
and the party would not long survive. Negro suffrage, the
politicians said, was a heavy enough burden for the young

party to carry at this time; add to it the unpopular load of woman suffrage and the party might break under the strain. By insisting on woman suffrage *now* the women would only be jeopardizing the Negro's chances to win the franchise now.

The women were torn. As abolitionists they could only rejoice at the fact that slavery was, at long last, abolished; but as advocates of woman's rights their cup of joy was mixed with the bitter pill of disappointment. As abolitionists they could only be proud at the thought that they had helped pave the way for the Thirteenth Amendment which said: "Neither slavery nor involuntary servitude . . . shall exist within the United States, or any place subject to their jurisdiction," thus dealing a death blow to slavery; but as champions of woman suffrage they could not overlook the fact that the two subsequent amendments, the Fourteenth and Fifteenth would deal a death blow to the enfranchisement of woman.

The conflict evolved around two words—"male" and "sex;" the one because it was included, the other because it was omitted. The aim of the Fourteenth Amendment was to make the Thirteenth meaningful; to enfranchise the Negro and raise yesterday's slave to the status of full citizenship. The women could have no quarrel with this. What they objected to was the following phraseology in the amendment: "But when the right to vote . . . is denied to any of the male inhabitants of such a State . . . the basis of representation shall be reduced in the proportion which the number of such male citizens shall bear to the whole number of male citizens twenty-one years of age in such State." Thus the word "male" was introduced for the first time into the federal Constitution. Later, when it became apparent that the Fourteenth Amendment would have to be buttressed by yet another amendment in order to plug the loophole of color, a Fifteenth Amendment was proposed, which read: "The right of citizens of the United States to vote shall not be denied or abridged by the United States or by any State on account of race, color, or previous condition of servitude."

As far as the women were concerned the inclusion of the word "male" in the Fourteenth Amendment and the omission of the word "sex" from the Fifteenth Amendment were devices calculated to block the path of woman suffrage by constitutional means. It was bad enough, they said, when for years their respective state legislatures had ignored their claim to the elective franchise; now their claim was to be denied by the federal Constitution itself! They were bitter and in a fighting mood. One has but to compare the following two statements by Elizabeth Cady Stanton to see how intense this bitterness had become. On May 12, 1864, speaking at the first anniversary of the Loyal League, she said, "Look not to Greece or Rome for heroes—to Jerusalem or Mecca for saints—but for the highest virtues of heroism let us worship the black man at our feet." But in December, 1865, when the administration's policy on the issue of woman suffrage was already apparent, she said, ". . . as the celestial gate of civil rights is slowly moving on its hinges, it becomes a serious question whether we had better stand aside and see 'Sambo' walk into the kingdom first."

It was in this twin mood of bitterness and belligerency that the women gathered at the Church of the Puritans, in New York, on May 10, 1866, to hold their eleventh National Woman's Rights Convention, the first such meeting in five years. Their "Address to Congress" which the convention adopted expressed both their plea and their determination to fight: "Crush not, we pray you, the million hopes that hang on our success." But a little later on they said, ". . . think you . . . we can stand silent witnesses while you sell our birthright of liberty to save from a timely death an effete political organization? No . . . our demand must ever be, 'No compromise of human rights'—'No admission in the Constitution of inequality of rights, or disfranchisement on account of color or sex.' "

But who would be their allies in this fight? On whom could they count for support? Why, the abolitionists, of course! Had not the leading abolitionists also been the most consistent advocates of woman's rights? The women were in for yet another shock. When they proposed to the Anti-Slavery Society that it merge with the Woman's Rights Society into one organization to be called the American Equal Rights Association their proposal was turned down. But why the duplication of effort, the women argued, when we have a common goal. The Negro and the woman are now the only two classes of people that have yet to achieve the status of full citizenship; with combined forces we can speed the attainment of that goal. The Society was adamant. Wendell Phillips, its new president, was an advocate of the "this-is-the-Negro's-hour theory" and he carried his followers with him. Garrison, Curtis, Higginson, Tilton, Gerrit Smith, Frederick Douglass, people who for years had been among the staunchest friends and supporters of the woman's rights movement, on this issue sided with the administration. For the women it was difficult to say which of the two was the harder blow—the betrayal of the Republicans or the abandonment of their friends. But their course of action was clear to them. They would not retreat one inch from the principle of universal suffrage. And if the Anti-Slavery Society refused to join forces with them they would find other allies; they would utilize their own resources to the utmost but they would not abandon the fight.

At this national convention, Ernestine placed herself unequivocally on the side of those who insisted that the demand for woman suffrage should not be delayed until the Negro was enfranchised but that both demands should be made together. She therefore supported the resolution proposed by Susan which read as follows:

> "*Resolved*, That as the time has come for an organization that shall cover the broad ground of universal suffrage, we shall be known hereafter as the American Equal Rights Association."

The resolution was adopted. The Republican Party and the abolitionists of the Wendell Phillips' wing did all they could to separate the Negro's claim to suffrage from that of woman's, but the women would not be torn from the Negro. They were determined to walk through that "celestial gate to civil rights" together.

At this stage of the controversy the situation was still fluid, and the issues involved were not yet sharply delineated. The holders of opposing views were still on friendly terms, and each side was trying to win over converts to its own position. It was still possible at this point for Frederick Douglass to be one of the vice-presidents of the newly-formed association, although the formation of this organization could not have had his wholehearted approval.

But as the rift between the Anti-Slavery Society and the Equal Rights Association grew wider, the tone of polemics became more bitter. The leaders of the Association openly campaigned against the Fourteenth and Fifteenth Amendments and countered the slogan of "manhood suffrage" with the slogan of "educated suffrage." If it is a matter of choosing between the two, they said, then they would rather that the educated white woman got the vote in preference to the uneducated black man, who only yesterday was a slave. Two million enfranchised Negro men, they argued, would only increase by that many the number of those who resist the granting of suffrage to woman, white and black.

In 1867 the embattled Equal Rights Association suffered two major setbacks in two different parts of the country, in New York State and in the young state of Kansas. Both states were holding constitutional conventions that year and the women were determined to take full advantage of the opportunities provided by such an occasion. If they could succeed, through constitutional amendment, in obtaining woman suffrage even in one state, what a triumph that would be! It might serve as an example and an inspiration for other states and territories to follow suit; it might even compel a change of heart in the adamant politicians in Washington!

In New York State the Republican Party was interested in expunging the word "white" from the constitution because it was an obstacle to the enfranchisement of the Negro. The women could only applaud this objective, but they were also quick to point to another word that should be stricken from the state constitution, the word "male," which had been part of that document since 1778. (New York had the dubious honor of being the first state to include the word "male" in her constitution.) Now was the time, argued the women, to remove both of these stumbling blocks to universal suffrage with one clean sweep.

Kansas held out an even greater promise. There both "white" and "male" were up for constitutional amendment, and some leading Republicans, including a Republican governor, urged that the word "male" be amended. Lucy Stone and her husband, Henry B. Blackwell, were dispatched to Kansas, while Susan, Elizabeth Cady Stanton, and a corps of other speakers, conducted the campaign in New York. Ernestine did all her poor health permitted her to do. Her physical condition forced upon her the passive role of elder statesman, counselor and advisor. She was too sick to make extensive trips away from home.

Neither Susan's well-organized meetings, nor Mrs. Stanton's eloquent pleas before the convention, were of any avail. The word "white" was stricken from the constitution; the word "male" was not. The women lost. And in the process they lost another valuable friend—Horace Greeley. Mr. Greeley had counseled the women to campaign only against the word "white" and to postpone their agitation against the word "male" for a later time. Of course they did not take his advice. "Well," said Greeley to Elizabeth Cady Stanton, "If you persevere in your present plan, you need depend on no further help from me or the *Tribune*." Mr. Greeley made good his threat. With the loss of the *Tribune's* support, and with the *Anti-Slavery Standard* treating them like stepchildren, the need for a suffrage publication which for many years had been an unfulfilled wish had now become an urgent necessity.

They failed in New York but there was still Kansas. Susan

and Elizabeth Cady Stanton hastened out to the prairie state
to pick up where Lucy Stone and her husband had left off.
They campaigned hard, as only two such veterans could; the
net result, however, was failure. Kansas, which held out the
brightest hope, yielded the biggest disappointment. Both
amendments were defeated. But the Kansas campaign was not
only doomed to fail; it was destined to become one of the
most hotly debated episodes in the history of the suffrage
movement. The principal characters in that episode were
Susan B. Anthony and George Francis Train. Two more dissimilar individuals one could hardly imagine.

George Francis Train was a financial wizard with a pro-
nounced adventurous streak, who had amassed a fortune from
various business enterprises. But Train, an Irish Democrat, was
a man whose interests were not always strictly financial. From
time to time he would venture into the realm of social reform.
At that particular time, in 1867, his fancy struck him to
espouse woman suffrage. As far as Susan was concerned his
fancy's timing was perfect. The Republican machine in Kansas was knifing the campaign in the back. The situation was
desperate. A successful appeal to the Democratic minority
and the state's Irish constituency might help turn the tide.
Train, it seemed to Susan, possessed the right qualifications
for this emergency and she accepted his offer to join the
campaign as a speaker. She was not oblivious to the repercus-
sions that such an alliance might evoke. But in her singleness
of purpose she brushed aside all hesitations; and Elizabeth did
likewise.

From that moment on Train became the main attraction for
the duration of the campaign. Large audiences flocked to the
meetings not so much to hear a lecture on woman suffrage as
to see the flamboyant Irishman perform. He would appear
dressed to the hilt, including lavender kid gloves, and amuse
his listeners with his colorful patter and salty humor. And
there was no more need for penny-pinching. Now they could
travel in comfort and the campaign received the best promo-

tion money could buy. At one meeting he made the startling announcement that henceforth the woman suffrage movement would have its own publication, and that he, George Francis Train, would be its financial guardian angel. He made his offer complete with title and editorial board. The paper would be called the *Revolution* and its editors would be Elizabeth Cady Stanton and Parker Pillsbury, former editor of the *Anti-Slavery Standard;* Susan would be the owner.

Susan and Elizabeth were beside themselves with joy. At long last the movement would have its own mouthpiece! To be sure, there was a string attached to Mr. Train's generous offer. In return for his financial support he expected some space in the *Revolution* where he could expound his views on such subjects as finance, politics, or any related topic that might require his urgent attention. At the moment this seemed a rather modest request compared to such overwhelming generosity.

With the Kansas campaign over, the trio went on a lecture tour through some of the major cities in the country, with Susan and Elizabeth speaking on suffrage and Train advocating his own candidacy for President of the United States!

In the meantime, back home, leaders of the Equal Rights Association and other prominent advocates of woman suffrage blushed with embarrassment at the Anthony-Stanton-Train alliance. Their initial reaction of disbelief changed to consternation when they learned that the news was not a hoax; then consternation gave way to bitter criticism. Lucy Stone, who was chairman of the executive committee, issued a statement, disassociating the Equal Rights Association from the Train alliance. And Garrison wrote a letter to Susan which reflected the sentiments of a good many other people as well:

January 4, 1868

Dear Miss Anthony:
    In all friendliness, and with the highest regard for the woman's rights movement, I cannot refrain from expressing my

regret and astonishment that you and Mrs. Stanton should have taken such leave of good sense as to be travelling companions and associate lecturers with that crack-brained harlequin and semi-lunatic, George Francis Train . . . The colored people and their advocates have not a more abusive assailant than this same Train . . . He is as destitute of principle as he is of sense, and is fast gravitating toward a lunatic asylum. He may be of use in drawing an audience, but so would be a kangaroo, a gorilla, or a hippopotamus.

Your old outspoken friend,
William Lloyd Garrison.

The *Revolution* began to appear on January 8, 1868, under the motto: "The true Republic—men, their rights and nothing more; women, their rights and nothing less." Almost from the very beginning the weekly paper had to struggle for its existence because Train's grandiose financial promises did not materialize. After its demise Susan had to tour the lyceum circuit for years in order to pay off, with lecture fees, a ten thousand dollar debt which the publication had incurred. Nevertheless she regarded the two years when the *Revolution* was published as among the happiest in her life.

George F. Train was not the only questionable ally the Equal Rights Association had acquired in its hour of desperation. When the Republicans were reluctant to present the women's petitions to Congress, they turned to the Democrats. From abolitionist circles came severe criticism and the cry of "copperheads." Their reply was that being compelled to choose between "the treachery of the Republicans" and the "hypocrisy of the Democrats," they chose the latter. They did so with their eyes open, knowing quite well that the Democrats were more interested in embarrassing the administration in power than in the promotion of woman suffrage. But whatever their motives, the women argued, the Democrats at least made it possible for the suffrage issue to be part of the current congressional debate, thus keeping their demand before the public eye, while if left to the mercies of the Republicans their petitions might not even see the light of day.

An alliance of an entirely different nature was the Association's brief flirtation with labor, specifically woman labor. In the 1860's the working women of America did try to make their own way in the world, but not through the path of suffrage. They were busy forging a bond of solidarity to protect their common interests; busy knocking on the door of organized labor for help, and organizing their own unions, with or without that help; busy trying to achieve their rightful place in the American labor movement. But to most seamstresses, textile workers, cigar makers, laundresses, printers, umbrella sewers, cap makers, collar workers and women in other trades, suffrage was a distant goal that bore little relevance to their immediate and pressing needs. What they were vitally interested in was protection from avaricious and unscrupulous employers who tried to do them out of their earnings; better working conditions and decent wages. For despite the increasing demand for their services during the Civil War, women's wages were appallingly low then, and were even lower in the post-war recession.

There had existed in New York, since 1866, The Working Women's Protective Union whose main function was to assist working women in obtaining jobs, learning new trades and collecting wages from unscrupulous employers through the legal aid supplied by this organization. But it had nothing to do with suffrage. In September 1868 the Equal Rights Association, under Susan's initiative, helped bring into being a new organization of working women, which, they hoped, *would* have something to do with suffrage. That this was an illusion became apparent at its very first meeting held in the offices of the *Revolution* on 37 Park Street, New York. Present at that meeting were two of the biggest names in woman suffrage, Susan B. Anthony and Elizabeth Cady Stanton. According to a report in the *New York Times*, "Mrs. Stanton thought it better to organize a Woman's Suffrage Association, with the view of obtaining the ballot," and in line with this thinking she suggested that the name of the new organization be the Working Women's Suffrage Association. But Miss Augusta Lewis, a typesetter and spokesman for the working women, disagreed with Mrs. Stanton. She visualized the new organization as concerning itself with the more practical needs of the working women and as making the ballot a secondary consideration. She even objected to the inclusion of the word "suffrage" in the proposed name because, she said, to many people suffrage was still synonymous with bloomers and short hair. Susan upheld the position of her friend, Mrs. Stanton, but in the end both reluctantly acceded to the wishes of the working women. On this shaky foundation of compromise a new organization was launched under the name: The Working Woman's Association.

On January 8, 1869, Ernestine was a guest speaker at one of the working women's regular meetings. She admitted that although she had addressed English workingmen at meetings as far back as 1833, this was her first experience in addressing a gathering of working women.

On the eve of its first anniversary the Working Woman's Association could boast of a membership of two hundred in New York, and of a number of similar organizations in other parts of the country; but despite these apparent successes the dominant theme of some of its leaders was that of failure. "This Association is useless and a sham, and has never done anything for working women," said Mrs. Norton, a founder of the Association. Susan took exception. "I admit," she said, "that this Working Woman's Association is not a *trades* organization . . . [it] is more upon the broad platform of philosophizing on the general questions of labor . . . The grandest work that some mortals can accomplish is to talk and thereby stir other people to do something . . ." In her reply, Susan, inadvertently, put her finger on the basic weakness of the organization. Talking and philosophizing in general about labor was not the platform on which a working woman's organization could long survive.

For a brief period of its existence the Working Woman's Association held the public spotlight when it came to grips with a concrete issue—the Hester Vaughn case. Hester Vaughn, an English working girl in her early twenties, was languishing in a Philadelphia prison, sentenced to be hanged for the murder of her own child, when the Working Woman's Association initiated a campaign to save her life. The campaign brought to light the true circumstances in the case. Hester Vaughn followed her husband to America only to learn, upon her arrival, that he had in the meantime acquired a new wife. Having no one to turn to in this country she found a job as a domestic and shifted for herself as best she could. In her loneliness she met a man who seduced her and then deserted her. Later she discovered she was pregnant. Half-frozen from cold and delirious with pain, she gave birth, unassisted, alone in a furnished room. When she was finally discovered the baby lay near her, dead. She was arrested, charged with infanticide, tried and sentenced to death. A crooked lawyer took from her whatever money she had and then abandoned her to her fate. She steadfastly refused to disclose her husband's name out of consideration for his new wife.

The Working Woman's Association initiated its own medical investigation, which discounted the charge of infanticide. The medical report stated that it was possible for Hester, in her state of delirium, to have injured the infant's head while actually trying to assist in its birth. The Association sent delegations to Hester Vaughn in prison, and to the Governor of Pennsylvania to plead for a pardon; it held public meetings and turned an almost forgotten case of an unfortunate girl into a *cause celebre*. At one such large meeting held at Cooper Institute, in New York, with Horace Greeley presiding, Ernestine Rose was one of the principal speakers. Thanks to the public clamor raised by the Working Woman's Association, Hester Vaughn was granted a pardon. She returned to England.

On January 19, 1869, the movement held its first suffrage convention in the nation's capital, but Ernestine was too ill to attend. Had she been able to go, she would have met delegates from about twenty states and sat on the same platform with Senator Pomeroy from Kansas, a staunch supporter of the Sixteenth Amendment which the women were now advocating, and which aimed at sweeping away the restrictions to woman suffrage contained in the Fourteenth and Fifteenth Amendments.

But since she could not be there in person she had to content herself with sending a message, which was read to the convention. It contained, among other things, a reply to Horace Greeley, who had recently said, "the best women I know do not want to vote." Without referring to Greeley by name Ernestine wrote: "The childish argument that all women don't ask for the franchise would hardly deserve notice were it not sometimes used by men of sense. To all such I would say, examine ancient and modern history, yes, even of our own times, and you will find there never has been a time when all men of any country—white or black—have ever asked for a reform. Reforms have to be claimed and obtained by the few, who are in advance, for the benefit of the many who lag behind. And when once obtained and almost forced upon them, the mass of the people accept and enjoy their benefits as a matter of course."

Four months later the conflict between the Anti-Slavery Society and the Equal Rights Association which had been brewing for some time came to a dramatic head. In May 1869, when the Association met for its annual anniversary in New York, both sides seemed to be prepared for a showdown. Ernestine was already a semi-invalid then, but despite her poor health she attended the meeting, served on its resolutions committee, delivered a speech and made a proposal of far-reaching consequences.

The meeting was one of the stormiest in years. Feelings ran high; emotion overwhelmed reason and the shrill note of bitterness was painfully audible in many of the speeches. Thus a woman like Ernestine Rose, who had devoted a lifetime to the struggle for human freedom, dignity and justice could bring herself to say: "Congress has enacted resolutions for the suffrage of men and brothers. They don't speak of the women and sisters . . . We might commence by calling the Chinaman a man and a brother, or the Hottentot, or the Calmuck, or the Indian, the idiot or the criminal, but where shall we stop? They will bring all these in before us, and then they will bring in the babies—the *male* babies."

But Ernestine was not the only leader who in her bitterness descended to this level of argumentation. Elizabeth Cady Stanton, whom Ernestine fully supported in this struggle, frequently resorted to the same reasoning. "It isn't merely giving suffrage to the black men," Elizabeth would say, "but giving it to ignorant men of every color landing on our shores." At the first Washington convention she said: "Think of Patrick and Sambo and Hans and Yung Tung, who do not know the difference between a monarchy and a republic, who cannot read the Declaration of Independence or Webster's spelling book, making laws for Lucretia Mott, Ernestine Rose and Anna E. Dickinson."

And Susan said, ". . . if you will not give the whole loaf of suffrage to the entire people, give it to the most intelligent first."

At this meeting Frederick Douglass mildly rebuked Elizabeth Cady Stanton for her use of the word "Sambo" and other expressions deprecatory of the Negro, and spoke stirringly in support of the "Negro's hour" point of view. "I must say," he said, "that I do not see how any one can pretend that there is the same urgency in giving the ballot to woman as to the Negro. With us the matter is a question of life and

death, at least, in fifteen States of the Union." Although his
words were warmly greeted, the prevailing sentiments in the
hall was against him when he called right then and there on
the Equal Rights Association to come out in favor of the
Fifteenth Amendment as "one half of our demands," and
pledged "to redouble our energy to secure the further amendment guaranteeing the same sacred rights without limitation
to sex."

What an ironic twist of history! At that moment Douglass
may very well have recalled that twenty-one years ago, at
Seneca Falls, it was his eloquent plea in behalf of woman suffrage that had turned the tide of opinion at that first woman's
rights convention. Elizabeth Cady Stanton had stood all alone
then. Even the fearless Lucretia Mott had hesitated to endorse
so radical a demand as the enfranchisement of woman. At that
time it was he, Douglass, who had stepped forward boldly
and saved the day for woman suffrage. Now, at the most
critical point in the struggle for Negro independence, this
same Elizabeth Cady Stanton, and those who were standing
with her, were unmoved by his plea for their support of the
Fifteenth Amendment.

Again and again Douglass pleaded the case for the Negro.
"When women," he said, "because they are women, are
hunted down through the cities of New York and New
Orleans; when they are dragged from their houses and hung
upon lamp-posts; when their children are torn from their arms,
and their brains dashed out upon the pavement; when
they are objects of insult and outrage at every turn; when
they are in danger of having their homes burned down over
their heads; when their children are not allowed to enter
schools; then they will have an urgency to obtain the ballot
equal to our own."

The women, though staunch abolitionists all, were not
swayed by Douglass's stirring words. On the question of
woman suffrage the chasm between them was too wide to be
bridged by the moving eloquence even of so loyal and con-

sistent a friend as Frederick Douglass. No wonder Douglass came to the conclusion that this was more a Woman's Rights than an Equal Rights meeting, and said so. Before the meeting was over his charge seemed to have been substantiated when Ernestine Rose, at the conclusion of her speech, made the following proposal: "I suggest that the name of this society be changed from Equal Rights Association to Woman's Suffrage Association." Had a bombshell been thrown into its midst the effect on the convention could hardly have been more startling. Even the Anthony-Stanton forces seemed to have been taken by surprise. Lucy Stone leaped to her feet and said, "I hope you will not do it." She urged that the proposed change of name be postponed until after the Negro had obtained his vote.

The convention was thrown into a turmoil of debate. Ernestine assured the gathering that she had no intention of abandoning the fight for the Negro; that she had suggested the change of name merely to clarify woman's position in her struggle to obtain suffrage. But her explanation failed to soothe the ruffled tempers of her agitated audience.

Susan seized at the idea and lost no time in bringing Ernestine's proposal to an early realization. Brushing aside parliamentary formalities Susan effected the change on the first evening after the meetings were over, at a reception given for the delegates. From that moment on events moved with lightning speed. Five days later the *Revolution* announced the formation of the new organization, its new officers, its constitution and the text of its petition to the Senate and House of Representatives. Elizabeth Cady Stanton was President. Ernestine Rose together with Susan B. Anthony and two other women formed the Executive Committee. The key article in the constitution stated clearly and briefly the purpose of the new organization: "Its object shall be to secure the Ballot to the women of the nation on equal terms with men."

The fact that not a single man was included in the leadership of the new organization was not an accident; it was a reflection of the frame of mind the women were in at that moment. Their experience with men in the past several years had not been a happy one. If men like Garrison, Phillips, Douglass, Higginson, Greeley, Curtis, Beecher, who only yesterday, it seemed, had been among their staunchest allies and supporters, were now on the opposite side of the battle line, then how, they asked, can man be trusted in this struggle? At a crucial point he is bound to betray us. No, woman must fight her own battles; from now on she must rely on her own resources.

But why exclude them only from leadership, some argued. If men are not to be trusted why not exclude them from membership as well? They were ready to go that far. Ernestine was strongly opposed to this narrow, sectarian approach. "I want an organization," she said, "that would not exclude my husband from membership."

Ernestine won her point. But when the names of the officers were published it was still an all-woman list. Significantly absent from that list was the name of Lucy Stone who, since the very first national woman's rights convention of 1850, had been one of the movement's top leaders. Lucy was steaming mad. So was her husband, Henry B. Blackwell. So was the entire wing of New England abolitionists. They were angry at the way the National Woman's Suffrage Association had been formed. There had been no advance public notice of the impending event. As far as they were concerned the Anthony-Stanton-Rose faction had engaged in a quick tactical maneuver to bring the suffrage movement under its own control. As they saw it there was nothing left for them to do but to form a rival suffrage organization and go their separate ways. This they did when they formed the American Woman Suffrage Association with headquarters in Boston. If the "National" had not a single man in the leadership, the leadership of the "American" was studded with men, including the very president of the organization—Henry Ward Beecher. And if the "National" had its *Revolution*, the "American" had a suffrage weekly with the more restrained title of the *Woman's Journal*.

The rift could hardly have come as a surprise to either of the two factions. It had been building up since 1866, when the movement resumed its activity after the Civil War. The Train episode accelerated its coming; and by May 1869 the atmosphere within the ranks of the movement was so charged that a mere spark could set off the explosion. Inadvertently Ernestine supplied that spark with her proposal to change the name of the organization. During those three years the conflict, originally rooted in ideological differences, and ostensibly fought on this basis, had progressively deteriorated from a struggle over principles to a clash of personalities, with the former often overshadowed by the latter; and the latter often mistaken for the former.

In the second volume of the *History of Woman Suffrage* which appeared in 1882 there is this reference to the more subjective aspect of the conflict: ". . . there were some personal hostilities among the leaders of the movement that culminated in two societies . . ." The editors of the *History*, Susan B. Anthony, Elizabeth Cady Stanton and Matilda Joslyn Gage, all partisans in this struggle, were discreetly brief and general on the subject. But Paulina Wright Davis, in a letter to Gerrit Smith, dated November 7, 1869, was more specific. She pleaded with Smith to lend his support to the "National" and not to the Boston Group "whose *purpose aim* and *object* is to destroy Elizabeth C. Stanton and S. B. Anthony." As one who had not taken sides with either party in this conflict, she said, her urge to write him was motivated by "a strong desire for right and truth to prevail." Before casting her own lot with the "National" she had made a personal investigation of the whole matter. She had gone to Boston for that purpose and had come away "sickened and disgusted with . . . the cowardly stabs in secret . . ." although the stated opposition against Susan B. Anthony and Mrs. Stanton was their approach to the Fifteenth Amendment. She found that in Boston

Susan's "integrity and honesty are constantly assailed." She wrote to "entreat you not to let Elizabeth Cady Stanton be sacrificed to envy and jealousy—to the pettiness of a clique." She spoke of a "feud personal and narrow," and of a "Procrustean spirit . . ."

Thus a movement was split in two; and a leadership which had held together for twenty years against all odds and opposition was now hopelessly divided at a time when unity was the crying need of the hour. This may well be characterized as the most tragic chapter in the history of the woman's rights movement. It was not until twenty years later that the gulf was breached, and unity restored.

Fortunately for Ernestine, she was spared the pain of being too close to the scene of debacle. Three weeks after the stormy May meeting she was on the high seas, with her husband, sailing for Europe. For the past several years she had been suffering intensely from neuralgic and rheumatic pains which put severe restrictions on her habitually active life. Once again the doctors recommended a trip abroad to restore her health.

Her devoted friend, Susan B. Anthony, though very busy setting up the new National Woman's Suffrage Association, found the time to arrange a farewell testimonial for her at the woman's literary club, Sorosis, which held its meetings at Delmonico's restaurant. At this party Ernestine was presented with many gifts, including a substantial sum of money which was collected, at Susan's initiative, from Ernestine's friends and admirers; and a basket of June roses. She sailed on June 8, 1869. Susan was disappointed that she could not see her off. She wrote to Lucretia Mott: "Was it not a little funny that this unsentimental personage should have suggested the thing and stirred so many to do the sentimental, and yet could not even take the time to go to the wharf and say good-by? I spent Sunday evening with her and it is a great comfort to me that I helped others contribute to her pleasure."

The editors of the *Boston Investigator* also surprised Ernestine with "a handsome testimonial in money" which they hastily collected from her friends and admirers as soon as they learned of her plan to go abroad.

Among the many farewell messages and public expressions of tribute which Ernestine received prior to her trip abroad was one from an unexpected source. The *Hebrew Leader*, a weekly for conservative German Jews printed partly in English and partly in German, and edited by Rabbi Jonas Bondi of Congregation Ansche Chesed, New York, gave her front-page notice in its issue of May 21, 1869, two weeks before her departure. Referring to her as the "earliest and noblest among the workers in the cause of human enfranchisement . . . ," and expressing "the hope that her foreign tour may restore her to perfect health," the *Hebrew Leader* went on to say: "Among all the advocates of human freedom and moral and social progress, who have labored in this country for the last twenty-five or thirty years, none have exhibited more constancy, devotion, sacrifice, earnestness and ability, than Ernestine L. Rose, and but for the fact that such genuine reformers are never suitably appreciated in their day and generation, she would now be the most popular, as she has long been the best female lecturer in the United States."

On June 17, the *Revolution* reported Ernestine's departure, stating that, "Mrs. Rose has long been an invalid, but has never ceased working for the enfranchisement of woman." And on June 22, that same paper announced Ernestine's safe arrival in England "in the short space of nine days and six hours; one of the quickest passages ever yet made across the Atlantic."

The story of Ernestine's life would not be complete without touching on yet another of her strong interests—peace. She had once said, "I trust that if ever woman touched the sword it would be to sheath it in its scabbard forever." On another occasion she said, "War is a terrible enemy of man, a terrible school for man." When the Universal Peace Society was founded in Providence, R.I., in May, 1866, Ernestine was soon in its ranks. She spoke at its meetings and was once its delegate abroad to an international peace congress.

But she was not a pacifist. Her devotion to peace did not exclude the waging of war against oppressors who maintained their tyrannical rule over peoples with the aid of their military might. In 1830 she had tried to return to Poland, ready to join the fight against the czarist oppressor of her native land. It was only the force of the Austrian authorities at the border that had prevented her from manning the barricades side by side with other Polish patriots. In her book, *Heroines Of Freethought*, published in 1876, Sara A. Underwood, who had attended a peace meeting where Ernestine spoke, gave this first-hand account of her speech when she alluded to Poland: "I remember well how she startled and electrified the members of the Universal Peace Society . . . by her description of the sort of peace *she* advocated . . . with eyes flashing, her pale cheeks flushing, and her voice thrilling, she declared how she longed to plunge, with her own hand, if need be, the dagger to the hearts of the enemies of her country's liberty and rights."

One of Ernestine's last public appearances in the United States before she went abroad was at a meeting of the Universal Peace Society held in Dodworth Hall, New York, on May 14 and 15, 1869, at the same time that the Equal Rights Association held its own last and stormy anniversary in another hall.

When Ernestine and William left for England they did so as citizens of the United States. Yet it was not until May 22, 1869, only 17 days before her departure, that Ernestine actually became a citizen, whereas William had obtained his citizenship in 1845, 24 years ahead of Ernestine. Why had she waited so long? Since we do not really know the answer the following explanation seems plausible. For William citizenship meant the possibility of expressing himself through the ballot; for Ernestine there was no such incentive. As a passionate fighter for woman's rights, her delay may well have been a conscious protest against a government that denied woman her full legal equality.

Once again she watched her beloved Empire City recede into the background as their ship steamed slowly out of New York's busy harbor. Thirteen years ago, when she had gone abroad, she had still been in her prime. Then she merely went for an extended vacation to mend her health and return to the fray, the struggle which was her life. Now, nearing sixty and very ill, she could no longer look forward to such a return. She was too wise not to know that after thirty-three years of nearly uninterrupted reign the Queen was stepping down from the platform.

PART THREE: 1869–1892

"All that I can tell you is, that I used my humble powers to the uttermost, and raised my voice in behalf of human rights in general, and the elevation of woman in particular, nearly all my life."

ERNESTINE L. ROSE—IN A LETTER

TO SUSAN B. ANTHONY

". . . one of the most remarkable women of the age; . . . as the advocate of the rights of her sex, she has no superior."

WILLIAM LLOYD GARRISON

Chapter XXIII

THE LAST YEARS

S HE FOUND HER BELOVED PARIS even more beautiful than
ever. To be sure, the city had undergone many changes
since her last visit in 1856 but these were all changes for the
better. Paris in June, after a smooth and pleasant ocean voyage!
Could one think of a better way to begin a period of con-
valescence? But it was a short stay, only five days. They had
heard of a wonderful little spa named Luxenill, about 330
miles from Paris. Physicians recommended it; and patients
who had benefited from its variety of springs and hot and
cold waters sang its praises. And so to Luxenill they went.

The spa was all that it was said to be, and even more. She
was delighted with its beautiful parks, its excellent bathing
facilities, its air of antiquity. The springs, she learned, were
over two thousand years old; once the Romans had strolled
through these parks and Luxenill still preserved some relics of
that period. One of these, an old house, containing Latin in-
scriptions and various statues and figures, was said to have
been the residence of Julius Caesar. And yet this spa was
practically unknown to the general French population. In
the United States, she said, a resort like Luxenill would "by
advertising and puffing, be made known and renowned all
over the world."

And who would have thought that in this out of the way
little town she would find people from foreign lands who
knew the name Ernestine Rose, and what it stood for! She
was so astonished by this coincidence that she wrote home

about it to the *Investigator:* "We have met with very interesting company here—a Greek and Egyptian family, and two gentlemen from Rome, one a Senator in their Congress, and the other a military man. They speak good English and, being posted up in American affairs, knew my name and heretical proclivities, which gave rise to very interesting conversations and discussions on religion and woman's rights. Is it not too bad that I cannot go anywhere without being found out?"

After five weeks in Luxenill, which they thoroughly enjoyed, Ernestine and William went to the Lake of Lucerne, in Switzerland, "to get braced up among the mountains . . ." They took walks; did a little mountain climbing, and feasted their eyes on the majestic grandeur of the snow-topped Pilatus and Riga, each over six thousand feet high.

At this moment their itinerary was fluid. They had no definite travel plans; no fixed destination. They knew that eventually they would settle in England for an extended stay; the immediate objective, however, was the restoration of Ernestine's health. Travel seemed to be the perfect medicine for that. Already it had markedly improved her condition. So they would travel whenever the mood would strike them, and to wherever the urge would take them. Right now they were in that frame of mind.

But the world has a way of intruding itself into one's plans, definite or indefinite, and compelling a revision of either. In September 1869 Europe found itself in the lengthening shadow of another war. Bismarck was dreaming expansionist dreams of empire, while Louis Napoleon III, already the ruler of a far-flung colonial empire, was straining to maintain that rule. The Franco-Prussian War, the Paris Commune and the subsequent bloodbath unloosed by Thiers, were less than two years away. Some liberal forces of Europe were mobilizing for peace and liberty. In September 1869 a Congress of Peace was to be held in Lausanne, Switzerland, with Victor Hugo presiding. It would have been unthinkable for Ernestine to be so close to the Congress and not attend it, even though cool reason dictated that congresses and conventions were hardly conducive to the restoration of her health. And so to Lausanne they went; and if the Congress imposed a physical strain, it was easily offset by the immense satisfaction of participating in an important social event. The reformer's conscience was put at ease. She was not merely loafing and abandoning the world to its own fate, but together with other fellow reformers she was on guard against the ravages of war and the subversions of human liberty. The high point at the Congress came when Victor Hugo delivered his closing address. As a life-long utopian socialist she was thrilled to hear the great Frenchman say: "Socialism is vast and not narrow; it embraces all human problems . . . it proclaims the inviolability of human life, the abolition of war . . . it proclaims woman equal to man . . ." It was a definition of socialism she fully endorsed.

They continued traveling—France, Italy, Germany. Their second visit to Paris lasted seven weeks and when it came time to leave they did so gladly. During this time Ernestine nearly undid all she had accomplished for her health. Life was too hectic for her in the city she liked so much. Seeing old friends and meeting some of the foremost reformers of France was always a pleasure. It was the walking and sightseeing that imposed the strain. The streets and boulevards of Paris had an irresistible lure for her. There was no limit, it seemed, to the ever new wonders the city possessed and she wanted to see them all. ". . . There is so much to be seen," she said, ". . . that if you are not strong you may walk yourself almost to death; and this was nearly my case, with a lame foot into the bargain."

She felt much better in Nice, Italy, but after they left that city she fell ill again, so they tried another place that was famous for its waters. And so it went throughout their travels. She never really succeeded in consolidating her physical gains for any considerable length of time; there was always the relapse. But on the whole her health had vastly improved since she had left the States.

Somewhere in the midst of her European tour she learned

from an editorial in the *Boston Investigator*, which was sent along to her, that the charge that she was an advocate of "free love," which had originated at the Rutland Convention, had once again been revived. Shortly after she had sailed for Europe there appeared a book entitled: *Woman: Her Rights, Wrongs, Privileges and Responsibilities*, by L. P. Brockett, M.D., which contained the following reference to Ernestine: "Some of the leaders of the woman suffrage movement, Mrs. Ernestine L. Rose for one, we believe, take even stronger ground than this. They avow that marriage has not even the sanction that belongs to an ordinary partnership, that 'every woman has a right to choose who shall be the father of her child,' 'that true marriage, like true religion, dwells in the sanctuary of the soul, beyond the cognizance or sanction or State or Church,' and scoff generally at the idea of any permanence or sanctity in the marriage tie."

The editor of the *Investigator* castigated the author for his slanderous attack on the good name of Mrs. Rose and regarded his remarks as, "foolish, inexpedient, injurious . . ." Whereupon the author promptly replied, admitting that, "I have no personal acquaintance with Mrs. Ernestine L. Rose, never saw her in my life, and never heard her speak in public." He said he drew his information about her views on marriage from newspaper accounts of her speeches at woman's rights conventions. If Mrs. Rose herself would produce evidence to refute these charges, then "I will cheerfully make the correction both in my book, and in your paper."

Ernestine did supply the evidence all the way from Nice, Italy, where she was at the time. It was a copy of the letter she had sent to the *New York Times* in 1858, refuting the same charge. In addition to the letter Ernestine sent some remarks aimed at her slanderers: "I have always spoken out so plainly on every subject I take an interest in, that people must be more than ordinarily stupid to misunderstand me, or more than ordinarily malicious to misinterpret me." The author, thus pushed to the wall, apologized. In a letter to the *Investi-*

gator, where the entire controversy was aired, he wrote, "I cheerfully accept Mrs. Rose's denial of the statement or formula as conclusive, and have directed her name to be stricken from the paragraph in all subsequent editions of the book . . . It seems," he added, "that she had been repeatedly charged with the advocacy of these views, and I do not wonder that she should have felt indignant at the repeated attribution of sentiments to her which she did not believe."

With Ernestine out of the country the *Investigator* became the zealous guardian and protector of her reputation. It defended her not only against the attacks of her enemies but also against the injustices of her friends. One day in the summer of 1870, the editor of the *Investigator*, scanning the *Revolution*, came upon the following statement: "First of all there is Lucretia Mott . . . then Elizabeth Cady Stanton . . . then Paulina Wright Davis . . . then Lucy Stone . . . then Susan B. Anthony . . . then, later, Anna E. Dickinson . . . noble, cultivated, gifted women, who are now apprenticing their best energies to the enfranchisement of their sex." Incredible! he thought, only one year away from home and already forgotten! Perhaps he had overlooked the name? He read the item over again carefully. No, the oversight was not his. "So goes the world," he muttered, philosophically, "especially with the unpopular; and this is their reward. Out of sight, out of mind."

But he didn't leave it at that. He sat down and wrote an editorial entitled: "Mrs. Ernestine L. Rose" in which he said: ". . . to omit *her* name from the catalogue, is like playing Hamlet with the character of Hamlet left out . . . These are all able women, but not one of them has done any more for the cause of woman than Ernestine L. Rose, if indeed as much. But they are eulogized and she neglected, though sacrificing her time, talent, means, and health to promote their cause."

And Ernestine, in turn, remained steadfastly loyal to the *Investigator*, her only strong link with the free thought movement in America. Writing was always difficult for her. She was the virtuoso of the spoken word. A roomful of people, the faces of men and women; the living contact with her fellow beings; these were the magic powers that could open the floodgates of her oratory, evoking a torrent of words. But the torrent would shrink to a bare trickle before the impersonal coldness of a blank sheet of paper. With pen in hand she was inhibited; she could not forget that English was not her mother tongue but an acquired language. Words which on the platform came with an easy naturalness here had to be painstakingly freed from the paralyzing grip of self-consciousness. That was why she never wrote out her speeches. And that was why she wrote infrequently for the *Investigator* even at the height of her active life. It was therefore a measure of her great loyalty to that paper when she continued to write an article from time to time even when the mere holding of the pen in hand imposed a physical strain on her.

In the summer of 1869, when Ernestine had arrived in France, the women of Great Britain had just won their first major victory—their right to vote in municipal elections. Not all the women, only those who met certain property qualifications could avail themselves of that right. Nevertheless the victory was significant for it gave thousands of women in England's larger cities, for the first time in their lives, a voice in the affairs of their government. In this respect the British women had outdistanced their American sisters to whom they had, only yesterday, it seemed, been looking for leadership and inspiration. True, they could not yet boast of a married woman's property bill or of other legislative gains which the American women had already won; but with regard to the ballot, which the American suffrage leaders regarded as the magic key to the kingdom of woman's equality, they had scored a major triumph. One could detect a note of understandable envy in the opening words of an editorial in the *Revolution*, greeting the British victory: "While in this country the great West as well as the East is all alive with woman's conventions, here, there and everywhere, the plucky women of England have actually taken Old John Bull by the horns, and are voters today."

But before the year 1869 was over Ernestine learned the cheering news from home that in America, too, some women had come into possession of the magic key, the ballot. This happened in the Territory of Wyoming, which in size was larger than all of Great Britain. This new Territory laid the foundation of equality of the sexes at the very beginning of its existence. Its very first legislature passed the woman suffrage act, raising woman to the level of full citizenship on a completely equal basis with man. On December 10, 1869, Governor Campbell affixed his signature to the act and it became the law of the Territory. It should be pointed out, however, that though the fruit had blossomed forth in Wyoming the seed had been planted elsewhere and over a period of many years. Largely responsible for the Wyoming suffrage act was the existence of a woman's rights movement and its continual agitation in the face of all odds and opposition. Ernestine Rose, now mending her broken health somewhere on the continent of Europe, had something to do with the passage of this law in Wyoming. Her numerous woman's rights lectures in New York State, New England, Michigan and other parts of the country had left their mark.* The same was true of Susan B. Anthony, Elizabeth Cady Stanton, Lucretia Mott, Lucy Stone, Paulina Wright Davis and the other pioneers. Among the eastern women who had accompanied their husbands to Wyoming to settle in that western territory were some who back home had fallen under the sway of woman's rights agitation. Now, in their new home, it was they who had sparked the campaign for the Wyoming suffrage act.

---

* In recent years some writers have claimed that Ernestine L. Rose was directly involved in obtaining suffrage for the women of Wyoming. This writer failed to discover any evidence that would substantiate this claim. The mere fact that the Territory of Wyoming was organized in May 1869, only a few weeks before Ernestine departed for Europe and when she was already too ill to engage in any campaigning would tend to militate against this claim.

As it was the first Territory in the nation to pass such a law, the eyes of the country were on Wyoming, watching closely the experiment. The enemies of woman suffrage predicted its failure in advance, while its advocates waited with bated breath for a practical demonstration of the justness of their claim. Neither side had long to wait. In 1870 women began serving on juries. They performed their new duty so admirably well that they won high praise from the Chief Justice of Wyoming. That same year a vacancy for Justice of the Peace of South Pass City was filled by Mrs. Esther M. Morris, the first woman in the modern world to hold such a post. Not a single one of her decisions had to be reversed by a higher court. Then came the most crucial test of all, election day, and here too the advocates of woman suffrage were completely vindicated. The usual violence and rowdyism that accompanied an election were either gone or reduced to a minimum. The day passed off quietly and peacefully, proving that women *could* have a refining influence at the polls. The leaders of woman suffrage had hoped that Wyoming would serve as as example for other States and Territories to emulate. Except for the state of Utah, where for a brief period women enjoyed the right of the franchise, Wyoming remained that proverbial single swallow that did not make a suffrage summer. It took another half a century of struggle before the wisdom of Wyoming became the wisdom of the entire nation.

After wandering around for nearly a year and a half Ernestine and William settled down in England. In December of 1870 they were in Bath and planned to spend there the entire winter. The chief attractions in Bath were its hot and cold springs, and Ernestine's health did improve there considerably. Another advantage was the low cost of living. For two large furnished rooms with excellent service and good food they paid two pounds and six shillings per week which in American money amounted to a little over $11. "In New York, to live the same way," Ernestine observed, "would cost us from $30 to $40." A disadvantage of their stay in Bath was their loneliness. In London they had many friends but here they knew no one. In a letter to the editor of the *Investigator* she wrote, complainingly: "Every denomination can be found in Bath, but I greatly fear *not one* Freethinker." For a while she considered the thought of giving a lecture and startling Bath out of its dull and complacent existence. "I should very much like to try it," she wrote, "but lecture rooms are rather high, and to get an audience to listen to anything out of the way, particularly from a woman, it ought to be free."

Ernestine, however, was not entirely deprived of the pleasure of stirring up a little excitement in Bath. In a correspondence from London to the *Cincinnati Commercial*, Moncure D. Conway relates the following incident: "Mrs. Ernestine Rose of New York, has been staying with her husband in the dignified and fashionable old town of Bath. By a local journal I learn that a startling episode occurred at a public meeting concerning the new School Board held there. An amiable lady, who disapproved of women being on the board, sent up to the chairman, to have read, a silly letter, written by Miss Burdett-Coutts, reproving the female aspirants for places on the board. Whereupon a fine-looking, middle aged lady arose, ascending the platform and, with that practiced ability which those who know Mrs. Rose will easily imagine, made a speech on the woman question generally, which fairly revolutionized the meeting."

London did not have hot and cold springs to soothe her rheumatic pains but it had the warmth of old friends to cheer her spirits. George Jacob Holyoake, veteran leader of England's co-operative movement, was such a friend. Another was Charles Bradlaugh, well-known freethinker, pamphleteer and editor of the *National Reformer*. And there was her friend and admirer Moncure D. Conway, the liberal American clergyman from Virginia, now minister of the South Place Chapel in London. And there were the leaders of England's suffrage movement who would pay their respects to the gray-haired lady from America, whose oratorical virtuosity and devotion to the cause of woman's rights had become legend on both sides of the Atlantic.

Under the heading "A Lioness in London" the following item about Ernestine appeared in the Philadelphia *Evening Star* (June 23, 1871) sent from England by Moncure D. Conway: "Mr. Conway writes that Mrs. Ernestine L. Rose is something of a lioness in London. On a recent Sunday, South Place Chapel was crowded with a thousand people to hear her address upon Robert Owen, and so completely did she charm the audience that three times applause began and had to be checked." The reporter for the *National Reformer*, in his account of that same lecture, wrote: ". . . I doubt if Mrs. Rose has her equal among the lady orators of the present day." The last time she had addressed an English audience of comparable size was some forty years ago when Robert Owen himself had invited her to address some of the large meetings held in his London palladium.

The women of England, having scored a victory on the municipal level, were now trying to extend that victory to the level of Parliament. In May 1872 the House of Commons rejected their Woman's Disability Bill. The women replied by holding a large protest meeting in the Hanover Square Rooms in London. Ernestine was there to address the meeting. The *Daily Telegraph*, listing the names of the speakers, commented: ". . . no wonder our M.P.'s fear to meet them in debate."

A letter arrived from Scotland. The Edinburgh Branch of the National Society for Woman Suffrage was planning a whirlwind campaign: three public meetings in three successive nights, to be held in January 1873. Would Mrs. Rose please come and address all three meetings? It would mean so much for the movement if she would. It was clear what the answer should be. Edinburgh in January was not London in May. There was the cold to consider, and the strain of the trip; not to mention the strain of addressing the public meetings three nights in a row. But all these were very sane and practical considerations of health. Ernestine wrote back that she would be very glad to come to Edinburgh and address all three meetings.

She did, and her wit delighted her Scottish audiences as it had her American ones for more than three decades. Replying to a member of Parliament who objected to woman suffrage because woman, he claimed, was not logical, Ernestine said: "I am not standing here to prove that woman is logical. I merely want to say that this is an exceedingly illogical argument. For the franchise was not given for logic. Had it been based upon logic I doubt whether that member of Parliament would ever have been in his place."

More than four years had now passed since Ernestine had left the States in 1869 to go abroad for her health. At home the National Woman Suffrage Association continued to list her name on its Executive Committee. At the time of her departure the farewell messages from her friends expressed the hope not only of a speedy recovery but also of a speedy return. No one had expected her to stay abroad that long. Why then had a trip that, at the most, was to have lasted six months, extended to over four years? Once again we can only speculate.

The trip abroad may have served a two-fold purpose. In addition to the stated aim of regaining her health, Ernestine and her husband may have seriously considered the possibility of living out their remaining years in England, whether for reasons of health, or economics, or both. Hence the time needed to assess and weigh the relative merits before making a final decision. By the summer of 1873 the decision must have been made in favor of England, for in September of that year they came back to the United States to liquidate their old home and return to their new home in England. The winding up of their affairs took about eight months, much of which time Ernestine was forced to spend in bed. Two months after her arrival Ernestine was expected in Boston for a lecture but could not come. Explaining her absence the *Investigator* wrote, ". . . we hear with much regret that she is so seriously ill that she has not been able to leave her room for some weeks, or even to sit up long at a time . . ."

But she had saved up enough strength for the most important event since her return, the annual May anniversary meeting of the National Woman Suffrage Association. It was a thrilling experience, after four years of absence from the American scene, to sit once again on the same platform with the veterans of her generation, Susan B. Anthony, Elizabeth Cady Stanton, Paulina Wright Davis; and to see the faces of a new generation that had risen from the ranks to leadership. She appeared calm and serene. It was a calm that came after the storm; a storm that had lasted for nearly four decades. Even the *New York Herald*, which was always more kind to her intellect than to her looks, now referred to her as: "Mrs. Ernestine Rose and her full large face, gentle as a child and framed in with waving white ringlets."

The few short steps from her chair to the rostrum were taken slowly and haltingly, but once she began to speak she was recharged with a new vitality; she was once again the Queen of the Platform, down to the very quaintness of her accent which had delighted her vast audiences for many years. First she gave her reply to a previous speaker who despaired at the slow progress the movement was making. "The wonder," she said, "is not that we have not accomplished more, the wonder is that we have accomplished so much." As if to underscore her words she told her listeners that in England nearly two hundred members of the House of Commons were ready to grant suffrage to the women of Britain. Then came the moment in her speech when even her clear-ringing voice cracked under the strain of emotion. "I shall forever cherish the memory of this day with you," she said, as though she were carefully weighing each word. "In the years that are still allotted me the remembrance of this day will both comfort and cheer me. Ill health prevents me from ever again taking the platform. I am not retiring from the battle; only from the battlefield. This has been my last public appearance." There was a long hush, as though the entire audience had fallen under the spell of this solemn declaration. But presently the silence gave way to a long and thunderous ovation. Two months later, in July 1874, Ernestine and her husband returned to England.

Her declaration that she was quitting the public platform may have been formal, but it was not final. In Europe, whenever the occasion arose, and when her health was up to it, she continued to speak. Sometimes months and sometimes years would go by between one public appearance and another, but speak she did for almost a decade more after the declaration. One such occasion came soon after her departure from America. They were in Brighton, England, for the waters that year, and one evening, on an impulse, she and William decided to attend one of the missionary meetings that were held in town at that time. One of the surprises of the evening was a clergyman's harangue against woman's rights, with copious quotations from the Bible to prove his point. This was all very familiar and quite natural. How else would a clergyman argue against woman's rights? But when he said: "During the French Revolution of '92, the women of Paris cut off the heads and legs of men, and ate the flesh, and all this was owing to Infidelity and Woman's Rights," Ernestine had had more than she could stand. "I never listened to any discourse with such perfect disgust, as to that one," she said afterwards. As soon as the clergyman had finished she was on her feet and asked for permission to say a few words. The unsuspecting chairman granted her permission. Whereupon Ernestine, directing herself to the previous speaker, said: "You thought there was not a single woman's rights woman in this hall. Well, sir, you were mistaken. I plead guilty to being a woman's rights woman; and listening to you I wondered why you had not also ascribed the Massacre of St. Bartholomew to

Infidels and Woman's Rights." She held the floor for fifteen minutes and to her great surprise was well received by the audience.

Ernestine was living in England but her heart was in America. So strong was her longing for America that although she had burned all bridges behind her and publicly announced her intention to take up permanent residence abroad she seriously entertained the thought of returning to the United States.

On July 4, 1876, when America was celebrating the centenary of its independence, she wrote to Susan:

My Dear Susan: ". . . This being the centenary of American independence, I must write a few lines, if but to let the friends know that though absent in body I am with you in the cause for which, in common with you, I have labored so long, and I hope not labored in vain . . . The glorious day upon which human equality was first proclaimed ought to be commemorated, not only every hundred years, or every year, but it ought to be constantly held before the public mind until its grand principles are carried into practice. The declaration that 'All men (which means all human beings irrespective of sex) have an equal right to life, liberty, and the pursuit of happiness,' is enough for woman as for man. . . . We need no other declaration . . .

"I hope these few lines will fill a little space in the convention at Philadelphia, where my voice has so often been raised in behalf of the principles of humanity. I am glad to see my name among the vice presidents of the National Association. Keep a warm place for me with the American people. I hope some day to be there yet. Give my love to Mrs. Mott and Sarah Pugh. With kind regards from Mr. Rose,

Yours affectionately,
Ernestine L. Rose."

Several months later she expressed similar sentiments in a letter to her friend Mendum: "I am terribly home-sick and hope to be there yet—and though nearly 70 (you see I am so unfashionable as to tell my age!) I *would* like to lecture a little more . . ." Though her longing for America continued, her dreams to return came to naught.

Toward the close of 1876 Ernestine received a letter from Susan B. Anthony informing her that she was gathering material for a history of woman suffrage and asking her, as one of the pioneers of the movement, to send in her personal reminiscences for inclusion in the first volume. Susan, with characteristic thoroughness, had also written to Robert Dale Owen for his reminiscences of Ernestine, since he knew her through her long, close association with his father. His reply was as brief as it was frustrating. "As for Ernestine Rose," he wrote, "I think it is probable that you know more about her than I do." Like his father in his later years the son was now an ardent spiritualist and so he added that Ernestine was "a skeptic as to any future beyond the grave, greatly opposed to Spiritualism."

Ernestine's own reply, dated January 9, 1877, though it contained some facts, could hardly have satisfied Susan. What she had hoped to get was a biographic sketch of her life and work; what she received was a letter saying: "Believe me it would give me great pleasure to comply with your request, to tell you all about myself and my past labors; but I suffer so much from neuralgia in my head and general debility, that I could not undertake the task, especially as I have nothing to refer to. I have never spoken from notes; and as I did not intend to publish anything about myself . . . and did not expect that a Susan B. Anthony would wish to do it for me, I made no memorandum of places, dates, or names . . . and therefore I have not anything to assist me or you . . . Yet in spite of hardships, for it was not as easy to travel at that time as now; and the expense, as I never made a charge or took up a collection, I look back to that time, when a stranger and alone, I went from place to place, in high-ways and by-ways, did the work and paid my bills with great pleasure and satisfaction; for the cause gained ground, and in spite of heresies I had always good audiences, attentive listeners, and was well received wherever I went . . ." She went on from there to cite some of her activities in behalf of the married woman's property bill, and to name some of the states and cities she had lectured in over the years.

Susan may have been disappointed with Ernestine's scanty reply but not surprised. Those who knew her knew how reluctant Ernestine was to speak or write about herself. As far back as May 1856 there had appeared in the *Liberator* a short biographic sketch of her by a contemporary, L. E. Barnard, which concluded with the following revelation: "The history of her life and experience, as disclosed to the limited circle of her friends, is said to be highly interesting and instructive; but hitherto she has uniformly resisted all their solicitations to give it to the world. They are not without hope, however, that she may, at some future day, consent to do so." To the best of our knowledge that future day never came.

She had always been an avid reader of the press and in these days of enforced retirement, when even writing a letter was a physical strain, reading became an all-absorbing activity. Holding a newspaper in hand was like feeling the pulse-beat of the world of which she felt herself so much a part; like hearing the heartthrob of nations and peoples about whom her curiosity never flagged. But when the *Boston Investigator* arrived it was as though a dear old friend had come for a long and leisurely visit. It brought news of the free thought movement in America; of people she knew; of places she had been. It gave her life a sense of continuity, a feeling of motion at a time when, physically, she was condemned to a static existence. Thus, she was delighted to read that Walt Whitman was the principal speaker at the 140th anniversay of Thomas Paine's birthday, held in Philadelphia, in January 1877. Speaking of the author of *Common Sense* the poet said: "I dare not say how much of what our Union is owning and enjoying today—its independence, its ardent belief in, and substantial practice of, radical human rights and the severance of its government from all ecclesiastical and superstitious dominion—I dare not say how much of all this is owing to Thomas Paine, but I am inclined to think a good portion of it decidedly is."

Sitting in her London flat in the bleak of winter, it was cheering to know that the Thomas Paine anniversaries, initiated by the shoemaker-freethinker, Benjamin Offen, and continued by the silversmith-freethinker, William Rose and herself, were now a permanent institution in America, and attracting poets like Whitman to their ranks!

In June 1878, after a winter of severe illness, Ernestine emerged from her retirement to enjoy a brief spell of public activity. She had accepted an invitation from Moncure Conway to participate in a two-day General Conference of Liberal Thinkers to be held at his South Place Chapel. Sitting near her on the platform was an old friend from America, Col. Thomas Wentworth Higginson, who had achieved that military rank in the Civil War, leading a Negro battalion against the Confederacy. She spoke briefly and even so she had to admit at the conclusion of her remarks that "my strength is very nearly exhausted." But as the following quotation indicates, even in this weakened state she could still speak with rare force and clarity. "My friend, Col. Higginson," she said, "had no pocket for the old definition of religion. My pocket is so full of humanity alone that I have no pocket for anything else. I go for man . . . All the emotion we can possibly possess, all the feeeling of which human nature is capable, all belongs to man. If there be one God or ten thousand gods, they do not need it, but man does and woman does, and to me it is stealing from man what belongs to man to give to a god, and to render to him things that cannot benefit him . . . Our life is short and we cannot spare an hour from the human race, even for all the gods in creation."

In New York, meanwhile, the National Woman Suffrage Association was preparing for a big celebration. That summer marked the thirtieth anniversary of the Seneca Falls convention. Instead of holding their usual May meeting in New York the women decided to meet in Rochester in honor of that historic event. Susan sent Ernestine an invitation. Ernestine replied: "Oh, how I should like to be with you at the anniversary . . . and speak of the wonderful change that has taken place in regard to women. Compare her present position in society with the one she occupied forty years ago, when I undertook to emancipate her from not only barbarous laws, but from what was even worse, a barbarous public opinion. No one can appreciate the wonderful change in the social and moral condition of women except by looking back and comparing the past with the present . . . I will therefore only say to the friends, 'Go on, go on! halt not and rest not.' "

In August Ernestine went with her husband to Paris to the World Exposition, which she found "grand and magnificent beyond description." They remained in Paris for five weeks and in September attended the International Peace Congress also held in that city. The congress which lasted four days had represented in it all the countries of Europe except Russia. The only other woman delegate from America was Mrs. Julia Ward Howe. Many of the leading initiators of the congress remembered Ernestine's participation in the Lausanne congress seven years ago. Quite unexpectedly she was called upon to address the congress as a representative of the New York Peace Society. She spoke in French and only for several minutes. After mentioning some of her own and her husband's activities in the peace movement both in America and abroad, she concluded with these words: "In every country, in every nation, I have concerned myself with those subjects which touch upon reform and the improvement of mankind." It was not only her shortest speech in her long career as public speaker but, as far as is known, it was also her last public utterance.

On January 25, 1882, Ernestine was struck by tragedy. That day William had gone out to the city on a business er-

London May. 17. 1880.

Dear Mrs Stanton.

You know me
too well to require my
assurance that it would give
me great pleasure to be with
you at your meeting on the
occasion of June. But as that
is impossible, I send my
voice across the Atlantic
to plead for Human rights
without distinction of sex.
and to uphold the grand chorus
in the demand of Justice

right to the suffrage and
proclaim her a citizen.
But the suffrage is
not only a badge of
citizenship but

a mental and moral elevator
which raises the pauper to
self-respect and dignity,
and prepares him for greater
usefulness and higher and
nobler aims in the progress
of Humanity.

Always to our cause
and love to the Friends
devoted to it.

Yours affectionately
Ernestine L Rose.

Reproduction of a letter from Ernestine L. Rose to Elizabeth Cady Stanton on the occasion of a special woman's suffrage convention held in Chicago, June 2, 1880, to coincide with the nominating convention of the Republican Party.

rand and did not come home again. He suffered a heart attack while walking in the street, and although he was rushed to St. Bartholomew's Hospital at once, he died on the way. He was sixty-nine years old. As soon as their close friend, Charles Bradlaugh, heard the sad news he hurried to the Rose residence and found Ernestine "very brave but very heart-broken at the loss of her faithful partner." At Highgate Cemetery where William was buried Charles Bradlaugh delivered the funeral oration and supported the widow at the graveside. Moncure D. Conway also spoke. Afterwards Bradlaugh wrote to the *Boston Investigator:* "Mr. Rose was a very worthy man in all relations of life . . . He was a genuine and intelligent Liberal, made so by reading and reflection, and, although quiet and unassuming, yet his upright example and kind deeds spoke louder than words of his mind and heart."

With the passing of William there came to an end a marital relationship of rare beauty, harmony and devotion. Ernestine never fully recovered from the shock. His death marked the beginning of the final phase of her life, a phase characterized by extreme loneliness and almost complete withdrawal from the outside world.

But the withdrawal was a physical one; mentally she clung to the world with all the faculties at her command. She continued reading; kept up an infrequent correspondence with Susan in New York and J. P. Mendum in Boston, and followed the fortunes of the woman suffrage movements in the United States and in Europe with unflagging interest. Thus in the summer of 1882, the first summer without William in nearly fifty years, lonely and despondent, she was cheered by the news that the British Parliament had at long last passed a Married Woman's Property Act! How surprising and unexpected were the twists and turns of the paths to human progress! The women of England had been voting on a municipal level for twenty-two years before they won this property bill; but the American women, who had won that same bill thirty-four years ahead of their British sisters, were still not voting even on a municipal level, (except, of course, in the Territory of Wyoming). Yet the world moved forward, as she was fond of saying, even when its course was at times bafflingly uneven and unpredictable.

Commenting on the passage of the Married Woman's Property Act, the weekly edition of the *London Times* stated: "Measures that effect the family economy are apt to be 'epoch-making'; and probably when the most talked of bills of the session are clean forgotten this obscure measure may be bearing fruit." Who in all of England at that time could have had a keener appreciation of those words than Ernestine who for years had watched the fruit that this bill had borne for millions of American women. She read the news and rejoiced. Yes, the world did move forward!

The outstanding event in Ernestine's life in 1883 was the cheering experience of speaking face to face with her old friends Susan B. Anthony and Elizabeth Cady Stanton, who had come to Europe for an extended period of time. Their several visits to Ernestine were a great comfort to her in her present state of loneliness. On March 22, Susan wrote home to her sister: "Saturday we went again to Bayswater to see Mrs. Rose—found her very lonely because of the death of her devoted husband a year ago. She threw her arms around my neck and her first words were, 'O, that my heart would break now and you might close my eyes dear Susan!' She is vastly more isolated in England because of her non-Christian views than she ever was in America. Sectarianism sways everything here more now than fifty years ago with us." The two tried to persuade her to come back to America where she would be near friends who would look after her, and they almost succeeded. In that same letter Susan describes another visit to Ernestine three days later, this time without Mrs. Stanton: "Tuesday morning I went again to Mrs. Rose's and finding her bonneted and cloaked for a chair ride, I walked beside her, holding her hand, through Kensington Park. I hope and almost believe she will go back to America with me. I feel sure that we, who have not forgotten her early and wonderful work for woman and for freedom of thought, will do all in our power to smooth her last days." In June, when Ernestine was in Turnbridge Wells, seeking relief from the waters, Susan traveled out thirty miles to see her. But in the end her efforts to get Ernestine to come home with her failed. It was Ernestine's wish to be buried in the same grave with her husband. Sentimental as this might be for a woman like Ernestine, nevertheless, this wish figured largely in her decision to remain in England.

1883 was a most difficult year, the first without William. Susan and Elizabeth departed and with them the momentary joy their visits had brought into her lonely existence. Mendum wrote from Boston, prodding her to write something for the *Investigator*. She wrote back saying she would like to but was too ill to write. ". . . Even now I can hardly hold the pen . . . In my lonely condition the dear old *Investigator* which I value very highly helps to keep me alive, if I may call my present inaction life, which I don't, for action only is life . . . But I must stop, as my hand trembles too much to allow me to write any more."

On June 3, 1886, one of those rare occasions when she was able to sit up and hold a pen in hand, she wrote to her friend J. P. Mendum:

". . . I am deeply interested in all the affairs of America. May the Great Republic, 'now known and honored throughout the earth,' as Daniel Webster said of its beautiful Starry Flag, always and forever be the home and asylum of Liberty, mental and political, and may kings and tyrants soon learn from its grand example that the only true or legitimate power to rule is in the People and not in any pretended 'right Divine.' But I really didn't intend, when I began my letter, to give you a Fourth of July oration, yet as that great day is drawing nigh, my thought is of the famous land beyond the sea where 'the eagle screams' for equal rights for men and women.

"Remember me to all inquiring friends, and accept for yourself and family, and for Brother Seaver, the kind regards of
Your affectionate sister,
Ernestine L. Rose"

Horace Seaver died in August 1889 but she was so ill that it was not until October that she was able to pen a few words to Mendum, saying: "It is impossible for me to describe to you my grief and sorrow when I heard that our dear friend, Horace Seaver, had died, and how sorry I was and am for you to have lost your fifty years' companion and friend." Since the death of Paulina Wright Davis in 1876 hardly a year had passed without bringing the sad news that some dear friend had died. Garrison, Lucretia Mott, Wendell Phillips, William Henry Channing, Mathilda Anneke, Sarah Pugh, people whose lives were so inextricably woven into hers—they had all departed. She wondered when her own turn would come and hoped it would be soon. To her close friend Hypatia Bradlaugh Bonner, daughter of Charles Bradlaugh, she would say: "Give my love to dear father, and tell him that I hope the time will soon come when he will take charge of me . . ." She did not fear death. In 1877 she had written a note of condolence to Garrison on the death of his wife, Helen, in which she said: "A time comes to all of us to submit to the inevitable." That philosophy sustained her to her very last days.

But the severest blow came in 1891 when two of her closest friends, Charles Bradlaugh and J. P. Mendum, died within days of each other. It was in her own house that Mendum had married her friend and protege, Elizabeth Munn of New York, in 1847. Their only son, Ernest, was named after Ernestine.

She hardly ever left the house now and depended entirely on the occasional visits of friends for human contact. But even in her state of extreme loneliness she would not compromise with principle for the sake of companionship. Once, while she was being visited by another one of Bradlaugh's daughters, a lady, a dear old friend, also came to see her. Ernestine introduced her friend to Miss Bradlaugh, who left soon afterwards. When she had gone the lady turned to Ernestine and asked: "Did you say that was Miss Bradlaugh—you don't mean any relation to *the* Bradlaugh?"

"Yes," said Ernestine, almost defiantly, "his daughter."

"Then," said the lady, striking a self-righteous pose, "you cannot expect me to come and see you, Mrs. Rose, if you have such people as that here, and I run the risk of meeting them."

Ernestine's face flushed. "In this case, my dear," she replied, "you must stay away." The lady did just that. Weeks went by and she didn't show up. Ernestine was annoyed by the incident. She missed her friend but would have none of her narrow-mindedness. Miss Bradlaugh, seeing her unhappy, suggested that perhaps it would be better if she stopped coming to the house.

"Nonsense!" Ernestine said, with finality, almost hurt by the suggestion. "That I shall never agree to." As it was, friendship triumphed over prejudice; after a while the old lady resumed her visits to Ernestine.

Now her world was rapidly receding from her, leaving her stranded alone on an island of twilight existence where life was growing dimmer with each passing day. The voices of the few pioneers of her generation that were still alive came echoing from across the Atlantic ever so faintly. It was comforting to know that after twenty years of bitterness and much wasteful duplication of energy the breach in the suffrage movement was, at last, healed, and that the movement, now renamed the National American Woman Suffrage Association, was at long last whole again. And it was gratifying to know that still standing at the helm of the combined organization were the two veterans, Susan B. Anthony and Elizabeth Cady Stanton. True, they were more the elder statesmen than the actual leaders of the movement. But that was as it should be at their age. A new generation had grown up since the day when she began to plead the cause of woman's rights, and from its ranks new leaders had emerged, young, confident, strong, reminiscent of her own young days when the movement was still in its infancy. And what she, and her generation, did not succeed in winning, the franchise, the magic key, they, her young successors, some day would. Of that she was confident.

As for herself, she was ready to depart. "It is no longer necessary for me to live," she would say to visiting friends. "I can do nothing now. But I have lived," she would add with a thoughtful nod of the head, "I have lived."

That longed-for day of deliverance came on August 4, 1892, when she was in her eighty-third year. Charles Brad-laugh was not there to take charge of her; he had died the year before.

Ernestine died in Brighton where she usually went in August for her summer holiday. Her friend Hypatia Brad-laugh Bonner gives this account of her last days: "On Monday August 1st she was taken ill, and on Tuesday became partially paralyzed and almost entirely unconscious. On Wednesday I was sent for but the summons did not reach me until six o'clock Thursday evening. I left by the next train for Brighton but was too late to see Mrs. Rose alive. Mrs. Rose had greatly dreaded that during her last illness she would be invaded by religious persons who might make her unsay the convictions of her whole life when her brain was weakened by illness and she did not know what she was doing; so it had been a long-standing agreement that when she fell ill she was to send for me and I would come to her wherever I might be. But al-though, as I have said, I was not able to be with her, she was fortunate in having a kind and able doctor and a devoted attendant, and her last hours passed away peacefully and were quite untroubled by any thoughts of religion . . . For Mrs. Rose's own sake I cannot regret that kindly death has at last come to relieve her long-contained sufferings, and bring to an end her many years of pain . . ."

Her desire to be laid to rest in the same grave with her hus-band, and her wish that her friend George Jacob Holyoake deliver the funeral oration, were both fulfilled when she was buried at the Highgate Cemetery in the presence of friends and relatives. Standing at the graveside, Holyoake said: "The grave at which we assemble is that of Mrs. Ernestine L. Rose . . . More than comely in features, which had dignity of contour, Mrs. Rose had a voice which at once arrested attention by its strength and melody. She spoke with easy accuracy, and with eloquence and reason. . . . In her youth her dark hair and gleaming eyes showed she had the fire of Judith in her . . . Like her great co-worker in the anti-slavery movement, Lucretia Mott, Mrs. Rose took truth for authority, not authority for truth . . . The slave she helped to free from the bondage of ownership, and the minds she had set free from the bondage of authority were the glad and proud remembrance of her last days."

On December 31, 1892, Ernestine's last will and testament * was probated. Among her bequests was one to her namesake in America Ernest Mendum, to whom she left "my gold watch with chain and key as worn by me."

Two years after Ernestine's death the aging Frederick Douglass, one of the few of her generation still alive, listed her among "the best of mankind," together with Lucretia Mott, Angelina Grimké, Lucy Stone, and other departed veterans of the woman's rights movement, and said: "No good cause can fail when supported by such women . . ."

On December 30, 1899, on the very threshold of the twentieth century, Susan B. Anthony, now President of the National American Woman Suffrage Association, sat in her office, 17 Madison Street, Rochester, N. Y., pondering a query from a Committee Chairman who was preparing a "Roll of Honor" of suffrage workers during the nineteenth century. Would Miss Anthony be so good as to suggest the names of

---

* For text of Mrs. Rose's will see Appendix pp. 289-90.

pioneers who should head the Honor Roll? Susan was still lost in thought when she picked up her pen and wrote:

"Dear Mrs. Colby:
"Generally I should say begin with Mary Wollstonecraft as your first Great Champion—then Frances Wright—then Ernestine L. Rose—they all spoke and demanded (suffrage) prior to Lucretia Mott, Mrs. Stanton, etc."

This then is the chronology in the evolution of the woman's rights movement: An Englishwoman; a Scottish noblewoman; and a Jewish woman from Poland, a child of the ghetto.

The novelist and lecturer, Lillie Devereux Blake, a younger woman who picked up where Ernestine had left off, called her "the Patrick Henry of the movement," and once said something about the older leader that might very well be a fitting epitaph to Ernestine's life: "The liberal laws which we now live under are due to the tireless exertions of this gifted woman, and never ought the women of New York to forget the debt of gratitude they owe to Ernestine L. Rose." To make the epitaph more complete one must add: and the women of Massachusetts, Michigan, Ohio, Illinois, Indiana, Wyoming, California; indeed, the women of the whole country, from the largest city to the smallest hamlet of America.

APPENDIX

ACKNOWLEDGMENTS

NOTES AND BIBLIOGRAPHY

INDEX

APPENDIX

All the speeches and writings included in this section are abridged versions of the original texts.

SPEECH OF ERNESTINE L. ROSE AT THE INFIDEL CONVENTION, NEW YORK, MAY 4, 1845

My Friends: . . .

There are many reforms; this is an age of reform; every one acknowledges that society is in a wrong state, and ought to be reformed. What makes man act wrong? Is it his desire to do it? We have been and are yet told that the heart of man is wicked and in accordance with this, such arrangements have been made in society as to fulfill the prophecy and make him bad indeed.

It is the greatest libel that has ever been put upon nature. Every human being has a tendency to do good, but the fundamental error, that man forms his own opinions, feelings and acts, has made him bad. He was considered as a being independent of every man around him; hence followed the isolated condition of society. These two fundamental errors are the cause of all evil; they make every man an enemy to his neighbor. Tell me, my friends, will the preaching "thou shalt love thy neighbor as thyself," as long as isolated interests exist, avail us anything? So long as the precept exists—everyone for himself and some supernatural power for us all—how much can you love your neighbor?

There is a great deal of poverty in the world; but is there any necessity for poverty? Is there any collective poverty? There is no such thing as poverty; there is ten times more in the world than would maintain all in yet unknown luxury. Yet how much misery there is in our midst; not because there is not enough, but owing to the misdirection of it. Those who create the most, get the least; those who build the largest castles often have not where to lay their heads; and then we say that man is bad by nature, because if he has not a crumb to eat, he will take some from his neighbor.

Why is it man has never been placed in a position to make himself happy? Isolation of interest is the cause—the contrary is the remedy. I have thrown out these few hints for you to reflect on. We must inquire what sort of beings we are, and are we rightly situated? Ponder over these questions. The welfare of the race depends upon them, and the application of the remedy is the reversion of the present arrangement of society. Ignorance is the evil—knowledge will be the remedy. Knowledge not of what sort of beings we shall be hereafter, or what is beyond the skies, but a knowledge pertaining to *terra firma*, and we may have here all the power, goodness and love that we have been taught belongs to God himself.

SPEECH OF ERNESTINE L. ROSE AT THE THOMAS PAINE ANNIVERSARY CELEBRATION, NEW YORK, JANUARY 29, 1850

My Friends:

I hope that everyone present is acquainted with the life and character of Thomas Paine—with his disinterested devotion to the cause of liberty and with the fact that . . . when in secret council with Washington, Franklin, Rush and Adams, Thomas Paine first spoke the magic word of Independence, the four sages looked with amazement at the audacity of giving utterance to a term which even their minds were unprepared to grasp and realize. But it was done!—the walls had ears and tongues!—the charmed word was echoed and re-echoed and through the length and breadth of this country, *Independence* became the watchword! Thus the offspring of obscurity gathered strength and power and by the fostering care of Thomas Paine grew into maturity, the fruits of which we enjoy this evening.

While we assemble to honor the memory of Thomas Paine, it would be well to remember that Paine, Lafayette, Kosciusco and many other noble minds who enlisted in the cause of right over might, were foreigners; and that, in addition to the plea of humanity, this country owes a debt of gratitude which now is the time to pay . . . .

If this country wishes to deserve the name as the place of refuge for the martyrs of freedom, let them contend for the adoption of Kossuth, Bem and Mazzini.* It is said that seven ancient cities contended for

---

* Louis Kossuth (1809-94) Hungarian patriot and orator. Became President of Hungarian Republic in 1849. Later, when Russia came to Austria's aid he was compelled to flee Hungary. He fled to Turkey. In 1851 visited U.S.A.

Joseph Bem (1795-1850) Polish general who participated in the Polish insurrection of 1830, then fled to Vienna where he joined the Hungarian insurgents and conquered Transylvania for them. Later was compelled to flee to Turkey where he saw service in the Turkish armed forces.

Giuseppe Mazzini (1805-72) Italian patriot and revolutionist. In 1849 he became a member of a triumverate that ruled briefly in the Republic of Rome. That same year he went into exile in Switzerland.

Homer dead; let us contend for living heroes that have done what
Homer wrote . . . and in so doing we will indeed honor the memory
of Thomas Paine, of Jefferson, and of Washington.

And now allow me to ask you, my sisters, shall we remain idle
spectators at the death struggle of Freedom because an ignorant and
degrading opinion prevails that participating in a noble act is out of
the sphere of woman? Do you want precedents and examples where
woman has burst her fetters, and stood in defense of humanity? . . .
Look at Poland, Rome and Hungary, and you will see that in the hour
of need, in the contest between freedom and despotism, woman, deli-
cately-brought-up woman, gave her aid to the cause of liberty! . . .

I mention this not, my friends, because I would wish to see woman
thus engaged; for I deplore the necessity for it alike in man or woman
. . . I trust that the time will come when the causes that transform our
fair earth into one great battlefield and charnel house will be removed
—when the present state of slavery and violence will be superseded by
freedom based on human rights, without distinction of sex, class, party,
country or color.

. . . I wished to show that woman is wanting neither in strength of
mind, courage, nor perseverance . . . But she must do something to
break the chains that ignorance and superstition have woven around
her and tied into a Gordian knot. She must untie it with the sharp
points of reason, dissolve the links by the light of knowledge, and
thus bursting the unholy fetters, she must claim her rights equal with
man and then indeed will she be a woman . . .

Finally let me say to all: deserve the name of friends to Thomas
Paine. The admirers of his moral courage, we must like him fearlessly,
oppose error wherever we find it, in church or state; never encourage
in word or deed those things that are obstacles to human progression;
never sacrifice principle for popularity, for it is unworthy of an honest and noble mind; court truth only, for it is the noblest impulse to
all our actions; and with truth as our guide, let us work on for the
emancipation of man, not only from his physical but mental bondage,
and hasten the glorious time when tyranny and oppression will cease
and union, directed by knowledge and affection will allow man to
dwell in harmony, security and peace.

SPEECH OF ERNESTINE L. ROSE AT THE SECOND
NATIONAL WOMAN'S RIGHTS CONVENTION,
WORCESTER, MASS., OCTOBER 15, 1851

(Mrs. Rose published this speech at her own expense and it was widely
circulated.)

. . . But need we wonder that France, governed as she is by Russian
and Austrian despotism, does not recognize the rights of humanity in
the recognition of the Rights of Woman, when even here, in this far-

famed land of freedom . . . woman, the mockingly so-called "better half" of man, has yet to plead for her rights . . . In the laws of the land she has no rights; in government she has no voice. And in spite of another principle recognized in this Republc, namely, that "taxation without representation is tyranny," she is taxed without being represented. Her property may be consumed by taxes to defray the expenses of that unholy, unrighteous custom called war, yet she has no power to give her vote against it. From the cradle to the grave she is subject to the power and control of man. Father, guardian, or husband, one conveys her like some piece of merchandise over to the other.

At marriage she loses her entire identity, and her being is said to have become merged in her husband. Has nature thus merged it? Has she ceased to exist and feel pleasure and pain? When she violates the laws of her being, does her husband pay the penalty? When she breaks the moral laws, does he suffer the punishment? When he supplies his wants, is it enough to satisfy her nature? . . . What an inconsistency, that from the moment she enters that compact in which she assumes the high responsibility of wife and mother, she ceases legally to exist and becomes a purely submissive being. Blind submission in woman is considered a virtue, while submission to wrong is itself wrong, and resistance to wrong is virtue, alike in woman as in man.

But it will be said that the husband provides for the wife, or in other words, he feeds, clothes, and shelters her! I wish I had the power to make every one before me fully realize the degradation contained in that idea. Yes! he *keeps* her, and so he does a favorite horse; by law they are both considered his property. Both may, when the cruelty of the owner compels them to run away, be brought back by the strong arm of the law and, according to a still extant law in England, both may be led by the halter to the market place and sold. This is humiliating indeed, but nevertheless true; and the sooner these things are known and understood, the better for humanity. It is no fancy sketch. I know that some endeavor to throw the mantle of romance over the subject and treat woman like some ideal existence, not liable to the ills of life. Let those deal in fancy who have nothing better to deal in; we have to do with sober, sad realities, with stubborn facts.

Again, I shall be told that the law presumes the husband to be kind, affectionate, and ready to provide for and protect his wife. But what right, I ask, has the law to presume at all on the subject? What right has the law to intrust the interest and happiness of one being into the hands of another? And if the merging of the interest of one being into the other is a necessary consequence on marriage, why should woman always remain on the losing side? Turn the tables. Let the identity and interest of the husband be merged in the wife. Think you she would act less generously toward him, than he toward her? . . .

Man forgets that woman can not be degraded without its reacting on himself. The impress of her mind is stamped on him by nature, and the early education of the mother, which no after-training can entirely efface; and therefore, the estimation she is held in falls back with double force upon him. Yet, from the force of prejudice against her, he knows it not.

Not long ago I saw an account of two offenders, brought before a Justice of New York. One was charged with stealing a pair of boots, for which offense he was sentenced to six months' imprisonment; the other crime was assault and battery upon his wife: he was let off with a reprimand by the judge! With my principles, I am entirely opposed to punishment, and hold that to reform the erring and remove the causes of evil is much more efficient, as well as just, than to punish. But the judge showed us the comparative value which he set on these two kinds of *property*. But then you must remember that the boots were taken by a stranger, while the wife was insulted by her legal owner!

It is high time . . . to compel man by the might of right to give woman her political, legal and social rights . . . She will find her own sphere in accordance with her capacities, powers and tastes; and yet she will be woman still . . . Away with that folly that her rights would be detrimental to her character—that if she is recognized as the equal to man, she would cease to be woman! Have *his* rights as a citizen of a republic, the elective franchise with all its advantages, so changed his nature that he has ceased to be man?

Such is the superficial mode of reasoning, if it deserves that name, that is brought against the subject. It reminds me of two reasons given by a minister of Milton, on the North River. Having heard I had spoken on the rights of woman, he took the subject up the following Sunday, to prove that woman ought not to have equal rights with man, first, because Adam was created before Eve, and secondly, man was compared to the fore wheel of a wagon! These reasons are about as philosophical as any that can be brought on the subject . . .

But, say some, . . . would you expose woman to the contact of rough, rude, drinking, swearing, fighting men at the ballot box? What a humiliating confession lies in this plea for keeping woman in the background! Is the brutality of some men, then, a reason why woman should be kept from her rights? If man, in his superior wisdom, cannot devise means to enable woman to deposit her vote without having her finer sensibilities shocked by such disgraceful conduct, then there is an additional reason as well as necessity why she should be there to civilize, refine, and purify him, even at the ballot box . . .

Do you not yet understand what has made woman what she is? Then see what the sickly taste and perverted judgment of man now admires in woman. Not health and strength of body and mind, but a pale delicate face; hands too small to grasp a broom, for that were treason to a lady; a voice so sickly, sentimental and depressed, as to hear what she says only by the moving of her half-parted lips; and, above all that nervous sensibility that sees a ghost in every passsing shadow—that beautiful diffidence that dare not take a step without the arm of a man to support her tender frame, and that shrinking (mock) modesty that faints at the mention of the leg of a table . . . Oh! the crying injustice towards woman! She is crushed in every step she takes, and then insulted for being what a most pernicious education and corrupt public sentiment has made her.

SPEECH OF ERNESTINE L. ROSE AT THE THOMAS PAINE ANNIVERSARY CELEBRATION, NEW YORK, JANUARY 29, 1852

. . . The infancy of the year 1852 is prophetic of the most important events in the annals of human history. Life, liberty and happiness is on one scale, dark despotism, Siberia, the guillotine, Austria's galling chains, and the Papal inquisition in the other. And who that has human blood flowing in his veins, who that ever felt the warm gush of affection thrill his being, can hesitate whether to throw his weight into the balance of life and freedom, or that of chains, oppression and death?

But our wise men in Washington tell us that our policy is non-intervention . . . When we struggled to cast off our yoke we asked for and obtained active intervention. Men from all parts of Europe fought our battles. France sent us a large fleet with millions of money, without which we might yet be an appendage to Great Britain. But then we were weak and prostrate, and therefore believed in intervention, but now that we are strong and able to stand alone, we think non-intervention is the best policy for us. And as long as we do not aid the destroyer of human freedom, and profess to be the friend of human rights, we can lay the flattering unction to our souls that we are very good republicans . . .

Non-intervetion! There is no such thing as non-intervention. Silent influence is often far more powerful than active; and to him who fears only your opposition, but requires no personal aid, silence is consent. And silence where life and liberty is at stake, where by a timely protest we could stay the destroyers hand, and do not do so, is as criminal as giving actual aid to the oppressor, for it answers his purpose, he can achieve the foul deed . . . I hope the people will release those poor members of Congress from their burdens, and compel them, by the force of public opinion, to vindicate the character of this republic, and act worthy of a Washington, Jefferson and Paine.

REVIEW OF HORACE MANN'S TWO LECTURES BY ERNESTINE L. ROSE, NEW YORK, FEBRUARY 1852

(The following passages are extracted from the pamphlet and presented here in the form of the debate which Mrs. Rose wanted to have with Horace Mann but which never took place. In the pamphlet the statements attributed to Horace Mann appear in quotation marks, but an examination of the published version of Mann's lectures reveals that Mrs. Rose was not quoting him verbatim but paraphrasing him. In his preface to the lectures, published a year later, Mann takes note of Mrs. Rose's pamphlet by citing it as an example of severe criticism of his views by "a distinguished advocate of woman's rights.")

H. M.: The human soul and feelings were created male and female as much as their bodies . . . The structure is entirely different in the sexes; there is not one single organ in structure, position and function alike in man and woman, and therefore there can be no equality between the sexes.

E. R.: Suppose, then, that the structure of the sexes is different—that the heart, lungs, liver, stomach, or any other of the organs requisite in the human economy are larger, smaller, situated a sixteenth of an inch higher, or lower, more to the right or the left, in man or woman, what then? Does it follow that woman cannot, or must not be socially, civilly, and politically his equal?

H. M.: As well might knives and forks, hooks and eyes, buttons and button-holes claim equality as man and woman.

E. R.: I will not presume to comment on this philosophical simile, it being the product of the "higher intellect of the sterner sex . . ."

H. M.: It is true woman has been oppressed and degraded by man, and it is not to be wondered at; when we see her run to the extravagance of calling conventions, and under the banner of woman's rights appear on the forum and make speeches, she unsexes herself and loses the grace and delicacy of her sex, and gains none of the superior powers of the other.

E. R.: That is as modest as it is consistent. He admits woman is oppressed and degraded by man, but to claim and vindicate her right to call conventions and appear on the forum where she would have a chance to be heard then "she unsexes herself," etc. . . . But what does the Honorable Lawgiver really mean by that term? I fear we will have to send it to Washington for congressional deliberation.

H. M.: What have been the rank and influence of woman for 6,000 years? Man has immensely degraded her; she has been little more than the mother of a race—such a race! that it might be doubted if its increase would be a benefit to the world.

E. R.: What else, Mr. Lecturer, *could* have been the rank and influence of woman than to be the mother of just *such* a race, bad as it may be, judging from some specimens, when she has been "immensely oppressed and degraded by man?"

H. M.: For four thousand years the Jewish women did nothing but give birth to a race of unmerciful, stiff-necked men.

E. R.: ... unmerciful and stiff-necked as the Jews are they still are the authors and originators of his religion, and a Jewish woman was the mother of his Redeemer. Well, gratitude is a virtue; and seeing how corrupt the race is, it is quite refreshing to find one mother's son possessing the amiable virtue of gratitude to God's (His God's) chosen people.

H. M.: Joan of Arc commanded an army but she brought her sword back pure without a blood-stain, still the best place for woman is at home with her family; for a man to take care of children would be like an elephant hatching chickens.

E. R.: Perhaps if woman had more to command, fewer swords would be stained with human blood, until they finally might be made into plowshares.

H. M.: ... The greatest pride of woman should be as a housekeeper, as a scientific cook, to enable her to cook a good breakfast, and keep it nice and hot till her husband is ready for it, to take care of the wardrobe, and keep the buttons where they belong; but her greatest duty is at the cradle, to take care and educate the children.

E. R.: If men and women were educated in accordance with their predilections and tastes, it might so happen that some men might have the best capacity for the science of cooking and some women for the science of government. And as for "buttons," every girl ought to know how to sew on buttons, and I am quite willing to give the same privilege to men, particularly to the bachelors. But the lecturer can certainly not insist that . . . the Creator assigned the wardrobe to woman, for according to the Bible, "Did the Lord God make coats of skins buttons and all and clothed them?"

Genesis iii 21

H. M.: The law is not at all suited for woman. She lacks that hard, dry, calculating spirit . . . she lacks the unflinching nerve demanded in a judge, the endurance required in a juror.

E. R.: That the law is a dry subject I doubt not; but seeing how soft most lawyers are it does not appear to require a very hard head to master it, though it may require a very hard heart to carry it out . . . Has the lecturer ever found a woman flinch from a trying position? Let him point her out, and she will be as great a curiosity as his arguments.

H. M.: Fancy to yourself one husband's wife locked up in the jury room with another's wife's husband and see them marching two and two after the court martial to and from the jury room.

E. R.: Let him remember—*Honi soit qui mal y pense!* The lecturer, I ask pardon, was not as wise as a certain mayor of a country town who, on apologizing to a prince who visited the town, for not firing cannons, gave eighteen reasons; the first was, the town had no cannons with which reason the prince was so well satisfied that he dispensed with the other seventeen. Had we had the last of the above series of reasons first we might with royal magnanimity have saved the lecturer the trouble of giving, and us of hearing the other seventeen.

H. M.: Politics! politics! that any person could ever wish to see woman embarked upon this Stygian lake, is incomprehensible! ... the political and legislative bear-garden ... [is] the deepest and darkest sink of corruption, and hence woman ought not to have anything to do with government.

E. R.: I have not the least idea of disputing the lecturer's opinion on government, particularly as he can speak from personal experience. But that such a description would have the effect to reassure and satisfy woman that she is quite safe in leaving her best and dearest interests in the hands of such a "set of animals" is rather doubtful, particularly as it might suggest itself to her mind that as the government is in such a lamentable, disgraceful condition would it not be well, even as a mere experiment, to send these legislative gentlemen home to be tamed, and let women take their places.

REPLY OF REV. AMORY BATTLES TO REV. G. B. LITTLE BANGOR, MAINE, DECEMBER 17, 1855

(This letter appeared in the *Whig and Courier* of Bangor, Maine in defense of Mrs. Rose's appearance as a lecturer in that city for the Independent Course, a series of anti-slavery lectures.)

Monday, Dec. 10, 1855

Dear Sir: . . .

You inquire 'if it is irrevocably fixed that Mrs. Rose is to appear in the Anti-Slavery course?' Why should she not? . . . We live in an age and country where free thought and free speech are acknowledged in theory as they should be in practice; and you will pardon me if I fail to discover in the facts to which you refer with so much sensitiveness, anything that disqualifies one for lecturing in our Course. I cannot see how one's theological opinions should fit or unfit one for speaking upon Moral Reform. According to my humble judgment, an irreproachable character, intellectual ability, and an acquaintance with the subject are the qualifications demanded in a lecturer upon such subjects; and that Mrs. Rose has these, in an eminent degree, has never been denied, to my knowledge except by a single individual, imported into our city to malign one too pure and noble for him to appreciate . . .

During the revolutionary war, Thomas Paine offered upon the altar of freedom his talents and his pen. Infidel though he was, the Christian patriots of that day did not disdain the offering. They were all engaged in a common cause—the cause of human liberty—and they welcomed the labors of any one who had a heart to work. History mentions with praise the aid Paine rendered the revolutionary struggle, and the Legislature of Pennsylvania voted him twenty-five hundred dollars for his pamphlet on 'Common Sense.'

To-day, more than three millions of our fellow-men are suffering a bondage, 'one hour of which outweighs the misery,' to use the language of Mr. Jefferson, 'a century of that against which our fathers rose in rebellion;' and not only are they suffering, but the tyrannical power which forged their chains has laid its bloody hand on us, and filled the land with oppression, and a pure-minded, gifted, and self-sacrificing woman,—like Paine, of foreign parentage,—offers her talents and voice to help strike off the shackles; and shall we be less catholic than our revolutionary fathers, and say to her, because she has presided at a Paine festival, and sympathizes with Paine's religious sentiments, that we want none of your help? Would the slave thus speak? I submit that such a procedure is to allow our bigotry to rule humanity, and to govern our sense of justice. If your house were on fire, and an atheist should offer to carry a pail of water, could you spurn his kindness because your religious opinions might receive a 'violent shock' to have your house saved by heretical hands? . . .

If a woman, who is called 'infidel,' proposes to speak here upon the same American slavery, she is denounced and vilified. But a clergyman who advocates the infamous and infidel Fugitive Slave Bill, is freely admitted into a Bangor pulpit; . . .

But I grieve most of all to know that any who profess faith in God and Christ should attempt to make them apologists for slavery . . .

In behalf of my associates, I thank you for your caution against 'pride' and say, that it is not pride, but principle, that influences our action . . . Providence permittting, Mrs. Rose will appear in the 'Independent Course.'

Respectfully yours,
A. Battles.

LAST WILL AND TESTAMENT OF
ERNESTINE LOUISE ROSE

This is the Last Will of me, Ernestine Louise Rose, formerly of the City of New York in the United States of America and now residing at No. 18 St. Petersburg Place, Bayswater in the County of Middlesex, England. Widow. I appoint Philip Syng Justice and his son Philip Middleton Justice, both of No. 55 and 56 Chancery Lane in the County of Middlesex, England, to be the Executors of this my will and I hereby revoke all my former wills and codicils.

I give and bequeath unto my niece Jeannette Pulvermacher nee Morganstern now residing at number 4 Spanish Place, Manchester Square in the County of Middlesex, England all my clothing, books, letters, papers and personal effects not otherwise herein named.

I direct that my said executors shall pay all my funeral expenses and just debts as soon after my decease as may be and that they shall have full power to sell and convert into money all and any of the bonds, shares, securities or property of which I may die possessed when and as they may deem proper.

I give and bequeath unto Ernest Mendum of Boston in the State of Massachusetts, United States of America, my gold watch with chain and key as worn by me. I give and bequeath unto Philip Middleton Justice, one of my executors, the sum of one hundred pounds sterling and I direct that all legacy duties on my bequests shall be paid out of my residuary estate. I direct that the balance of my cash remaining in the hands of my executors as well as any bonds, shares or securities which they may not have converted into money as well as all the rest of my property of which I may die possessed, whether the same be in Great Britain or any other Country, shall be divided into three equal parts as near as possible so to do, one part of which I give and bequeath unto my niece Mrs. Jeannette Pulvermacher nee Morganstern, now residing at No. 4 Spanish Place, Manchester Square, County of Middlesex, England; one part I give and bequeath unto my niece Mrs. Ernestine Radjewski nee Morganstern, now residing at 43 Dragoner Street, Berlin in the Empire of Germany; one part I give and bequeath to my niece Miss [sic] Bertha Sigismund nee Morganstern, now residing at No. 324 East 74th Street in the City of New York in the United States of America. In case any of the aforenamed persons should predecease me then their share shall be paid to their next of kin.

I request that my executors shall not permit my body to be taken into any Chapel or Church but to carry out my funeral in like manner generally as that of my late husband William E. Rose.

In witness whereof, the said Ernestine Louise Rose, have hereunto set my hand this sixth day of January in the year of our Lord One thousand eight hundred and ninety.

[Signed] Ernestine L. Rose

Signed by the above named testator Ernestine Louise Rose as and for her last will and testament in the present and at her request and in the presence of each other have hereunto subscribed our names as witnesses.

Washington Epps, Physician, 89 Great Russell Street W.C.
Howard R. Justice, Consulting Engineer, 55/56 Chancery Lane, London W.C.

On the 31st Dec. 1892 Probate of this will was granted to Philip Middleton Justice, one of the Executors.

[Text of Will copied from a photostat of the original document, supplied by Morris U. Schappes]

ACKNOWLEDGMENTS

I AM GREATLY INDEBTED to the Emma Lazarus Federation of Jewish Women's Clubs for the grant that made this book possible.

I am most grateful to historian Morris U. Schappes, a pioneer in research on the life of Ernestine L. Rose, for generously placing at my disposal his entire file of notes, photostats and correspondence, the accumulation of many years' work.

I also wish to express my thanks to publicist and editor Bernard Postal, another pioneer in this subject, for letting me see all of his material on Ernestine L. Rose.

I am especially thankful to Mrs. Miriam Young Holden, publicist and book collector, for giving me the unlimited use of her library, one of the largest private collections on the subject of women in the country, and for her warm interest in my work on this book.

I wish to express my deep appreciation to Mrs. Rhoda Miller da Silva; Mrs. Elizabeth Goldman; Mrs. Virginia Rosen and Mrs. Rita Ochman for their valuable assistance in my research.

I am thankful to Miss Jean Karsavina for assisting me with translations from the Polish and to Rabbi Abraham Bick for assisting me in translations from the Hebrew.

I am also grateful to Mrs. Ruth Selly for her careful typing of the manuscript and to Harry Pollack, a dealer in rare books, for going out of his way to secure for me books vital to this subject.

My warmest thanks and appreciation are due to the following institutions and their staffs for their prompt, efficient and courteous response to my inquiries: Bangor Public Library, Harvard University Library, Grosvenor Library (Buffalo), Rochester Public Library, Syracuse Public Library, Onondaga Historical Society (Syracuse), Library of the State of New York, New York Public Library, Columbia University Libraries, New York Historical Society, Jewish Scientific Institute (Yivo), Brooklyn Public Library, Free Library of Philadelphia, Swarthmore College Library, Enoch Pratt Free Library (Baltimore), Library of Congress, National Archives, Chicago Historical Society, Detroit Public Library, Indianapolis Public Library, and Henry E. Huntington Library. My special thanks are due to the staff of the American Antiquarian Society and its director, Dr. Clarence S. Brigham; Mrs. Margaret S. Grierson, Director, Sophia Smith Collection, Smith College; Mrs. Richard Borden, Director, The Women's Archives, Radcliffe College; Mr. Lester G. Wells, Curator of Special Collections, Syracuse University; and Mrs. Belle H. Waterman, Librarian, Skaneateles Library Association.

My deepest appreciation I reserve for my wife, Isabelle. Her assistance in the research for this book was invaluable; her belief in its meaning was inspiring; her faith in my ability to write it sustained me through many a difficult period in my work.

NOTES AND BIBLIOGRAPHY

THE MAIN SOURCES for this biography are the speeches and letters of Ernestine L. Rose that appeared in the various publications of her time, and the writings about her by her contemporaries.

L. E. Barnard's "Ernestine L. Rose," *History of Woman Suffrage*, I, cited below, and Jenny P. d'Hericourt's "Ernestine L. Rose," the *Revolution*, September 16, 1869, are the two primary sources about the early European period of Mrs. Rose's life.

The most important single source for all aspects of Mrs. Rose's life from the 1840's until her death is the *Boston Investigator* (1831-1904), a free thought weekly to which Mrs. Rose contributed regularly though infrequently for nearly fifty years.

The most important source of information about all aspects of the woman's rights movement and Mrs. Rose's role in it is the *History of Woman Suffrage, 1848-1900*, Rochester, 1881-1902, 4 vols. I-III were edited by Elizabeth Cady Stanton, Susan B. Anthony and Matilda Joslyn Gage; Vol. IV, by Susan B. Anthony and Ida Husted Harper. Other valuable sources on this subject are: Ida Husted Harper's *The Life and Work of Susan B. Anthony: A Story of the Evolution in the Status of Woman*, Indianapolis, 1898, 1908, 3 vols., and the published proceedings of the conventions Mrs. Rose attended, which are listed below.

The only three official documents related to the Roses that were found are: the *Seventh Census of the United States, 1850*, manuscript schedules of the Sixth ward of New York City; the records of the Roses' citizenship on file in the Special Term, Part II, Room 315, 60 Center Street, New York; Mrs. Rose's last will and testament (see Appendix).

The only known manuscript materials consist of a few scattered letters of little importance. The Chicago Historical Society has two; the Garrison Collection, Sophia Smith Collection, Smith College Library, has one; Miss Alma Lutz owns five.

EXTANT WORKS OF ERNESTINE L. ROSE (published in pamphet form):

Speech of Mrs. Rose, a Polish Lady, at the Anniversary Paine Celebration, in New York, January 29, Year of Independence, 74th—Christian Era, 1850. New York, 1850.
An Address on Woman's Rights Delivered Before the People's Sunday Meeting, In Cochituate Hall, on Sunday Afternoon, October 19, 1851. Boston, 1851.
Review of Horace Mann's Two Lectures Delivered in New York, February 17th and 29th, 1852. Privatey printed, n.d.
"Speech of Mrs. E. L. Rose at the Woman's Rights Convention, Held at Syracuse, September 1852," in *Woman's Rights Commensurate With Her Capacities and Obligations: A Series of Tracts*. Syracuse, 1853.

Two Addresses Delivered at the Bible Convention, Hartford, Conn. in June 1853. Boston, 1888.

A Defence of Atheism, Being a Lecture Delivered in Mercantile Hall, Boston, April 10, 1861. Boston, 1881.

LITERATURE ABOUT ERNESTINE L. ROSE:

Ditzion, Sidney. *Marriage, Morals and Sex in America: A History of Ideas.* New York, 1953.

Foner, Philip S. *The Jews in American History, 1654-1865.* New York, 1945.

Friedman, Lee M. *Pilgrims in a New Land.* Philadelphia, 1948.

Lebeson, Anita Libman. *Pilgrim People.* New York, 1950.

Lewis, Henry. "Ernestine Rose—First Jewish Advocate of Woman's Rights," *Jewish Daily Forward,* June 19, 1927.

O'Connor, Lillian. *Pioneer Women Orators: Rhetoric in the Ante-Bellum Reform Movement.* New York, 1954.

Schappes, Morris U. *A Documentary History of the Jews in the United States, 1654-1875.* New York, 1950, rev. ed., 1952.

——. "Ernestine Rose, Queen of the Platform," *Jewish Life,* March, 1949.

——. *The Jews in the United States: A Pictorial History, 1654 to the Present.* New York, 1958.

——. "To Be Included," *Morning Freiheit,* March 13, 1948.

Sillen, Samuel. *Women Against Slavery.* New York, 1955.

Simonhoff, Harry. *Jewish Notables in America, 1778-1865.* . . . New York, 1956.

Underwood, Sara A. *Heroines of Freethought.* New York, 1876.

Williams, Mary Wilhelmine. "Ernestine Louise Siismondi Potowski Rose," *Dictionary of American Biography,* Vol. XVI. New York, 1935.

Yoakam, Doris G. "Woman's Introduction to the American Platform," *A History and Criticism of American Public Address,* ed. by William N. Brigance, Vol. I. New York, 1943.

JEWISH LIFE IN POLAND: 1810-1826

Dubnov, S. M. *An Outline of Jewish History.* Vol. III. New York, 1925.

Feinkind, Mojżesz. . . . *Dzieje Żydów w Piotrkowie i Okolicy od najdawniejszych Czasów do Chwili obecnej.* Piotrków, 1930.

Mahler, Raphael. *Haskole un khsides in galitsie in der ershter helft fun neintzenten jor-hundert.* New York, 1942.

Nadler, Samuel, ed. *Sefer ha-yovel likhevod ha-rav Meir Shapiro.* Lodz (Poland), 1930.

Pollak, Gustav. *Michael Heilprin and His Sons: A Biography.* New York, 1912.

Raisin, Jacob S. *The Haskalah Movement In Russia.* Philadelphia, 1914.

Shatzky, Jacob. *Di geshikhte fun yidn in varshe.* Band I. New York, 1947.

EUROPE: 1826-1836

Ewen, Frederic. "Heinrich Heine: Humanity's Soldier," in *The Poetry and Prose of Heinrich Heine,* selected and ed. . . . by Frederic Ewen. New York, 1948.

Halevy, Elie. *A History of the English People, 1830-1841*, trans. from the French by E. I. Watkin. New York, n.d.
Kridl, Manfred, ed. *Adam Mickiewicz, Poet of Poland.* . . . New York, 1951.
Kuczynski, Jürgen. *A Short History of Labour Conditions Under Industrial Capitalism.* Vol. III, Part I. London, 1945.
Morton, A. L. *A People's History of England.* London, 1948.
Ogg, Frederic Austin. *Economic Development of Modern Europe.* . . . Rev. ed. New York, 1926.
Palmer, R. R. *A History of the Modern World.* New York, 1950.
Pascal, Roy. *The Growth of Modern Germany.* London, 1946.
Robinson, James H. and Beard, Charles A. *Readings in Modern European History.* Vol. II. Boston, 1909.
Scott, Jonathan F. and Baltzly, Alexander. *Readings in European History Since 1814.* New York, 1930.

ROBERT OWEN AND OWENISM

"American Women in Europe," *Golden Age*, March 25, 1871.
Cole, G. D. H. *Socialist Thought: The Forerunners, 1789-1850.* London, 1953.
Haynes, Fred E. *Social Politics in the United States.* Boston, 1924.
Laidler, Harry W. *A History of Socialist Thought.* New York, 1927.
Lockwood, George B. *The New Harmony Movement.* New York, 1905.
Manual of the Association of All Classes of All Nations. . . . No. 2. London, 1836.
Owen, Robert. *The Life of Robert Owen.* . . . Reprinted, New York, 1920.
Podmore, Frank. *Robert Owen: A Biography.* 2 vols. London, 1906.
Rose, Ernestine L. [Remarks at Albany Woman's Rights Convention] in the *Una*, II (1854), 243.

UNITED STATES, 1830-1850:

Beard, Charles A. and Beard, Mary R. *The Rise of American Civilization.* One vol. ed. . . . New York, 1930.
Dulles, Foster Rhea. *Labor in America.* New York, 1955.
Ernst, Robert. *Immigrant Life In New York City, 1825-1863.* New York, 1949.
Fish, Carl Russell. *The Rise of the Common Man, 1830-1850.* New York, 1927.
Foner, Philip S. *History of the Labor Movement in the United States.* Vol. I. New York, 1947.
Hone, Philip. *The Diary of Philip Hone, 1828-1851,* ed. Bayard Tuckerman, 2 vols. New York, 1889.
Howland, Edward. *Annals of North America.* . . . Hartford, Conn. 1877.
McMaster, John Bach. *A History of the People of the United States.* . . . Vols. VI-VIII. New York, 1906, 1910, 1913.
Minnigerode, Meade. *The Fabulous Forties—1840-50.* New York, 1924.
Morris, Lloyd. *Incredible New York.* . . . New York, 1951.
Parrington, Vernon Louis. *Main Currents in American Thought.* Vol. II. New York, 1927.

Spiller, Robert E. and others, eds. *Literary History of the United States.* Rev. ed. in one vol. New York, 1953.
Stokes, I. N. Phelps. *The Iconography of Manhattan Island, 1498-1909.* Vol. V. New York, 1926.
The Traveller's Guide Through the State of New York, Canada, etc. . . . New York, 1836.
Tyler, Alice Felt. *Freedom's Ferment: Phases of American Social History to 1860.* St. Paul, Minn., 1944.

Newspapers:

Anti-Slavery Examiner, August 1836 [Anti-slavery petitions].
Liberator, May 21, 1836 [New York City description].

MARRIED WOMAN'S PROPERTY BILL, 1836-1848:

Herttell, Judge [Thomas]. *Remarks Comprising In Substance Judge Herttell's Argument In The House of Assembly of the State of New York, In The Session of 1837, In Support of the Bill To Restore To Married Women "The Right of Property,"* . . . New York, 1839.
———. "Remarks of Mr. Thomas Herttell, in the House of Assembly of New York, May 20, 1836, on the Resolution Offered By Him Touching the Rights and Property of Married Women," in the *Condition, Influence, Rights and Appeal of Women.* 4th ed. Albany, 1847.
New York State. *Documents of the Assembly of the State of New York.* Albany, 1842, 1844.
———. *Journal of the Assembly of the State of New York.* Albany, 1836-1848.
———. *Journal of the Senate of the State of New York.* Albany, 1836-1848.
———. *Laws of the State of New York, Passed at the Seventy-First Session of the Legislature.* . . . Albany, 1848.
Rose, Ernestine L. "Woman's Rights," *Boston Investigator,* April 11, 1860.

THE SKANEATELES COMMUNITY (1843-1846):

Douglass, Frederick. *Life and Times of Frederick Douglass.* . . . Reprinted New York, 1941.
Hillquit, Morris. *History of Socialism in the United States.* New York, 1903.
Holloway, Mark. *Heavens on Earth: Utopian Communities in America, 1680-1880.* London, 1951.
Noyes, John Humphrey. *History of American Socialisms.* Philadelphia, 1870.
[Proceedings of the New England Social Reform Convention, Held in Boston, Mass., May 28-31 and June 1, 1844], in *Social Pioneer and Herald of Progress* (Boston) July 1844.
Wells, Lester Grosvenor. *The Skaneateles Communal Experiment, 1843-1846.* Syracuse, N.Y., 1953.

Newspapers:

Boston Investigator, June 12, 19 and July 17, 1844.
Communitist (Skaneateles Community, Mottville, N.Y.), 1844-1846.
Herald of Freedom (Concord, N.H.) August 16, October 6, 13, 20, 27, November 3, 17, and December 1, 1843.

Liberator, January 12, May 17, December 27, 1844.
New York Tribune, December 6, 1843.
Onondaga Standard (Syracuse), November 22, 1843.
Skaneateles Columbian, November 19, 1843.

FREE THOUGHT, SOCIAL REFORM AND OTHER ACTIVITIES: 1837-1869.

*Address of the Universal Peace Society to All Persons, Families, Commu-
nities and Nations.* Philadelphia, 1866.
Barker, Joseph. *Modern Skepticism: A Journey Through the Land of Doubt
and Back Again.* Philadelphia, 1874.
Bennett, D. M. *The World's Sages, Infidels and Thinkers: Being Biograph-
ical Sketches of Leading Philosophers, Teachers, Reformers. . . .* New
York, 1876.
The Common School Almanac. . . . New York, 1839.
Foner, Philip S., ed. *The Complete Writings of Thomas Paine. . . .* 2 vols.
New York, 1945.
McCabe, Joseph. *A Biographical Dictionary of Modern Rationalists.* Lon-
don, 1920.
Macdonald, George E. *Fifty Years of Freethought. . . .* 2 vols. New York,
1929.
"Minutes of the Proceedings of the Infidel Convention, Held in New York
City, May 4, 5, 6, 1845," in *Meteor of Light* (Boston) June 1, 1845.
Parrington, Vernon Louis. *Main Currents in American Thought.* Vol. I.
New York, 1927.
Post, Albert. *Popular Freethought in America, 1825-1850.* New York, 1943.
*Proceedings of the First Anniversary of the Universal Peace Society, Ma-
sonic Hall, New York, May 8 and 9, 1867.* Philadelphia, 1867.
*Proceedings of the Free Convention Held at Rutland, Vt., [June] 25, 26
and 27, 1858.* Boston, 1858.
Proceedings of the Hartford Bible Convention. . . . New York, 1854.
Putnam, Samuel Porter. *Four Hundred Years of Freethought.* New York,
1894.
Robertson, John M. *A History of Freethought in the Nineteenth Century.*
London, 1929.
Rose, Ernestine L. "The Jews . . . ," *Boston Investigator,* February 10, 17,
24, March 2, 9, 16, April 6, 13, 1864.
———. "Letters . . ." [her trip abroad], *Boston Investigator,* May 7, 1856;
July 30-December 10, 1856.
Strong, George Templeton. *The Diary of George Templeton Strong,* ed.
Allan Nevins and Milton H. Thomas. Vol. II. New York, 1952.
Taylor, J. Orville. *The District School.* New York, 1834.
———. *Satirical Hits on the People's Education.* New York, 1839.
Waterman, William Randall. *Frances Wright.* New York, 1924.
Wheeler, Joseph M. *A Biographical Dictionary of Freethinkers of All Ages
and Nations.* London, 1889.
Whitman, Walt. "Notes and Fragments Left By Walt Whitman," *Com-
plete Prose Works,* ed. Dr. Richard Bucke. Vol. IX. New York, 1902.

Newspapers:

Boston Investigator, 1840-1869.
Jewish Record, February 19, 1864. [Re: Mrs. Rose's defense of Jews].

Liberator, June 17, 1853 [Hartford Bible Convention]; August 27, 1858 [Rutland (Vt.) Convention].
New York Beacon, November 5, 1836-October 21, 1837 [Moral Philanthropists]; December 23, 1837 [Broadway Tabernacle Meeting]; August 10, 1844 [Thomas Paine Celebrations].
New York Commercial Advertiser, December 13, 1837 [Broadway Tabernacle Meeting].
New York Correspondent, February 2, 1828 [Early Paine Celebrations].
New York Herald, December 16, 1837 [Broadway Tabernacle Meeting]; May 5, 1845 [Infidel Convention]; May 4, 1858 [Mrs. Rose on 1837 Broadway Tabernacle Meeting]. December 28, 1858 [Speech on Owen's death]; May 16, 1868 [Universal Peace Society].
New York Tribune, May 5, 7, 1845 [Infidel Convention].
Rutland (Vt.) Herald, June 24, and July 1, 22, 1858 [Rutland Convention].

ANTI-SLAVERY ACTIVITIES: 1847-1865.

Garrison, Wendell P. and Francis J. *William Lloyd Garrison, 1805-1879: The Story of His Life Told By His Children*. Vol. III. Boston, 1894.
Korngold, Ralph. *Two Friends of Man: The Story of William Lloyd Garrison and Wendell Phillips*. . . . Boston, 1950.
Proceedings of the Meeting of the Loyal Women of the Republic Held in New York, May 14, 1863. New York, 1863.
Schappes, Morris U. "Ernestine L. Rose: Her Address On the Anniversary of West Indian Emancipation," *Journal of Negro History*, XXXIV (July, 1949), 344-355.

Newspapers:

Bangor (Me.) Daily Evening Mercury, November 10, and December 15, 1855.
Bangor (Me.) Daily Journal, December 20, 1855.
Bangor (Me.) Daily Whig and Courier, November 3, 6, 15, 19, and December 17, 19, 24, 1855.
Boston Investigator, December 12, 19, 26, 1855 and January 16, 1856 [Bangor, Me. controversy]; February 20, March 13, 1861; February 5, June 4, 1862; December 1, 1869.
Liberator, May 10, 1850 [Rynders' Mob]; August 19, 1853 [West Indian Emancipation speech]; June 8, 1855 [New England Anti-Slavery Convention]; January 4, 1856 [Bangor, Me. controversy]; February 15, 1861 [Albany meeting].
National Anti-Slavery Standard, August 13, 1853 [West Indian Emancipation speech and report].
New York Herald, August 5, 1853 [West Indian Emancipation Celebration]; May 16, 1863 [Women's National Loyal League.]
New York Tribune, August 5, 1853 [West Indian Emancipation Celebration].

WOMAN'S RIGHTS ACTIVITIES: 1836-1869.

Anthony, Katherine. *Susan B. Anthony: Her Personal History and Her Era*. Garden City, N.Y., 1954.

Blackwell, Alice Stone. *Lucy Stone: Pioneer of Woman's Rights*. Boston, 1930.

Blackwell, Henry B. "Life and Work of Miss Anthony," *Woman's Journal* (Boston), March 11, 1899.

"The Champions of Woman's Suffrage," *Harper's Bazar*, June 12, 1869.

Dall, Caroline H. *Woman's Rights Under The Law*. . . . Boston, 1861.

Davis, Paulina W. *A History of the National Woman's Rights Movement . . . From 1850 to 1870*. New York, 1871.

Declaration of the Rights of Women of the United States. [Philadelphia], July 4, 1876.

Dorr, Rheta Child. *Susan B. Anthony: The Woman Who Changed The Mind of a Nation*. New York, 1928.

Greeley, Horace. *Recollections of a Busy Life*. New York, 1868.

Hallowell, Anna Davis, ed. *Life and Letters of James and Lucretia Mott*. Boston, 1884.

Holley, Sallie. *A Life For Liberty: Anti-Slavery and Other Letters of Sallie Holley*, ed. John White Chadwick. New York, 1899.

Irwin, Inez Haynes. *Angels and Amazons: A Hundred Years of American Women*. New York, 1933.

Lutz, Alma. *Created Equal: A Biography of Elizabeth Cady Stanton, 1815-1902*. New York, 1940.

Mann, Horace. *A Few Thoughts on the Powers and Duties of Woman*. Syracuse, 1853.

Mansfield, Edward D. *The Legal Rights, Liabilities and Duties of Women . . .* Salem [Mass.], 1845.

Michigan. *Journal of the House of Representatives of the State of Michigan, 1846*. Detroit, 1846.

Ossoli, Margaret Fuller. *Women in the Nineteenth Century*. Boston, 1855.

Proceedings at the Presentation to the Hon. Robert Dale Owen of a Silver Pitcher on Behalf of the Women of Indiana on 28 of May 1851. New Albany, Ind., 1851.

Proceedings of the First Anniversary of the American Equal Rights Association, Held at the Church of the Puritans, New York, May 9 and 10, 1867. New York, 1867.

Proceedings of the National Woman's Rights Convention . . . [at] Worcester, 1850, 1851; Syracuse, 1852; Cleveland, 1853; New York City, 1856, 1859, 1866.

Proceedings of the Woman's Rights Convention . . . [at] Seneca Falls and Rochester, 1848; New York City, 1853.

Quarles, Benjamin. *Frederick Douglass*. Washington, D.C., 1948.

———. "Frederick Douglass and the Woman's Rights Movement," *Journal of Negro History*, XXV (1940), 35-44.

Rose, Ernestine L. "Female Reformers—A Speech by Mrs. Rose" [at the Tenth National Woman's Rights Convention], *Boston Investigator*, October 3, 1860.

Smith, T. R., ed. *The Woman Question*. New York, [1918].

Stanton, Elizabeth Cady. *Eighty Years and More*. New York, 1898.

Stanton, Theodore, and Blatch, Harriot Stanton, eds. *Elizabeth Cady Stanton as Revealed in Her Letters, Diary, and Reminiscences*. 2 vols. New York, 1922.

Swisshelm, Jane Grey Cannon. *Half a Century*. Chicago, 1880.

Thompson, William. *Appeal of One Half of the Human Race, Women, Against the Pretensions of the Other Half, Men. . . .* London, 1825.

Walker, Timothy. "Legal Conditions of Women," *Western Law Journal,* I (1849), 145-159.

Wollstonecraft, Mary. *A Vindication of the Rights of Women.* New York, 1845.

"Woman," *Godey's Lady's Book,* January 1836.

The Woman's Rights Almanac for 1858. Worcester, Mass., [1858].

Working Women's Protective Union. *Annual Reports.* New York, 1878, 1888.

Newspapers:

Alexandria (Va.) Gazette and Virginia Advertiser, March 31, 1854.

Boston Journal, October 24, 25, 1850.

Buffalo Commercial Advertiser, October 1853.

Cleveland Plain Dealer, October 4-10, 1853.

Hebrew Leader, May 21, 1869.

Indianapolis Daily State Sentinel, October 24, 1855.

Indianapolis Journal, October 22, 23, 24, 1855.

Liberator, October 8, 1852; April 7, 14, 1854; January 12, 1855.

National Intelligencer (Washington, D.C.) January 21 and September 20, 1852.

New York Herald, 1850-1860 [Woman's rights conventions].

New York Times, 1850-1860 [Woman's rights conventions].

New York Tribune, 1850-1860 [Woman's rights conventions].

North American and U.S. Gazette (Philadelphia), October 19, 1854.

Philadelphia Evening Bulletin, October 18, 19, 1854.

Philadelphia Public Ledger and Daily Transcript, April 12, 15, 1854; October 19, 1854.

Revolution, 1868-71.

Rochester Daily Democrat, June 18, 19, 21, 1851; October 10; December 2, 3, 1853.

Rochester Daily Union, January 16, 1855.

Syracuse Daily Journal, September 9-13, 1852.

Syracuse Daily Standard, September 9, 13, 16, 1852.

Una, 1853-55.

Washington (D.C.) Sentinel, March 29, 1854.

Worcester Daily Spy, October 23, 24, 1850.

Manuscripts:

Susan B. Anthony Scrap Books, Library of Congress.

Garrison Collection of Letters, Sophia Smith Collection, Smith College Library.

Letter of Paulina Wright Davis to Gerrit Smith, November 7, 1869, *Smith MSS.,* Syracuse University Library.

Letters of Ernestine L. Rose to Mr. C. H. Plummer, December 23, 1854—January 29, 1855, Miss Alma Lutz, Boston, Mass. [Copies supplied by Morris U. Schappes].

Elizabeth Cady Stanton's Intimate Papers, Library of Congress.

THE LAST YEARS: 1869-1892.

Brockett, Linus P. *Woman: Her Rights, Wrongs, Privileges and Responsibilities.* Hartford, Conn., 1869.

Congrès Internationale des Sociétés des Amis de la Paix, tenu à Paris, les 26, 27, 28 et 30 Septembre, et le 1er Octobre, 1878. Paris, 1880.

Conway, Moncure D. *Autobiography, Memoires and Experiences.* Vol. II. Boston, 1904.

"A Legend of Good Women," *Golden Age,* July 1, 1871.

Rose, Ernestine L. [Speech at] *General Conference of Liberal Thinkers, June 13 and 14, 1878, South Place, Finsbury.* . . . Women's Service Library, Oxford, England.

———. [Speeches extracted from the] *Report of the Fifth Annual Meeting of the Edinburgh Branch of the National Society for Women's Suffrage, January 27, 1873,* Women's Service Library, Oxford, England.

Stanton, Theodore. *The Woman Question in Europe.* New York, 1884.

Theiss, Lewis Edwin and Mary Bartol. "Wyoming—The Pioneer of Suffrage States," *Pictorial Review,* October 1913.

[Woman's Suffrage Meeting at the Hanover Square Rooms], *Graphic* (London), May 25, 1872.

Newspapers:

Boston Investigator, 1869-1892.
Brighton (Eng.) Herald, August 13, 1892.
Edinburgh (Scotland) Daily Review, January 28, 31, 1873.
Freethinker (London), August 14 and 18, 1892.
London Daily News, August 9, 1892.
London Times, August 6, 1892.
National Anti-Slavery Standard, October 16, 1869 [V. Hugo's speech].
National Reformer (London), May 7, 28, and June 11, 1871 [Owen centenary]; August 14, 1892.
New York Herald, May 16, 1874.
New York Times, May 15, 16, 1874.
Woman's Journal, August 13, 1892 [Lucy Stone's obituary of Mrs. Rose].

Manuscripts:

Letter of Ernestine L. Rose to William Lloyd Garrison, January 22, 1877, *Garrison Collection,* Sophia Smith Collection, Smith College Library.

Letter of Susan B. Anthony to Mrs. Colby, December 30, 1899, [Copy supplied by Morris U. Schappes from materials sent him by Mrs. Una R. Winter, in 1948, Upland, California].

INDEX

(ER indicates Ernestine L. Rose)